There and Then

Personal Terms 6

Frederic Raphael was born in Chicago in 1931 and educated at Charterhouse and St John's College, Cambridge. His novels include *The Glittering Prizes* (1976), *A Double Life* (1993), *Coast to Coast* (1998) and *Fame and Fortune* (2007); he has also written short stories and biographies of Somerset Maugham and Byron. Frederic Raphael is a leading screenwriter, whose work includes the Academy Award-winning *Darling* (1965), *Two for the Road* (1967), *Far from the Madding Crowd* (1967), and the screenplay for Stanley Kubrick's last film, *Eyes Wide Shut* (1999). The first volume of *Personal Terms* was published by Carcanet in 2001, with subsequent volumes in 2004, 2006, 2008 and 2011.

Frederic Raphael

There and Then

Personal Terms 6

CARCANET

First published in Great Britain in 2013 by

Carcanet Press Limited
Alliance House
Cross Street
Manchester M2 7AQ

A CIP catalogue record for this book is available from the British Library

ISBN 978 1 84777 140 7

The publisher acknowledges financial assistance from Arts Council England

Set in Monotype Bembo by R. J. Footring Ltd, Derby
Printed and bound in England by SRP Ltd, Exeter

Contents

Introduction

In his diaries of the *entre-deux-guerres*, Evelyn Waugh reports just one remark made by my namesake, Enid Raphael: 'I don't know why they call them "private parts", *mine* aren't private.' Who was she? What became of her? Who knows? How wise she was, possibly, never to say anything else! As prolific as a writer may be, few of his remarks are likely to survive the winnowing of time. A man or woman may compile a ponderous *oeuvre* and yet remain, so to say, out of cite. This does not entail that none of their works are worthy of posterity's attention: 'Remarks are not literature,' said Gertrude Stein. Indeed; but who can quote (or enjoy) anything much that she wrote, apart from 'a rose is a rose is a rose'? She did also say of Oakland, California, where she lived as a young girl (and went to Hebrew classes), that 'there's no there there'. These tautologous triplets might as well have been her only progeny. Yet her fat aura still sits, as irrevocably sedentary as Whistler's mother, in today's Paris; the mature, just slightly rancid, eidolon of Daisy Miller, the American girl who never went home again.

Enid Raphael's shameless observation was an augury of what has come to pass. With the advent of the internet, and its derivatives, what is now private? There is no veil of modesty between the electronic flasher and publication, whether of erotic images, confessional boasts, wild opinions or asterisked obscenities. The new media truncate language and turn clichés into cute, sometimes cryptic acronyms. Speed being of the essence, any attempt to be original, or even considered, is anachronistic. The response goes before we have time, or inclination, for second thoughts. How many e-mails are read through by the sender? Misprints, omissions and solecisms fly away unchecked. No wonder 'flout' and 'flaunt' are, according to the latest dictionaries, accepted alternatives.

Today's reader of e/pistles misses the surge of anticipation which used to accompany the arrival of the post. The individuality of the handwriting on an envelope, and the thickness of its contents, promised, when they did, a 'proper letter'. Once a letter was opened, hurriedly or with delicious care, the nuances of stationery presaged its quality. Nothing one wanted to read could be written on lined paper. Green ink warned of monomania. The slope of a correspondent's script, his ability to avoid the slouch of the lines on the page, the use of exclamation marks or underlining, whether or not the pages were numbered, the paragraphing, even the charge of ink on the pen, the blots, the corrections, all such things were silent witnesses which alerted the reader to the character and merit of the sender. Even the way in which the date was inscribed (whether the month was announced in numerals or abbreviated or set out in full) told us something of the letter's provenance and pretensions.

Part of what was valuable in correspondence was its privacy. The opening of the envelope promised, if you were lucky, something which might confirm what Robert Graves called 'the meum–tuum sense'. To read other people's mail was a breach of decency. A US Secretary of State forbade the secret service to steam open the mail of the German and Japanese embassies on the grounds that 'gentlemen don't read other people's letters'. Alec Douglas-Home, I am promised, had the same wincing attitude when, in the early 1970s, MI5 disclosed how they had come on the evidence of widespread Soviet spying in Great Britain.

Somerset Maugham wrote a short story (not *The Letter*) in which a lonely planter, in Malaya, is so jealous of the many letters which his colleague receives that he buys one of them from him, unopened. The addressee presumes that once it has been read, the letter will later be handed to him for second-hand perusal. When its purchaser insists on keeping it to himself, it is the original recipient's turn to be murderously jealous. Only Dorothy Parker had the brazenness to claim that, never mind the personality of the sender, the most acceptable letter was one containing the words, 'Cheque enclosed'.

How many handwritten envelopes does anyone now see on the mat? The chances are that, even if there is one, the enclosure will be mechanically rendered. As for books, whose today are not composed directly on a PC? One freezing Boxing Day, more than forty years ago, my daughter Sarah and I went to visit the poet George MacBeth. He was living in a large rectory in Norfolk with Lisa St Aubin de Téran, whose portrait he wanted Sarah to paint. The damp and cracked walls of their unheated living room were hung with old typewriters. In the 1970s, it seemed idiosyncratic. Most writers today have, whether literally or metaphorically, hung up their typewriters. The last one to be manufactured was produced in 2012.

There was a time when American universities bought up the manuscripts of ranking writers, for flattering fees. Even the least of their *obiter scripta* were solicited and stored. In the 1980s, it was said to be no very rare sight to come across some solicited celebrity copying out the text of his old novels into an exercise book in order to supply the original manuscripts, convincingly tortured with corrections, and flying balloons with Proustian second thoughts. Did the cleverest of such fabricators amuse themselves by interposing new variant phrases, nicely crossed out, or even heavily obscured, so that PhD students might later have the excited pleasure of decrypting them? In contemporary cases, if we seek an original text, we are likely to find that there is no there there.

Last summer, at what was billed as an academic conference, I gave a misconceived lecture. The overall subject of our symposiastic attentions was Biography. When invited, I took it that we were to consider the topic *sub specie aeternitatis*: what would a 'true' biography be and how could a writer best approximate to it? My unaggressive case was that there were lacunae, even in the best documented lives, which could be filled, or bridged, only by an imaginative reading of what we knew in order to divine what tact or indifference had left unrecorded. No archive, however ample, embraces the quick (or the dark) of a subject's life. I made a case for something like the intuitive, perhaps sly, precision which a picture-restorer brings to her work. In writing, the choice of tone and vocabulary, even when rehearsing facts, supplies a way of indicating how, in human lives, similar causes have different effects.

I took it that the 'crisis' in biography was to do with how literary portraiture might survive in a world of instant Facebookish facsimiles, soundbites and journalistic opportunism. If I was a little fancy, I assumed that was what was expected in the circumstances. It was not. The next speaker, a pale editor from one of the most influential London publishers, was not concerned with truthful depiction or nuance. His notion of a crisis was identical with that of the Chancellor of the Exchequer: a fall in revenue from the mercantile category under review. The suited delegate from the *gratin* of English publishing was no more than a sales manager in sententious drag. On his pragmatic calculus, profit-and-loss was the only aesthetic. He enlightened us about his anxieties by projecting a flow-chart on the lecture-room wall. It demonstrated perhaps a 0.7 per cent dip in the public appetite for his brand of canned goods. What was worth writing, we were led to suppose, was identical with what the writing was worth to him, Maecenas on the make.

During the lunch break, as we lined up for economic sand-wiches and cellophaned salads, the important editor asked me, with demanding deference, whether I would let him have a copy of my lecture; he would like to post it on his company's website. Having spent a full week composing a paper which I hoped would be erudite enough for the occasion, I saw neither honour nor advantage in supplying free pabulum to a man who had just declared that a sales chart proved how good a book was. 'Why,' I said, offering him the dirty end of his own *shtick*, 'would I find it profitable to give anything to you?' Ah, the sweet smell of burning bridges!

On the first available train to London, I resolved never again to play the pundit unless – in conformity with the current ethos – it had a resurgent effect on my economic flow-chart. As we passed through Esher, it occurred to me to wonder when the last pub-lished biography was composed in handwriting; and whether it mattered. Does it not? Handwriting refuses the instant scan, the seamless assimilation of a text into the machinery of production. It resists the prompt interpolation of editorial 'notes' and the sug-gested clarifications which give the progeny of Maxwell Perkins the last word in the boa-constricting process of turning a writer's work into 'our sort of book'.

Marshall McLuhan achieved instant, if perishable, fame in the 1960s as the prophet of the convergence of advertising, marketing and the arts. His annunciatory essay, *The Gutenberg Galaxy*, asserted that the means of production affect both the diffusion of ideas and then the ideas themselves. Movable type was, of itself, and whatever the intent, an emancipation and an incentive to vulgarity. Sacred texts, which had been clamped in the cloistered custody of the literate priesthood, became available for general scrutiny, and revision. Demotic versions and scholarly glosses replaced, or supplemented, dogmatic interpretations. As if by itself, print demystified religion.

It is said the Tibetan goddess Tara was once summoned up, in exquisite person, by an old man reciting his prayers to her in eighteenth-century Lhasa. Local theological pundits scrutinised the old man's text and declared it a faulty translation. They required him to learn and use only the authorised version. From that day forward, the goddess was never seen again. The demand that all texts, trivial or elaborate, be passed through the homogenising medium of the internet entails loss of literary personality. Learning to write no longer has anything to do with having a specific 'claw', as Winston Churchill called it, when he reproached a colleague for typing a personal communication.

Who can now afford to disdain the instant legibility (and speed of transmission) which personal computers supply? When it comes to articles, books and scripts, one has little choice. Yet there will always be something about manuscript which cannot be duplicated by mechanical means. The fingers which hold a pen contribute something unique. The medium, whatever it is, deforms or informs the message. To use pen and ink is a form of drawing. Each letter comes without mechanical mediation. The fingers do a kind of thinking; they run on with the line into a gloss, and a gloss on a gloss, quite as if they had access to a reservoir of energy and acquired intelligence which is not available to the typographer. A manuscript is a manuscript is a manuscript.

In the 2012 movie *Silver Linings Playbook*, personal letters play a significant part in the development of the story. Supposedly written by the hero's wife, whose affair with one of his colleagues has driven him at least halfway out of his mind, they would certainly have been depicted in handwriting in any film of the last century. Here, the message – when unfolded for the camera – is spelt out in the black legibility of a domestic printer. The intimate letters in *Silver Linings Playbook* have not an iota of individuality. Their content, supposedly heartfelt, is spelt out in platitudes. The producers took care not to alienate the audience by any unfamiliar usage. In an elevated version of the same nervousness, the editors of New York's fanciest literary journal, so I am told, tend to query any form of words which might cause the reader to look at it twice. All prose has to conform to the house style; in doing so, as if by chance, it also confirms the house ideology. In journalism, smoothness and abrasiveness become *de facto* synonyms.

An everyday aspect of depersonalisation can be seen, regularly, on television. When bereaved family members declare their grief in public statements, almost all of them appear incapable of announcing their feelings except in platitudes: all deaths are 'tragic' and are certain to leave the survivors 'devastated'. Quite often, such declarations of anguish are read out, haltingly, from pieces of paper. It is as if, without a menu of clichés, the speaker would not know what he or she was supposed to feel.

While it is understandable that, in cruel circumstances, people should be lost for words or too choked to express them, it is a sign of the times that the most convincing expressions of distress, the most seemingly sincere appeals for a missing person or child to return, or to be returned, quite regularly turn out to be have been uttered by their murderers or abductors. Such appeals are almost always delivered spontaneously, choked with the obligatory tears. Falseness now sounds and looks more authentic than genuine anguish. Electronic media, we are promised, provide a new means of education; and so they do: they have taught people how to lie. Such is the fruit of living in what Plato called a *theatrokratia*.

What is written, or depicted, on a computer is, in principle, instantly public, whether or not it was intended for publication. The risk of being hacked is an inescapable, not always wholly unwanted, part of the ostentatious narcissism implicit in the addiction to electronic media. Today's Greta Garbos will never be alone, not least because they do not want to be. The indignation of celebrities swells with the prospect of tax-free damages; but those who live by the media must expect to perish by the same means. The pain caused to famous vanities is not of the same kind, though it culls a higher rate of recompense, as that felt by the family of Milly Dowler and other 'ordinary' people.

It is the business, and the pleasure, of the writer to take passage in a boat against the current. The Pharisees are a misunderstood sect. In an age of mass illiteracy, how is there not some virtue in taking care not to be as other men? A true writer does not have a career; he need not solicit votes, or even readers; his duty is to do whatever will incline him to do his best work, even if it means that he does it in obscurity. I persist in writing in my notebooks with pen and ink (even a biro seems to detract from the personality of a text). To some extent, I am enough of an antique Tibetan to fear that if I were to switch to an electronic device, for the sake of speed or legibility, my personal *daimon* would cease to supervise my verbosity. I do not think that I write better because I write from margin to margin on my squared pages, nor more sincerely, but I do write *differently* with a pen between my fingers.

I cannot claim that, when it comes to preparing my notebooks for publication, I transcribe my dated thoughts or observations entirely untrimmed. I do, however, try not to do what Bertel Thorwaldsen did when he 'shaved' the valuable ancient patina from the fifth-century marbles from the temple of Aphaia on Aegina, when they were on their way to Munich. I limit myself to correcting solecisms and pruning banalities; but I do not doctor my opinions or observations with the benefit of hindsight or in the hope of popularity. The transcription of handwriting does, however, incline me to shorten sentences and to omit the kind of busking which, even in solitary circumstances, can dispose a writer to ramble to the end of the page. I have also cut whatever might cause pain where I should not wish it to do so. For the rest, let the chips fall where they may. As the man said, '*Ho gegrapha, gegrapha.*'

FREDERIC RAPHAEL
2013

1979

19.8.79. G. Steiner, looking like the world's umpire in a white linen cap, promises that the Swiss have a special unit whose duty, in the event of war, is to maintain a line of communication with the enemy. The Swiss boast an efficient military; but the authorities in Berne discovered that, at the end of World War II, the Japanese were already trying to surrender before the atom-bombing of Nagasaki took place. Later, it was realised they had been petitioning a deaf receiver. Hence the Swiss have resolved never to lose access to whatever powers might come against them, in case at some stage they conclude that they must throw in the towel.

More is decided by referendum in Switzerland than anywhere else. Universal conscription is the sole topic not open to such public question. The Jesuits, G.S. told us, have revived interest in their religion by advertising willingness to provide private space for just such a discussion.

On hearing that Shirley Williams was to be a fellow-guest at Lagardelle, G. tuned himself up with prefatory jibes. When she arrived, her politic deference rolled him over; that she is about to lecture at Harvard procured respect. She also has an imminent TV series and has been recruited by various research institutes and similar dispensers of emoluments. Her ministerial salary continued only one month after Labour's eviction from power. Divorced and not yet fifty, she proclaims friendship to be the most important thing in her life. She has settled for being one of those bustling aunts who abandon being attractive in favour of being full of beans.

When she was a young MP, on a parliamentary delegation to Brussels, a 'senior Labour MP', a notorious *coureur*, invited her for a drink in his suite after an evening session. He soon dodged into the other room and emerged, fat and unappealing, kilted in a towel. Although staying in the same hotel, she fled into the street, either in panic or because she reasoned that he would not have the nerve to follow her into the open. She ran round a corner of the deserted street into the arms of three Belgian policemen.

They accused her of being a prostitute and loaded her into a Black Maria. After she was allowed to go back for her passport, which proved that she was indeed a British MP, the police escorted her, with apologies, to her room. To be taken for an adventuress and a whore on the same night was some kind of an achievement.

A letter from Peter Levi, in reply to a question from me about dialogue in the ancient world. Beetle thought the handwriting on the envelope was that of a nut. Perhaps it was penned in the train. There is something warm as well as troubled there, a hectic ambition for excellence. Such a man implies that to work in the movies is degrading, but P.L. is not above having written a thriller in which he has his 'worst enemy stung to death by Cretan bees'.

21.9.79. On the way to lunch with Fred Zinnemann, I bumped into Stuart Lyons using the telephone at the Hilton. He told me that Ken and Liz have had 'a great shake-up'. They have always been a 'close family'. Tanya, their daughter of eighteen, has been having an affair with Elton John's manager. She came back to his place one day and found him in bed with another man. Stuart traced tears on his cheeks.

Geoffrey Kirk's *The Nature of Greek Myths*. I am somewhat sorry to find it an excellent piece of demystification. G.S.K. claims that the going orthodoxy, which argues for parallelism between myth and ritual, is unjustified. His case is but slightly weakened by scholarly uncertainty about what precisely happened in rituals. Its excellence lies in disentangling drama from religion. The essential feature of Attic theatre was that it was *theatrical*.

Tragedy played *against* its affinities with mythology; that was the link between them. The urge to devise prize-winning twists impelled playwrights towards 'truths' never mooted until the advent of dialogue and the liberty of impersonation. In *Agamemnon*, Aeschylus invents slow motion: Cassandra's predictions prolong the tension preceding the death of Agamemnon (and of herself). Her morbid prescience is more chilling than Agamemnon's *omoi* scream or the *post mortem* report of the messenger.

The centre for the distribution of Grand Marnier is the village of Neauphle-le-Château (Seine-et-Oise), the place of exile whence the Ayatollah Khomeini set out to impress vindictive Puritanism on Iran. The French hoped to benefit from having given him asylum.

When he reached Tehran, the stocks of Grand Marnier, along with all alien liquors, were smashed or poured down the drain.

4.10.79. Allingham on Byron: 'He was a lord and he wrote vulgarly and that is why he was popular'. And why he would be now: there is something modern in B.'s rakish vulgarity. The English, in their solemn moments (of which academic criticism is a repository), cast regular aspersions on self-centredness. The abiding charge against Byron is immodesty: he exposed himself. 'Poor dear me' was his abiding topic. No modish dandy, he had to *be* the fashion rather than to follow it.

B.'s maiden speech to the House of Lords, in defence of the frame-breakers in Nottingham, paraded his dilettantism. His prompt departure on his travels proved that he did not propose to live with the consequences of his trouble-making. Losing his parliamentary virginity too elaborately, he became a now familiar type: the yo-yo man, who plays the toff with the common people and the maverick with the quality. He reconciled his contra-dictions by being an actor who starred in his own show-off. Hence his emulous admiration for the flashy Edmund Kean, who generated indoor lightning. Regency audiences, like today's, expected genius to radiate both virtue and vice. Byron was never the type of mannequin that Brummell was; unlike the dandy, he actually did something. Yet since his work vaunts himself, critics have had difficulty placing it. Iconoclast and icon, Byron challenges categorical formalities. He *was* a kind of revolutionary: the conservative kind.

His fugues and boasts articulated the mutability of human character. When he announced himself 'Turk, Jew' and all the rest, he embodied everyone in his one-man band. The desire for recon-ciliation (especially of Greek with Turk) was his noblest quality. Vulgarity was graced by magnanimity. The lame boy imagined himself straight. His peerage, his eroticism and his exile planked an unsteady platform from which he sought, skittishly, to put a lever under English society. The chanciness of entitlement and wealth (granted by inheriting Newstead) primed his sense of the absurd. The lapsed Calvinist experienced everything as a fall. B. revelled, woefully, in the comedy of physical degradation, baldness and loose teeth. His sense of being damned – which lent fascination to the three executions which he made himself witness in Rome – required that he put as good a face on his own impending end as a gentleman player could contrive. With panache to rival that of Sir Walter Raleigh on the scaffold, B. welcomed the surgeons ('Come on, you butchers!') who came to bleed him to death in Missolonghi. His facetiousness has a gallant deposit: it gives heart to fellow-prisoners in the condemned cell which is life.

5.10.79. The scorn with which Plato confronts Aeschylus might be taken, by René Girard, to suggest the former's dread of his double. The case for social stability was made in dramatic form by Aeschylus; by Plato in philosophical.

7.10.79. How little we hear of the acting qualities of Vivien Merchant now that Harold Pinter has left her! Combining intensity with lack of beauty, she seemed to possess some clever secret, of which H.P.'s departure has docked her. His presence *was* the secret. How nice that a cricket enthusiast has now selected a woman who boasted that she slept only with the first eleven! I know Harold only from casual encounters and from having supplied him with a small part in *Rogue Male*. It seems that he held his marriage with V.M. together for as long as he needed it to hold him together.

When the *arriviste* becomes the lover of a woman who has had many adventures, he believes that he has taken possession of her history, like a *nouveau riche* who acquires a mature garden.

The Muse. A writer does his best work when confined within a strict marriage to an unglamorous woman; his least good when free of the supposedly falsifying constriction of rectitude. Zola lost his aggravated sense of social horror and pity after he had left his wife for a much younger mistress.

13.10.79. I am waiting to hear of my father's death. He had a serious infection, brought about by the inept replacement of the catheter which came out last weekend. Now he has pneumonia. He was not expected to survive last night, but did. I have long argued (money my argument) that he should be allowed to spend his last months, or days, in his own home. What has been killing him is exile in that hopeless hospital. I said to Beetle, and it was an involuntary confession, 'I never really liked him'. But then he once said to me, 'We love you, but we don't like you'. He spent more time than he wanted in teaching me the games which he himself enjoyed: bridge and golf. He never cared to learn anything from me, even on topics of which he liked to proclaim my knowledge to others. He had a cold appreciation of the world, the result – was it? – of his humiliating and painful physical condition. Did he regard it as punishment for his sexual misadventure with Molly?

As a boy, I respected him as much as I feared him; as a man, the less I feared him, the more affectionately I behaved. If I came to love him, it was when he was weak and I was rich enough to stand free of his judgment. In the nine years since the accident in which he all but died, I have been careful to allude, with due tenderness, to what we had in common, bridge hands above all. Politics were rarely mentioned; literature never. Cedric was clever and foolish, considerate and obstinate, emotional and cold. He took no joy in nature. When he danced, he honoured the beat, not the music. He wanted Christians to be Christian because he believed, or hoped, that they would then be charitable. As for the 'truth' of religion, he was less sceptical than indifferent. He rarely chose to be outspoken. Irony was its only vestige, as when he spoke of Pat Cotter being '*almost* the nicest man in the world'. He became aware too late of missed chances: lying in the hospital, he talked of learning Italian, a language of gestures and flourishes which, at the best of times, he could never have mastered. It will be sad when he is no longer there, brave, dry and resigned. The shameful truth is that he is dying at an inconvenient moment, when I am beginning to move well into the new novel, *After the War*. Shall I remember all his good qualities when he is dead? I should like to think so; but his virtues are mediocre: never violent or cruel, he encased Irene and me in suburban security. He wanted to be a good man, but he had to deny his own history in order to stay principled. His wish to be 'right', in the antique dealer's sense, turned him into a fake.

16.10.79. About three in the morning, 'he stopped breathing'. He timed it well; we shall be able to do all that is necessary and be back here at the end of the week. Stee will not miss more school than suits him and I shall be able to give another week to the novel before I head for NYC, San Francisco and LA. The dryness of this report is a reflection of my dry eyes. I cannot weep again for what was pitiful nine years ago and grew pathetic. He hated the Hospital for Incurables, the condition that took him and the circumstances that kept him there. He saw the light dying, but never summoned the force to rage. Death cancels his faults; we are left with a sense of his misfortunes. They began in the 1920s, with naïve belief in Teddy Schlesinger, whose surgical skills would gain him a knight-hood, many years after his apprentice ineptitude had wrecked his friend's life. As a result, Cedric endured frequent surgery and dilatations without self-pity. His consciousness was dominated by his urinary tract. He suffered years of pain and apprehension until Dr Johannsen's 'miraculous' repair of his urethra in the 1950s.

31.10.79. In the Michel Ange Houasse[1] show at the Grand Palais: a small painting of the drawing school, a nude model with his hand supported in a deictic gesture by a rope hanging from the raftered ceiling. Another nice image: Goya's Duchess of Alba, wearing a red sash, attended by a poodle at her feet, wearing a red bow around his left hind-leg.

13.11.79. Cedric was cremated on Thursday, the 18th of October. I never saw the body. I remember him in intensive care in Chertsey, swollen almost beyond recognition, on the night of the accident which tipped him into that long decline. I shed a proper tear when the Rabbi spoke in the little interdenominational set at Putney Vale cemetery. I used to cycle past the gates as a wartime schoolboy. Several people came to the funeral, although little is left of the family. I knew only Margaret Piesse and Jon Kimche, small and frail, soft-spoken, alert and charged with wary vitality (he is, among other things, a Swiss citizen). The Rabbi, David Goldberg, from the Liberal synagogue in St John's Wood, was an Oxford man (Lincoln, and no friend, it seemed, of John Patrick Sullivan, who was Dean there for a while). He pronounced the Hebrew so that its unintelligible generalities composed a verbal shroud. They rendered death a clean and universal condition; neither blessing nor affliction. I had asked him to remark on Cedric's habit of loyalty which he did in unaffected style. In private, he had something of the garrulous neatness of Freddie Ayer.

Goldberg was assisted by Mr Foreman, a weighty, bearded person who dealt regularly with funerals. He plays rugger for the Rosslyn Park third team. He told me that they were burying Leslie Grade that afternoon and perhaps overdid his lack of solemnity by observing that that was *really* name-dropping. He was very British; we were spared the feeling that, *en route* to Gehenna, Cedric had been delivered into the hands of funny foreigners. Some of the Gentiles in the congregation were so impressed by the beauty of

---

1 Michel Ange Houasse (1680–1730) was a French painter, most of whose career was spent at the court of Philip V of Spain, who summoned him to the court in Madrid in 1715.

the service that they stole the prayer books, for which they were pardoned by the Rosslyn Park forward. Adie Tutin, now eighty, announced as she got out of the car, 'I'm next!' We held a small wake at the flat, served by Beetle. The warmth of the gentle autumn day seemed to see Cedric off – oh those crematorium rollers! – under good, if vacuous, auspices.

13.11.79. Fine weather friends deserve more credit than they get. It is easier to like one's friends when they fail than when they succeed.

My American trip was less an adventure, more an absurdity; if positive things were achieved, none were achievements. I paid my planned visit to the Bantam offices. I could wish that there was a genuine rapport between me and Peter Gethers. I kept recalling that his mother runs a cookery course at *Ma Maison*, on Melrose Avenue in LA, the most overrated 'French' restaurant in the world. P.G. can hardly be blamed for his mother's dishes, but it is an uneasy omen so far as taste is concerned. The Bantam fraternity greeted me like the Messiah of the Week. It was, they said, unusual for them to publish an author whom they enjoyed reading.

The State of the Language. A day later, in San Francisco, I told the earnest English Speaking Union audience that the only thing that NY publishers were likely to commission was 'shit'. The Mark Hopkins hotel, at the top of cable-carless Nob Hill, is a thickset tower. Its cavernous conference room was filled with those prepared to pay over a hundred bucks to listen, for six hours a day for two days, to the 'presentations' of a panel of patronising and mostly unamusing experts. The British contingent had flown in thanks to Laker Airways. I met Raymond Quirk in the lobby on the eve of the big day, a neat, correct-looking and furious professor with a Crippen moustache. He had been on his way to a cocktail party in a smart suburb, but 'the fucking car broke down'.

The conference was opened by Ishmael Reed, a plump, moustachioed black poet, novelist and – what else? – professor. He spoke from a prepared text and at length. He accused and he lamented. His accusations were just and his lamentations righteous; but he was tedious and repetitious. He might have been presenting the treasurer's report for a very dull club. He was determined to be uncompromising in his demand that black writers be better treated by New York publishers. He lost me and he lost the audience. Finally a note had to be passed to Leonard Michaels, in the chair, from Christopher Ricks, who had secreted himself discreetly below the salt but knew when a pinch was needed.

The next speaker was Richard Rodriguez, a Chicano with a grand mahogany nose and a PhD. Reputed to be one of the most brilliant students his teachers had ever had, he expressed, with controlled passion, the anguish of the deracinated immigrant. Assimilation through school and college had been a process of graduated amputation. The nuns called him 'Richard'; his parents 'Ricardo'. He had been persuaded, with patience and generosity, to come over to the side that regarded his family as folkloric anomalies. He had the resigned clarity of someone falsely accused of a crime of which he is certain he will be convicted. It was difficult for an outsider to understand why he took it so signally amiss that Walter Cronkite[2] referred to his particular group as 'Chicanos' when that is how they speak of themselves. Is it analogous to a Jew's resentment when he is referred to as 'a/the Jew'? Rodriguez's well-phrased statement was oddly moving. Yet he was so isolated in his pain that he evoked more embarrassment than sympathy.

Leonard Michaels was next up. He is a short story writer and a professor of English. He said that when he told strangers of the latter activity, they always said, 'That was my worst subject'. And often their only one, I imagine, in view of the number of Americans who either study or teach it, or both at once. I sat at the long green-baized table, facing a thousand people, and wondered what the hell I should say when my turn came. Everyone else was equipped with notes and typescripts. Michaels gave the impression that, having come into academic office by administrative mischance, he feared lest one day he would be thrown back on his fictional talent. Pale and petitioning, he was a genteel Philip Roth, with no more than that naughtyish single volume, *Going Places*, to sustain his reputation and his confidence.

David Lodge, my neighbour, spoke after Ellen Hellerstein, a nervous, rather pretty 27-year-old, much younger than her age and on the verge of intelligent tears. She translates from Yiddish, which she learnt after being exposed to Donald Davie, who encouraged this 'regional' interest in her. Lodge is small, dark and Celtic-looking, like a refined J.P. Sullivan. He confessed to a tincture of Jewish blood, among other good things, and talked smart sense, in

---

2 A renowned American TV 'anchor' of whom my friend Joseph Epstein remarked, 'he had a face that only a nation could love'.

equally small measure. I was pitched quite promptly into frankness. Meaning no offence, I succeeded in offending Ishmael Reed by talking about Jews in New York publishing and how Jews, the outcasts *par excellence*, had somehow succeeded in crossing into the other camp. Doubting the value of the subsidies which Reed craved, I remarked that shit was more commonly and more richly commissioned than anything else. My petty impropriety was the first to be uttered during the long, tedious proceedings. When I followed it with a few sketchy imitations, I was accused of being a Shakespearian actor and accorded so rapturous a reception that I considered briefly declaring myself a candidate for the presidency. I asked them, during my number, please not to applaud too quickly and unanimously, since this led me to fear that I might have said the wrong thing. They loved it.

When the discussion was thrown open to the floor, an early speaker was a blind Catholic priest, whom I wished was sighted. I did make a mild, justified attack on the Church in a subsequent symposium (no drinks served), to which he replied with a cloying attempt to combine forthrightness with the all-embracing prayer that we 'love, live and give'. Raymond gave me his quirky smile.

I asked later what Richard/Ricardo did, since I had lost my brochure. I presumed that he was teaching somewhere. 'No,' I was told, 'he's a gigolo.' There was such dignified reproachfulness in his anguish that making love for money seemed an appropriate trade. Locked in articulate solitude, he could escape only by some act of intimate heartlessness. He lacked the muscle to be a pimp, with all the risks involved of keeping his girls and his territory, but the servicing of, presumably, white ladies made whores of them, without requiring him to take a businesslike stake in the world. That so brilliant a man should put himself on the streets (without having to go outdoors) seemed suddenly plausible.

Marina Vaizey looked almost young, still bulging, but with a shiny new face. She was emboldened by the presence of her brother, Peter Stansky, a professor of history at Berkeley; smug, belly-cosy, middle-European, never as slickly mid-Atlantic as her ladyship. Marina's pretentiousness is on a diet: she works to keep it light. She has achieved the American Jewish female's dream of being at once career-girl, mother, celebrity (of a negligible kind) and a Lady, if never a princess. We dined with Karlinski and some of the symposiastic audience, including a girl with great tits and the dress to advertise them. Her pneumatic presence passed unspoken comment on the whole middle-aged, middle-American occasion.

I was pursued by a nice LA woman, married, who worked for a TV company and looked remarkably like Beetle.

16.11.79. The highlight of the gala dinner, for which I had carried my dinner jacket halfway round the world, was a speech from Alistair Cooke. He performed impeccably, and not a bit better than that. He made some excellent jokes I should certainly always remember, had I not forgotten them. Grey and groomed, he catered to the taste of his audience. There is something depressing about the admiration one cannot withhold from those whom one does not at all admire.

There was a long line at the United Airlines check-in for LA. Only two clerks were on duty. I remarked to my neighbour that this was 'rather curious'. He said, 'Oh too rather spiffing, what?' 'Listen, mac,' I said, 'if you want to make something of it, we can always do that.' My American accent, praised by Dick Cavett no less (John Simon would say 'no fewer' perhaps), was quite effective. The guy never spoke again until we were past the desk. It took a long time. As well as the rest of his luggage, the man ahead of us was dragging three hunting guns in what looked like individual golf-bags. The clerk was Chinese, slow, correct and inflexible. The guns, he said, had to be checked through separately and could not go on our flight; they would follow later. The big, red-faced hunter had a 150-mile drive after he had landed in LA and asked for the guns to be waved through; who would ever know? The clerk said he would lose his job. The hunter pleaded; he insisted; he appealed. He asked the clerk please to be a good guy, and a pal. The clerk would have liked to be a good guy, and a pal, but the rules were right there in black and white; he could not contravene them in front of the whole airport. The guns had to go separately. The argument was long and so was the queue. The hunter had to yield, but he also had to lose his temper: 'You stupid asshole!' A woman called out, 'We've been waiting a long time.' 'You can go to hell, lady.' The hunter stormed away, only to return, soon afterwards, to supervise the loading of his armoury into foam-lined cardboard containers.

Ron Mardigian met me at LAX and lent me his black Alfa Romeo Veloce for my two days in town. 'Nice car you've got,' someone called out to me when I was on my way to Factor's for lunch with the Weissbourds on the Saturday. Over hot pastrami, Burt and Kathy were happy at the prospect of their imminent child. K. is not Jewish. The Weissbourd family consoled themselves with the observation that 'she looks Jewish'. Kathy's family were equally uneasy, but when they met Burt's mother, they too were somewhat consoled. 'Is she Jewish too? She *is*? Well, she doesn't look Jewish.'

Ron and Merle live on Las Palmas, down in Hancock Park, the flat area of 'old' LA between downtown and Beverly Hills; once an enclave of Wasps, its real estate values are now menaced by prosperous blacks. The house, beige stucco, in no way advertises the talents of Merle, an interior decorator who has her office in a little guest-house across the large bricked patio behind the house; no pool for the Mardigians; they do a lot of power-walking, salutary stones in their backpacks. They are having their bedroom enlarged, so the roof was off a quarter of the house. The builder telephoned on Saturday, when I was waiting for my cab, and asked if they had put plastic on the rafters: it looked like rain. They hadn't, so he came by a few minutes later, in a Cadillac, to take care of it.

Dinner at Giuseppe's, the new in-place run by the chef whom Leslie Linder lured away from Scandia for his ill-fated London Club, where you 'got the best lunch in town, but which was torpedoed by its own pretensions. Leslie insisted on people not coming in unless they were wearing collars and ties; so they didn't come in. The place now resembles a terracotta-tiled set, tricked out with plush chairs and flocked walls and cute sculpted forms. Giuseppe sat down at our table so often that I should not wonder if Ron had to pay a cover charge for him.

Thanks to Fox, I flew home first-class. My benchmate was Harold Vance, banking consultant, specialist in mergers. He came from Marina del Mar and kept a power boat; nearly sixty, tall, creased and lean, an ex-lieutenant-commander USN and then a professor at Harvard Business School until he decided to get rich. He was flying to Hamburg to merge some people. Aloof, ruthless and conservative, he liked his juniors to wear suits and ties and for the women in the office to sport bras; he didn't like them to 'jiggle'. He was used to being obeyed. His sense of responsibility towards his staff was compounded of duty and contempt. A bully who never raised his voice, a proponent of fair play, provided the dice were loaded in his favour, he was certain that Great Britain was 'finished', although he liked the English and respected their best brains. British industry was beyond redemption. The US was still the most efficient manufacturing nation. He could promise me that the dollar would recover.

The energy situation was not a serious threat to the future; there was enough gas available in the shale of the state of Colorado alone to last another hundred and twenty years at the present rate of consumption. The problem was ecologically acceptable exploitation and that was being licked right now by a process that could bake the ash into bricks and allow its practical re-use as foundations. As for the mid-East, there was always 'the 50,000 marines solution'. And what was that? Sending 50,000 marine advisers to Saudi Arabia to maintain oil supplies. What if the Russians would not allow such a neat answer to the Gordian knot? Might not they also have their eye on external sources of energy? 'That case, we'll split it with them 50/50.'

Mr Vance made no effort to be amiable, but he was being as amiable as he knew how. Careful with his diet and his investments, he is determined to live as long and as well as he can. He has a sailing and fishing pal who had been dying of cancer but was pulled round by a dietician; he now lives on a diet of 'squash'. He brings bags of the stuff on board when they go in search of marlin. The squash has to be put in the bilge because it can't be refrigerated. Vance has two young sons. I suspect that he is one of those men who, capable of stringent premeditation, marry a young wife at the moment when they fear that they themselves are about to be no longer young. One can imagine him running a plan for murder through his Phoenix, Arizona computer in case it could come up with a flaw he had overlooked. He has a ruthlessness from which his own performances are not exempt. Hardness in such a man is a matter of vanity: fucking literally and metaphorically are much the same for him. There *is* a capitalist class capable of dispassionate brutality.

He likes expensive toys. His tennis racquet, of the latest design, he calls an 'investment'. He has bought a tract of land down towards San Diego on which he expects to make a killing. What concerns him most, and buoys him, is a conviction that the world's course can be charted, and influenced. Intelligent guessing and taking prompt advantage of other people's weaknesses are the means by which to remain his own, and the situation's, master. To be a capitalist is a continuation of military command by other means. He cannot force young men to join his firm, but once they have, they must observe a quasi-official code of conduct and honour the uniform of an officer of the organisation. Their first duty is to generate trust; how can they deceive people otherwise?

The arts have no interest for him; they demand discrimination and disinterestedness. Unless there is an advantage to be taken, he cannot see the point of anything. He may not have been an anti-Semite, but no one was ever going to take him for a Jew. Yet he was, in obvious respects, the very instance of what the anti-Semite believes a Jew to be: loyal only to his own profit and the cultivation of wealth. He was content for the majority to be committed to rock music, junk food and casual sex. He incarnated perennial values, those of cash.

Across the aisle was a Saudi Arabian broker in the aeroplane business. He complained, at length, of having been searched, *twice*, at New York, even though he was a brother-in-law of the Crown Prince. He wore a pointed tuft of beard and smoked incessantly. In good English, voice strident with the expectation of deference, he said that he was going to announce his mistreatment to the royal family and that they would arrange for incoming Americans to be humiliated at Riyadh. I advised him not to take it too badly; after all, I wouldn't be admitted to his country at all, however many times I consented to be searched. Consumed with aggrieved vanity, he ignored my amiable charge. He had told the customs man at Kennedy that he would make sure that he was fired from his job, but it had made no difference. The discovery that there can be functionaries who are not intimidated by well-heeled braggarts was all set to threaten the balance of the world's economy. Mr Vance shrugged off the Saudi's threats (this was before the Iranian seizure of the US's Teheran embassy). Listen, he was never going to send any of his people any place where Americans were not welcome.

To do the right things for the right reasons is no recipe for satisfaction.

Oliver Taplin[3] assumes that implicit in Aeschylus's text is preserved the French's Acting Edition, in which every exit and entrance is pre-ordained. Even if Aeschylus, as scriptwriter, supplied instructions for every step and syllable, his genius can be expected to evade any singular reading, including his own. Once in rehearsal, he was bound to spot opportunities for improved readings. The actor also has a part to play. A question for O.T.: were tragic actors talented?[4] If so, their skill had to affect the meaning, i.e. the playing, of the play.

---

3 In *The Stagecraft of Aeschylus* (1977).

4 At least one was: Nikias freed one of his slaves who had had a rapturous reception for his performance as Dionysos. His liberation evidently recruited the fans' votes for Nikias.

The tension, heightened by whether Agamemnon will agree to step onto the crimson carpet spread before him by his tempting wife, domesticates sacrilege. Much learned ink has analysed the 'ritual' source of Agamemnon's fatal step on the royal drugget. In practice, through the king's hesitation before yielding to his wife's obsequious request, the play creates a moral crisis within its own terms. Aeschylus anticipates Pinter's hermetic scheme: the 'meaning' of a play just is the tension generated on the stage. Since its words and actions have no external sources, the audience is denied the digestive comfort of interpretation.

England is in another retrospective convulsion about 'security'. 1930s Cambridge is being scrutinised for signs of original sin. I suspect that the Apostles' homosexuality was less the means by which they were recruited (by impressive older men) than the fuel of their recklessness. They already lived an illicit life. Duplicity had long been both a social habit and an ingredient of their pleasure. To turn Red and deceive the prudish bourgeoisie for *moral* reasons was an additional spice. The sole visible and audible consequence was the amusing tartness that issued in 'camp'. What better cover for serious treachery than exhibitionist facetiousness?

20.11.79. The long-faced responses of Anthony Blunt (making a 'Sir Anthony' of oneself is already part of the rhyming slang current in the BBC) are enough to convince most people that he has been hounded by prejudice. Nice people liked to believe him when he claimed that he passed secrets to the Russians only when they were our allies against the Germans. Trevor-Roper asked the punctual question: what did Blunt think he was doing between 1939 and 1941, when Russia and Germany were allies and when he already had access to secret material? One might as well ask what the secret service was doing in enlisting him, since – as Hugh Sykes Davies indicated yesterday – he had hardly hidden his Communist sympathies. Did he owe his recruitment to another sympathiser? Philby? It was a petty relief not to hear that any Jews had been involved, but then someone called Samuel Kahane was said to have been the paymaster of the gentleman agents.

A version of E.M. Forster's dictum is widely repeated: better to betray one's country than one's queen. The standard condemnation of Blunt's treachery forgets that certain brands of patriotism can be no less poisonous. How about the Foreign Office luminaries who dutifully (if not gladly) connived at the destruction of European

Jewry? A man may be as callous as he chooses, and retire with inalienable honours, provided he is never tempted to rectify the vices of the government he serves. Diplomats go abroad to lie for their country; a civil servant need not pack a bag before proceeding to the salaried humbug known as 'public service'. There are also instances when any decent person might wish to subvert the policies of his country. The vanity of Winston Churchill Jr and of Hugh Trevor-Roper is that neither can imagine a clash between the interests of the ruling class and their own predilections. When Labour was in power in 1945, Evelyn Waugh was not voicing the view only of the crackpot fringe when he claimed to feel as if he were living in an occupied country. The loathing expressed by such Tories, for an elected government, suggests that some of them might well find it possible, if not obligatory, to do as the French Right did in 1940: betray their allegiance in order to confirm it.

A list is said, by Henri Amouroux, to exist of Englishmen who had either agreed to collaborate with the Nazis or could be expected to do so. Its publication (postulated fictionally by George Sims in *The End of the Web*) might balance the minds of those who would have us think that all pre-war treason was Moscow-oriented. When the fascist dictators offered practical rewards for defection and delation, there was no shortage of outstretched palms. Blunt's conscience was only more refined than that of the Londonderry clique whose biographers have creamed and sugared its defeatism into delectable British eccentricity.

Ted Heath is now regarded with sorry admiration on all sides of the House. Although the policy of the Thatcher government could as well be his, he is plummy with *Schadenfreude* at its ineptitudes. The discrediting of each party in turn, after up to five years in office, has led to the sporting alternation which is the pride of the democratic system. If the present government fails before the electorate forgets its predecessor, mayhem may replace the masochistic amnesia in which the British like to bask. Should the Labour Party be led by Tony Benn (disclosed, Tony King told us, by the polls as the least trusted politician in the country), voters may hanker after some strange gods. Is Roy Jenkins due for a comeback? He is too educated, and too fruity a Common Marketeer, to be a likely *rassembleur*.

22.11.79. In May we received a desperate letter from Harry and Charlotte, saying that they were going broke. H. had been looking for work in Barcelona and Madrid, but they did not know what they were going to do. I sent them a thousand dollars. They should call, reversing the charges, if they needed more. Meanwhile, I suggested that Char should regard the $1,000 as the basis of a commission for a pottery wall-hanging. We sent her the dimensions of the empty space above the fireplace in the Lagardelle kitchen. My intention was to avoid seeming charitable. It did not occur to me that I was entering into a contractual commitment. I did, however, tell them that I was very busy in the movies; I could afford my petty generosity. I must have left the impression that they could ask whatever seemed good to them for the finished product. They proposed to visit us for a fortnight (their anglicised term) at the end of August in order to instal it.

When we were in New York in June, Lee Friedlander guessed the wall-hanging would never be completed. In early August, C. called from Mijas to tell us that the clay had cracked in a freak hot wind in the days before it was due to be fired. They would have to postpone their trip. Lee's forecast seemed to be fulfilled. However, the next batch of clay dried all right. The firing was a success. They now wanted to come in mid-September, when Stee was due to begin a new term at Belvès and would be unavailable to play with their children. We managed to postpone their visit without seeming graceless.

After a while, a letter came from C. concerning the terms of acquisition of the sculpture. She hummed and whored and then asked for $8,000. Beetle could not believe her eyes and read the sum for $4,000. I had just resigned from the tripartite Katzka project and had lost my golden allowance. How could such a sum be asked for a wall-hanging destined for a kitchen in the Périgord? I should have flinched if its price had been attached to a fifth-century Attic vase. I replied that I had not intended to let myself in for a surcharge. I could not think it friendly that C. should continue with a piece so large (I assumed) that its price was going to exceed anything I ever had in mind. They can keep my money (they have done it before) and they can take their friendship and Charlotte's work elsewhere. They have for too long furnished my fantasy of an American couple with whom I could be unguardedly open. I have made a fool of myself with too many people, conscripting them into the Happy Few whom I needed and longed to join. Too eager to please, I have allowed myself to be divided, and ruled. I now realise that the middle ground is where they bury you.

When all passion is spent, there is always some small change.

25.11.79. Tom Conti has had a great success in New York. He took me to dinner at Elaine's, where smart people go to be seen and, I guess, to honour their diets in a showplace where not eating the food is no hardship. I lunched there ten years ago with Faye Dunaway, when I was going to direct her in *Guilt*. There are two long, narrow rooms, darkish walls brightened by muddy murals. The best moment is the one which procures you a table; it proves you have been recognised. Tom is recognised everywhere. Having waited a longish time for fame, he has got used to it quickly (everyone does). The second evening, we went to a preview of a play produced by his roguishly moustachioed patron, Manny Aizenberg, who is nothing like as much of a character as he is costumed to look. He was wary of me lest I might discourage Tom from becoming the tool of his ambitions, one of which is the not uncongenial wish to make Tom a fortune. The preview was of a play called *Devour the Snow*, a melodramatic slice of Americana about cannibalism during the trek to California. It was performed with amateurish obviousness which thumped the forgettable: 'That it should come to this!' Oh but it did! Without surprise or drama, confusing scandal with incident, full of terrible things that failed to terrify, protracted, humourless and deathy, the play was the lump's idea of tragedy. Tom knew how bad it was; tact required him to promise that it would be a hit. Manny had seen it at a 'workshop' and had been impressed. What except the subject of cannibalism can conceivably have left its mark? Afterwards, we went to Ted Hook's Backstage where entrance was even more restricted than at Elaine's. A pianist singer did his stuff and the host read the roll of celebrities in the place. We met up with Lucy Arnaz who is to be Tom's co-star in London when the Neil Simon musical *They're Playing Our Song* comes to town; a big, dark-haired, energetic, dull girl. They gave me a lift home in her limo.

30.11.79. I was re-typing *On the Black List*, on a sunny morning in a week of warm, still, blue days, when our neighbour Christiane Barat appeared at my door with a doleful face; full of dole indeed, since it is now two years since she borrowed 2,000 francs for a couple of weeks. I suspected that she was after some new subvention but her woe did not concern herself: our neighbour across the valley, the cheerful and *vaillant* Monsieur Lacombe, had been killed the previous evening. He was working with his son, Bernard, on the tractor, preparing the foundations of the big, new, ugly *hangar* which threatens to blight our view. Lacombe tried to adjust something while the machinery was turning at 2000 revolutions a minute. The button of his cardigan caught in the works and his arm was torn off and thrown across the field. He cried out and he was dead, almost before 21-year-old Bernard had time to cut the engine.

Lacombe was a short, cheerful man who used to shake our big walnut tree when it did not yet belong to us, bracing himself nimbly up there, legs splayed, and insisting on the nuts falling. He gave a football pitch to the village in 1978 and raised a scratch team of elders, including me, to play St Laurent's best. In a flat cap, a sleeveless vest and a pair of nylon drawers, he ran and ran in the August heat and the long grass, willing to be ridiculous, despite his lack of skill. I scored the only goal for our side. He came up regularly to Lagardelle in order to water his cattle from our *citerne*. He liked to go hunting with the men at the weekend, but we remember him with his wife, a handsome slim woman with a rectangular face, constantly in a good humour, as if she were recalling something that gave her pleasure. She brought us eggs at Easter. They seemed the most contented of the locals. Their broad meadows sloped gently to the valley bottom. They kept horses, although they had no use for them, because their beauty decorated the landscape. Even their cows shone. The family was integral to the Virgilian landscape. They were lucky and they knew it. Unlike the Barats, they had a son, Bernard, who was eager to learn the *métier* alongside his father. He was often warned of the dangers of working with tractors.

We went to the village church for the funeral. It was a cruelly fine autumn day. Three or four hundred people, dressed in their sometimes incongruous best: women in trousers, men in tartan shirts, Mexican-style cardigans, jeans. As the hearse came down from the house, there was a communal surge of pain and sympathy. He had been alive the day before yesterday. The death was an act of terrorism; people could not cope with it. We stood like penitents and intruders. The shuffling crowd followed the cortège into the church. The bell tolled. Friends and relatives shook hands without a smile. Outside the church, on the gravel slope down to the *mairie*, stiff leaves wore a border of whitish rime. The murmur of voices stilled, there was only the careful crunch of footsteps.

The family was already in the church. We did not see them. The white-surpliced priests went in. The service lasted a full hour. We stood in the golden cold. The waiting crowd outside lost its silent cohesion. Latecomers joined their friends. They lacked the solemnity of those who had been there since the beginning and produced the first, discordant, smiles. One pinched another behind the neck, a frivolity so habitual that it could not be restrained. We shook hands with our beastly little postman, a lonely figure in blue suit, brown shirt.

At last the ceremony ended. People who had been standing outside filed into the yellow-beige church, under the stone hoop of eroded carving, and came out again, saying or doing whatever people were supposed to say or do. Ritual lent dignity to conformity. They brought out the wreaths and the coffin. The flowers were lapped in a silk flag borne by mourners. The friends carrying the coffin included Norbert Barat. The family did not have to run the gauntlet of eyes. They must have gone through to the adjacent cemetery by the vestry door. The crowd was too great to fit in the walled enclosure. We waited against the church wall while the ceremony took place at the graveside.

Suddenly the son of M. Lacombe, a boy too tall for childhood, face halved, longitudinally, by the sideslip of his anguish, was carried, vertically, by his elbows, from the cemetery and hurried down the slope, a log of blanched agony, hair dislocated on his head like a replaced cap of lifeless stuff; the image of desolation. I was ashamed to witness such nakedness. I thought that he had been broken by a ceremony which others were having to endure even longer, but the rest of the cortège followed, down that trampled green slope, slipping and hurrying. Wrapped in mourning as if roused from sleep by some catastrophe, they were stunned by their common eviction from the ordinary. Madame Lacombe bore herself, and was borne, with silent, pale dignity. The daughters were as if floured, flesh the tone of uncooked pastry. As they came past, one cried out, 'C'est pas possible, c'est pas possible!' and then they were away towards the cars. I never saw anything so close that so clearly lent meaning to the word écœuré as those poor people went away to live with the impossible. Today in Sarlat, I saw it in the local paper: 'Un agriculteur tué à St Laurent-la-Vallée, happé par son tracteur'. Thus does one learn locutions françaises.

Christiane went into hospital for her long-awaited hysterectomy. Beetle said, 'If it weren't so awful to say it, I'd say that Christiane is quite upset that the Lacombes have stolen her thunder!' Tonight, a pale glaze of golden light falls like a heartless benediction across the valley. Skittish calves and pendulous cows stream up the green slope towards the Lacombe farmhouse.

At the Hotel St Albert in Sarlat there were smiles and bottles. A son has been born to Michel, the young *patron* who treats us with such generous good humour (we rarely fail to have a plate of asparagus slide in to supplement our *hors d'oeuvres*). His wife, Mireille, is beautiful: large, clear, well-set eyes, strong jaw, olive complexion, full, untinted mouth, skull distinguished by a strict hair-style. She could have modelled for Vermeer. She had been very big with her child and produced it three weeks early, luckily for her; he weighed seven pounds already, Thomas. As we drove back, we came upon another funeral, at a house at the crossroads by La Chapelle Péchaud where I called, during the summer, at 4 p.m., when they were still eating lunch, to ask for some water for Sarah, who was painting a water-colour in their field.

The 79-year-old Ayatollah is calling on young Iranians to prepare for war. The distinctness of our neighbours' pain contrasts with the indifference with which we observe horrors on TV. On the screen bad news is always good, in the sense that it is not near us. We watch a rapist shot in China. The trial has taken place in a sports centre. We could see the basketball lines. The Chinese are going to be admitted to the Olympic Games. The ringleader whom we saw shot in a field had taken part in 107 rapes; hardly a first offender. The execution was so callous that it seemed that some ultimate taboo had been breached; the unbearable was rendered entertaining. Compare the dismemberment of the family across the valley. The paper says that Bernard heard a bump, turned and saw his father being chewed by the metal. In China there is a new mood of 'de-liberalisation': the 'freedom wall' is forbidden to fly-posters.

2.12.79. The Brinsleys came to dinner last night. Beetle was in the kitchen most of the weekend. Amiable, voluble and appreciative, they arrived and left promptly. They have had a long painful time with their misshapen youngest child, Gloria; triumphal name for an ugly duckling with a golden cross hanging from her neck. They are less distressed by her than by their son, another Thomas, who is twenty-one, has a degree and is always at odds with them. It cannot be difficult. Meg is short, fat and over-made-up. She boasts of having come all the way to England from New Zealand by herself, quite as though she had emulated Captain Cook, although she was in her twenties and her place at RADA had already been booked. No actress, she now has silver-green eyelids and a RADA-modulated voice. She suspects that Tommy is sleeping with his French girlfriend in Norman's 'company flat'.

'Meg,' I said, 'sooner or later you're going to have to face the fact: everyone fucks.'

She and Norman have the idea that Tommy is searching for his 'identity' and is discountenanced by his father's success, as an accountant. They reproach the boy for being selfish and unhelpful, unlike his sisters who fit in so well with the household. Meg resents what has to be spent on them, which includes £1,100 (really?) on Penelope's flute. She likes to think of herself as 'enlightened' and scorns the complacency of those more complacent than herself. She was pleased to tell us that one of the local ladies in Royston had had her self-satisfaction punctured by the death of her son. 'They said of pneumonia, of course; no one mentioned *drugs.*' Her relish over a neighbour's bereavement would have been more apt if it had greeted the news that the boy had got a 2:1 instead of an expected First. 'Her life is completely shattered,' Meg said, quite as if her second-best tea set had fallen on the quarry tiles. There are many Catholics in their district. Meg asked one of them to lunch. In the prelude to sitting down (in the kitchen she had worked hard to clear up), Meg alluded to the courage of the Pope in taking a political stand in Ulster. Her guest was so distressed by this observation that she discouraged her hostess from putting the Grand Marnier soufflé in the oven. She then ate practically nothing. She goes to Mass every day, in the front row. A Catholic widow in the parish lives with a man called John. Someone saw her home after a party and John was asleep in her bed. He had had a few drinks. Gossip among the faithful held that he had been so drunk that he had not realised which bed he had fallen into. They chose to believe that the couple co-habited without having sex: 1979, in Royston.

5.12.79. My father would have been eighty today. A new member of the family arrived in the early hours: another daughter for Beetle's niece, Ruth. Had she had a son, my mother would doubtless have been offended if she had not called him Cedric. Loneliness bears down on Irene, even though she was often alone before, and by choice. She persuades herself that she has true friends in the Manor Fields widows who have only their financial waistlines to measure.

Stanley Donen asked if I would be interested in writing something for Diana Ross: a revamp of *Trilby*, say, or of *Camille*. I thought it unlikely, but I still thought about it. What about a photographer, call him Quinn, with a New York office and a plain secretary. He has decided on a life without attachments, feeding off the world without leaving teeth-marks. One day, after a fashion shoot in Chicago, he happens to meet a beautiful black girl at the airport. Fog has led to postponements and he decides to rent a car, dammit, and drive. The girl (Naomi?) is anxious to get to NY, so he offers her a lift. Quinn tells her how his parents were killed in an auto smash when he was twelve years old. Since then he has kept an eye on the world but never belonged to it. The police saw the boy covered with his parents' blood and assumed that it was his. He heard them say, 'They're all dead in there for Chrissake.' He watched them, open-eyed, as if it were true. Then he blinked and they pulled him out. Quinn (we never know his first name, as if he didn't know it himself any more) and the black girl have to drive slowly through the fog. Maybe they witness an accident. Quinn realises that they are going to have to stop. He turns off the main road and they check into a motel. They take separate rooms but wind up sleeping together. They make love with such abandon that it has to be, he tells her, that they need each other in that cold world. 'Yeah?' 'Look out the window, willya?' 'Like for what?' When they get to New York, he says 'When do I see you again?' She says, 'You don't.' She gets her kicks, so she tells him, picking up guys and fucking them. 'But...' 'What?' Quinn cannot believe that he has been summarily dumped (although he has done the same thing to quite a few women). He decides to forget her. He can't. He tries to get in touch, but who is she, Naomi? It seems like it has to be just one of those things.

Some time later, checking his messages, he finds one that asks him to call a number. It's Naomi. She wants to see him again. Again they make love. Quinn cannot believe that it doesn't 'mean something'. Once again she disappears without telling him how to get in touch. But some clue (he looks in her pocket-book maybe) enables him to discover that she is being kept – like a stolen masterpiece – by a rich man, of amiable ruthlessness, who will not allow her out of his possession. It could be that, a few years earlier, Milton (say) was her producer in a singing career; but it would be too obvious, and rob her of her mystery, if she had made a serious name. Better if she's been a singer in a louche club; a beginner who made trial discs only, and was then acquired by her protector. She imagined that she would use him and then ditch him, but there was something about being possessed that reassured her, just as treachery does, from time to time. Milton is pimp and sugar-daddy (cocaine his candy). He makes her feel safe, especially when she can cheat on him, a little. This time, she tells Quinn, is different because of what she feels for him, or likes to have him think she feels. Milton has made it a rule that she can fuck other men, but only one time each; and she has to tell him the details (when she does, that's when we realise the rule). Does she embroider? She just may. Quinn is the best, or so she enjoys saying.

When Milton finds out (or does she tell him?) that she has seen Quinn more than once, Quinn gets a call: 'You don't know me, but I'm your best friend, if you're smart.' As requested, Quinn goes to a bar and, in the stipulated corner, he sees a man wearing shades. He goes up to him and says, 'I think you have a message for me.' The man takes off his sunglasses and looks up at Quinn with blind eyes. 'See what he can do to people?' Quinn cannot accept that his beloved belongs to someone else. What kind of a man can impose his will like that? Naomi is frightened when Quinn refuses to lay off. Convinced that Milton is going to have him killed, she comes to the big scene where – to persuade Quinn to give up – she swears that her passion for him was a fraud. His claim to love her is, she tells him, just a cover for sexual inadequacy. 'Come on!' Quinn says. 'Oh,' she says, 'you thought you were good? That was because I was. Faking it.' She says that he doesn't really want her: 'Who really and truly wants to grow old with a black woman?' She makes herself as hateful as she knows how, but he tells her he wants her no matter what, if only because... He won't live without her. 'And you sure as hell won't live with me.' Maybe she simply can't make up her mind. He guesses that she can do without the luxury Milton supplies, but not the excitement. Has there been a man killed, much earlier, one of her casuals, about whom she feels guilty? She and Quinn part, inconclusively. She says she will call him at a certain hour, 'or as near as dammit', if she has decided that she wants to be with him. He waits. The precise hour passes. He is in his darkroom (aha!) when the telephone rings. The pictures in his 'bath' are ones that he 'stole' when she was asleep in the motel. The phone rings and rings. Why does he not go? We realise, he realises: he cannot quite bring himself to a commitment which might mean death. The phone remains unanswered. The images in the 'bath' bleach to nothingness. His life is blank. She sings one of her old songs over the ghost she has become.

The end of Romance comes when lovers are sure that they want each other, but not so sure that that is what they really want. Naomi is an orphan because 'black girls sing or dance or they're nothing'. It is important that, when the girl seems determined to break out, she 'accidentally' leaves clues so that Milton can follow and recapture (and punish?) her. Her escapades enhance his sense of power over her; and hers over him. She wants to be free so that captivity can retain its spice. Her protector needs to be strong enough to take her against her will; she is willing to be his as long as she can. The movie could start with Quinn shooting pictures of a woman on a high ledge. Does he want her to jump or to save her? How about both? He could tell Naomi about the episode in the car in the fog. He'll never forget her face as she jumped. It won him a prize. Naomi: 'Am I supposed to like you?'

We do not for a moment fear that Allah is really great or that anything 'true' lies behind the Savonarolan rant of the Ayatollah. We feel no spiritual pressure whatever. Muslim intelligence is limited by a sacred text with no stronger claim to respect than the Book of the Mormons. No one need question the beauty of Islamic art and architecture any more than we doubt the beauty of the rose-window of Chartres.

Communism has ceased to be attractive, not because of the revelation of its crimes but because they are no longer likely to deliver the goods. As long as Marxism threatened to be victorious, the ruthlessness of its clerks confirmed its validity. Only those who are sure to be right are entitled to have no conscience.

What appals us in the cruelties of religion is not the amount of blood shed; it is the discovery that spilling it has procured no divine dividends. Bertrand Russell's assertion that he could have no objection to the extermination of the Jews, if he had proof that such a massacre would lead to an earthly paradise, displays precisely why he *is* a Christian.

Refusal to admit that the world is all there is to the world has been the primer of man's ascent and the cause of his fall. Belief in belief as a form of higher intelligence is the source of Art and of Auschwitz.

When he sees the strength and cohesion of a credulous mob, Western man is torn between aversion and envy. Such envy is fatuous; the fracture of social unities is essential to a life worth living. There is nothing more exemplary in the fanaticism of the

Teheran mob than in the self-sacrificial gullibility of the inhabitants of Jonestown.

Hannah Arendt's attempt to show that 'the Jews' actively exacerbated the hatred of the Germans and others is calculated to preserve the scheme of cause and effect in the face of barbaric anomie: better that the world should continue to have a logic than that the Holocaust should not be 'somehow' the Jews' own fault.

The French may still fear the Germans, but they appear free of resentment. Whatever crimes Hitler's men committed, and despite the humiliation they inflicted, France was not for very long taken away from the French. The degradation of 1940–44 has been expunged by the myth of the Resistance and by the canonisation of the undefeated de Gaulle. The French have taken more revenge on the Americans and the British than on the Germans. They find it easier to embrace their enemies than to forgive their friends.

The worst thing said about Iran in the Western press during the Shah's regime was that it was unwise to drive a private car, especially a conspicuous foreign one, along the desert highways between the great sites. Iranian truck-drivers had the habit of driving deliberately into foreigners' cars, crushing them in the ditch and then robbing their passengers, often leaving them to die, if they were not dead already.

Platonic Dialogue. A post-tutorial conversation between a tutor and a 'twenty-year-older', about the latter's sexual and emotional problems. The tutor is a man approaching sixty; he is in love with the young man, who has no notion that such a distinguished and elderly academic could have desires anything like his own. His pupil puts the older man through hell without having any sense of how wounding his confessions are. The term 'twenty-year-older' derives from Gilbert Ryle's *Plato's Progress*, an unlikely *jeu d'esprit* which argues for Plato's development from the advocate of the Theory of Forms into a proponent of scientific speculation to which overarching metaphysics was irrelevant. Ryle postulates that Plato was arraigned for 'defamation' in 370 BC and that he agreed to abandon 'eristic' tuition in return for immunity. Ryle detects a coherent pattern in the whole of Plato's *oeuvre* by predicating an event for which, so far as I know, he has no text. Who but a registered pundit would dare to claim that Plato was taken to court for his contentious methods, when no source can be cited to show that such a prosecution was ever mooted?

'Can virtue be taught?' At the end of his academic studies, the young man thanks his tutor for proving that it is possible to distinguish specious from cogent argument, true character from its counterfeit, love from lust. The tutor has fostered the vanity of a young man who, in return, insists on wishing virtue on a man who wishes only that the twenty-year-older could perceive the desire and assuage the frustration which has made his teacher so sublime an influence. The latter would be glad to cash his pupil's gratitude for a single embrace. Such a proposal is beyond him; if he indicated, however politely, what he really wanted, he would (he fears) no longer qualify for even an abrupt handshake.

8.12.79. Juliana was thirty-nine in the autumn of 1959, when we were first in Fuengirola; vivid blue eyes, lean body enclosed in loose cotton; flesh slackening, beauty leaving her; and she knew it. Hans was three or four years younger. He had spent the war in Holland, under the assumed name of Johannes Piron. He confused being in the Resistance with stealing coal; but he did survive, which was indeed resistance, of a kind. He and Juliana must have married soon after the defeat of the Nazis; in 1960, their pretty, blonde daughter Claudia was already eleven. Hans took photographs of her naked and was pleased to show them around. Juliana's father was a German industrialist who had distanced himself both from the Nazis and from Germany. Living in Buenos Aires during the losing years, he escaped sanction when the Allies took over the German economy. He made himself useful to Juan Perón and so redeemed and amplified his fortune. Displeased when Juliana decided to marry a Jew, he cut her off without a pfennig. By the time we met H. and J., his aversion had abated to the point of lavishing presents on Claudia, which served to open, and widen, a breach between the girl and her father.

With his foppish bohemianism, his shampooed head of greying hair, embroidered shirts and courtly hand-kissing, Hans put on a handsome show which gave him some success with some women, despite being boss-eyed. His buffoonery stopped just short of clowning. As a professional translator, he took solitary fishing trips, to the Frankfurt Book Fair in particular, in order to drum up trade. Since Juliana had a young son, Juani, as well as Claudia, and little money, she stayed in Fuengirola when Hans went on the road. She suffered from asthma (the objective correlative of guilt over the gas which her father's company had manufactured?) and needed prompt oxygen in case of a severe attack. She and Hans lived next door, in the Calle Tostón, to Larry Potter, who also suffered from asthma and later died of heart attacks provoked by it. When Hans went to Frankfurt that October, Juliana went to bed with Larry. We were furtively scandalised. I could not see why the rather 'aristocratic' Juliana should want to sleep with Larry, although now it seems obvious: she would not go towards her father by leaving Hans, but she was chagrined by the latter's 'flirts'. How about she took revenge on the Jew by sleeping with a black man?

We were very nice to Larry, but I was not above thinking that it was very nice of us. Clever, well-read, a graduate (of Cooper Union), he was gallantly alone in his black solitude. Another inhabitant of our street was Paul Hecht, the poet son of a New York hack-driver. Paul was teaching himself Spanish and the guitar. He lived with a black girl. I asked Larry what she did. He said, 'Joan? She sleeps a lot.' After we had left Fuengirola in 1960, Larry went to Paris and became involved with *Négritude*; a character in Jimmy Baldwin's *Another Country* is clearly based on him. In Spain, he had had no interest in being black; he told us that he had more in common with Juan Gris than with African sculpture or Harlem. From Paris, he wrote to Harry Gordon that he was 'flat on his black ass'. He died not long afterwards.

13.12.79. The Literary Department of *The Sunday Times* is haunted by the ghost of its ousted headmaster, Jack Lambert. His exhortations to middlebrow mellowness continue to flavour the book pages. Exiled to a back office, he has been dubbed 'Chief Reviewer'. None of his quondam Indians care to know him. *School Play* might as well have been about a newspaper. The same jockeying for position and rank, the same urge to displace others in order to advance oneself, always for proper reasons, can be found in Thomson House as in any public school. The most effective way of depicting the Arts Department would be for its inmates to be played by schoolboys. Is J.W.L. monster (and comic) enough to hold the centre of the stage? Even at his sniffiest peak, he was in thrall to the unseen figure of arts supremo Leonard Russell. He was also somewhat overawed by those senior reviewers – Cyril, Raymond, Harold, and the others – who commanded space and by-lines. Only after their demise did he become redundant: he was no longer the keeper who alone had the knack of throwing accurate sops to difficult lions. Who could have guessed, from

Jack's articles, that such a lover of the comic muse was, in person, crusted with grievances and dragged down by fear of having missed something? Eternal verities provide no happy substitute for the meretricious.

John Peter was sure that his ascent had been blocked by Jack's public school narrow-mindedness. When Jack was ousted, J.P. was prompt to foster the promotion of John Whitley to his chair. This démarche, which I seconded, in handwriting, was a success. Once Jack's tenure had ended, however, the protective effect of his condescensions was revealed. J.P. discovered that there were worse kinds of petty authoritarianism than that of a head-prefect on the verge of superannuation. Within a short time, J.P. was given no place in the new broom closet. The period of the paper's closure[5] was inopportune for him: the journalists had nothing to do except to play musical chairs within the confines of the dormant paper. Offered free courses in any language they cared to study, not one of them accepted the chance. The energy dispersed in producing and editing copy went into manoeuvring for power. John Whitley had no need to play politics; being straight served him better than deviousness. The Arts Department pack was reshuffled in order to accommodate *la* Tomalin, about whom Harry Evans continued to feel guilty, on account of having sent Nick to his death on an assignment he had no wish to undertake. As for Claire, how mourning became her! She assumed the literary editorship trailing a coterie of chums, such as John Coleman, whose appearance scarcely rejoices me. In her *petit train*, a fresh *clientela* jostles for preferment. What professor does not yearn to lower himself to the base prints?

John Peter never guessed that Harry Evans might be the source of the querulousness which Jack Lambert relayed, in mitigated form. Jack referred to John P. and John Whitley as 'my boys'. In his treacherous way, he was loyal to them. Every replacement of the old brigade issues in the rise of upstarts more ruthless than those whom they displace. John P. was particularly stricken when James Fenton, a left-wing political columnist, and a poet already, parachuted in to replace Bernard Levin as drama critic. The latter presumed that he owed an explanation, *urbi et orbi*, of why he was absconding after only three years, quite as if the readers had

---

5   *The Sunday Times* was closed for several months in the late 1970s while the new proprietor, Rupert Murdoch, fought the print unions in a stand-off which ended with the capitulation of the latter.

been counting. As Bernard's understudy, John P. cherished the conviction that he would be the replacement. He misunderstood the usage: however applauded a stand-in's performance, a star always replaces a star. Fenton made an inauspicious beginning. Punchy opinions have little impact when expressed in weak prose (quite a habit with poets). F.'s faltering debut is unlikely to lead to the elevation of J.P. A witness had better have some leverage if he hopes to derive an advantage from seeing his boss get it wrong. What validates J. P.'s resentment also damages his prospects.

14.12.79. Charles Snow's sponsorship, viewed from *outre mer*, appeared to offer his *protégé* every chance of Cambridge eminence. In the event, G.'s brilliant prospects were dimmed by the dislike many felt for his sponsor. Rejection has scarcely dumped him on Lemnos. Who else would continue to be loudly wounded after being relegated to one of the most conspicuous professorships in Europe?

The success of *School Play*[6] tempts me to the rich subject of today's Bedales. Its inversion of values is mordantly modern: adult pupils, childish parents. The pupils are sophisticated and *dégagés*; the staff ill-paid and ill-favoured, apprehensive of the Press and of the consequences of the 'progressiveness' which was the fundamental *raison d'être* of the school. Today's parents expect academic results. They cleave, furtively, to the bourgeois values from which they are paying to liberate their offspring. The recent selection by the governors of Mr Nobody as headmaster is symptomatic of a regression in English society at large. His fawning on the princess and her children, when they arrived as pupils, was a perfect paradigm of the paperbacked snobbery of the 1970s. The declaration that he had 'always wanted to do this for a princess', as he lit Princess Margaret's cigarette, speaks for the wetness of the wet dreams of the clerks of today. Bedalians were prescient concerning the effect of the Royals' arrival: they guessed that, regardless of their specific

---

6 Despite memorable performances by Michael Kitchen, Jeremy Kemp, Denholm Elliott and Jenny Agutter, *School Play*, in which adult actors played the parts of overgrown schoolboys, was not regarded with good humour by the bosses of BBC television. When the producer pressed for it to be shown again, he was told that those in charge were well aware that it was a satire on the Corporation itself. In fact, my only conscious target was the Charterhouse I had known between 1945 and 1949. Some caps fit a surprising number of big heads.

personalities, they would, by their well-known presence, pervert the tenor of the school. The curiosity of the Press, its avidity for silly stories, made everybody anxious and unnatural. The unassuming show which the Princess and Snowdon mounted could not survive the welcoming compliments paid to them.

After the War. In the school section, Marsden should be a senior boy with covert homosexual and overt scholarly ambitions. He is attracted to Fairfax when the latter becomes one of the persecutors of Reiff, a red-haired refugee delivered to cruel asylum among the English. Fairfax is a curly-headed scamp who likes to run short singles. Marsden lacks his attractive devil. He is ungainly and 'only just' a member of the cricket house team, despite being older than Fairfax, who keeps wicket and who opened the batting in his first year. Might Marsden have a tincture of Jewish blood, enough for it to be a remote secret which weighs on him, even though it would scarcely excite the attention even of the Gestapo? He could harbour an embarrassing memory of a childhood visit to some strange stamp-collector in Streatham, who wore a black skullcap. The persecution of Reiff excites his sympathy and his disgust. Marsden wants to save the victim and yet he is excited by his victimisation. It is now that the idea of 'taking out' Fairfax occurs to him. He is enchanted by the boy's freckled grin and almost wishes (oh almost!) that he, not Reiff, could be the target of that blithe devil. Marsden, at seventeen, is apt to be enslaved by his junior. Fairfax has a sense only of the social opportunities and power which such a friendship might offer. Marsden's attention immunises Fairfax and thus gives incidental protection to Reiff, whom he dares not openly support. Conniving at the persecution which he imagines he would like to forbid, Marsden draws off one of the hounds of Reiff's hell, if only to make him his pup.

In school rules, the penalties for 'love' are more severe than those for hatred. Love separates lovers from other people; hatred is a team game. The persecutors of Reiff run no risk of sanction; only those who dare to find each other in desire are in danger. The ambition of the headmaster, like that of Bags Birley, to qualify for elevation to a grander school could be the clinching reason why Marsden is not expelled for loving Fairfax: it might get into the Press.

With little faith in his physical charm, Marsden has the brainy man's belief that subterfuge must play a part in getting what one wants. Unabashed desire is monstrous. A narcissus with mud in his pool, Marsden is as thrilled and appalled by himself as he can be enraptured by others. He likes to detect corruption because he senses it so strongly in himself. He might be disappointed when the chaplain fails to make an improper suggestion to him. To escape from self-disgust he needs the world to be foul.

The affair between the boys is in counterpoint to that between Pierrette and the *collabo* doctor in wartime Annecy. There again, but at a much more dangerous level, the enchantments of cruelty are at work, and play. That Pierrette should be discovered to be still in the doctor's power, long after the Liberation, balances Marsden's wish at once to detach himself from Fairfax and to keep the other somehow in his trophy cabinet. That Pierrette has been a prisoner, obliged to sexual submission (and enjoying the freedom it entails) in order to save her skin, makes Marsden so ardent as almost to be her rapist. The parallel with Fairfax (who, for Marsden, is a delicious double for Reiff) is so sweet that, at the moment when he 'rapes' Pierrette, he hardly knows who he or she stands for, or even which sex she is: sex impersonalises.

What about the English girl, Gillian, whose 'purity' Marsden has so unkindly honoured and whom he finally marries, almost in apology for the 'wrong' which he has done her when she at last succeeds in seducing him? If one then uses Steiner's gossip and has the diary of Marsden's secret life bequeathed to Gillian, many years later, as a piece of loving persecution, the whole thing can become a work of some elegance: a confession on the part of the narrator that he has never been able to be the man Gillian has supposed, while all the time she has been wanting the man he could have been, if only he had not been with her. The whole story is at once a love letter and a savage assault.

On the Pontic Shore. A local remembers Ovid after his recall from exile has come, too late: 'He won't be all that sorry not to have to go back to Rome. He was a cheerful character, old Publius, and didn't he love it down here?'

Coming of Age. A man and his son; the man feeling old (after the death of his father), having himself a son of twenty-one, about to have an affair with a German girl. It is a moment when the older man tries to assess his life and pass on what he knows, whatever that is. This could be a continuation of *Orchestra and Beginners.* Leonard can be distinguished from Cedric by having the leverage of a little money to dispose of. Mark becomes involved with a nice girl before he goes to France and meets Pierrette. He is 'betrayed' to Leonard by his mother, who has always seemed to be 'on his side' but who panics at the prospect of his being 'tied' to a woman older than himself with a child of dubious origin ('I don't believe in rape'). M. drops Pierrette, with a sense of anguished exaltation ('At last I've let someone down!') and marries the suitable girl, whose qualities are greater, he finds, than he ever guessed in his first heartless assault. She, however, is too straight quite to suit him; he has in him a desire for pain and its uses. Anaesthetised by his English education, he muses on the delights of cruelty. His marriage is unendurably happy. He sleeps with another woman out of vanity; not caring makes him feel like a real man. His wife discovers it, through the concerned malice of a third party (nice if it was Reiff!) and takes her time and her revenge with an American who just might later become the second husband of M.'s sister, Nancy.

When, many years later again, Mark discovers that his father is a quite different man from the one against whose 'morality' he has fought all these years, he recognises that he has been justifying himself before the wrong judge and living the wrong life, at odds with what he has failed to read correctly. He considers leaving his wife and children and then, if he does, he realises that all along, and despite everything, something of true value has been created.

Why is it so dark in here? He asks the question with a brave little smile, eyes wet with hope for an answer other than the one they give him: 'It isn't'. The day is dark with this time of the yearliness. There is nothing wrong with the room. He doesn't listen to their answer, but then he wouldn't, in his condition. The room is blanked off from the old ballroom (this used to be a famous house). There is a common cornice egging and darting all along the ward wall. The room is a rectangular slice of this old wedding cake. He was in a bed diagonally across from a long old baby who lay flat, and stayed flat, in a railed cot, mumbling wordlessly; a junked machine that would never again make sense. There was no point in giving him a light, because he could not read, could not even acknowledge a visitor. 'Company for you, Mr Clyde.' But he never saw anyone. They could get a brighter bulb, but aren't things dear these days? He smiles with recognition, although he has never been in this room or this place before. He smiles like a small boy who is supposed to deserve what he is getting, but knows something his betters do not. 'Why is it so dark in here?' When has he asked or heard that question before? It is the question that people ask of lovers when they break in upon them, a couple for whom the long day has darkened imperceptibly because both have the other so fervently in vision that no common light is needed. The third person cannot see them when he comes in and brings his commonplace question with him, turnkey with a last breakfast, casually breaking dreams, clumsy kitchen-boy. He has asked this question and he has been asked it and that is a man's life. Has he asked it of his parents, coming in from games a little earlier than expected, blood on the stripes of his jersey? He has known the answer even as he asks the question, even as he knows the answer here: this is where they have brought him to die. They know that he knows the answer, the little old new boy who is lucky to have this room, which isn't really dark at all. He has asked the question before, coming into dark laughter after business and finding that refugee doctor there, and his wife, and everything quite as it should be, no hurried movement, but the room quite sightless and the pair of them in the window looking out at the serried city. They blinked and laughed when the light went on and darling, it was him, so early, isn't that nice, and he knew he had been excluded, that she didn't want him there then, she was so welcoming. He shook hands with the enemy and wished this man had not escaped the killers to sit there with his wife, all these years ago with the lights on all over the city, across the crepuscular park where no one went at this hour. It was as if they had been part of that tenebrous ambush, bushes in which they had lain (oh lain!) in wait for him and done him down with their darkness. Their soundless club came down on him and made him the victim of their polite cruelty. Why was it so dark in there? Darling, we'd been sitting talking and we simply never noticed. Simple. There was the other time, which filled even the familiar with new shadows, his parents in the darkened flat, nothing to do with him, and now his wife and the refugee doctor. Here was the third time and everyone knew and no one said why it was so dark in there, because death was waiting in the room to make the third, loss of innocence, loss of faith, loss of life. That was why it was so dark in there. There is no need for light in a coffin, in this corner-cupboard of the ballroom with the pattern on the cornice that ran off through the plasterboard wall, as if it led to another world.

Wasn't There Another Child? A couple are condemned, by themselves, to wander the face of the earth because once, by mistake, they killed their own child and were married by the guilt they had to share. They keep moving because residence anywhere would involve questions about the past. 'You're so lucky,' people tell them, 'you two! You can live wherever you want.'

What did he really want? A writer receives a call from an actor whom he knows only slightly and who has been out of the country for some time, so he explains. The conversation, mostly about something some producer wants them both to do, possibly, is amiable but inconclusive. It is only when his actress wife asks 'What was that about?' that the writer realises that she and the actor must have been lovers. (This is based, baselessly, on a call to France from Norman Rodway, who has been approached with an 'availability check' re *Richard's Things* and wanted to know if the book was still in print, small reason for an overseas call, though I could find no other.)

Characters for Herbert Ross's *Glittering Prizes*, US-style: a Leslie Bricusse figure whose ascent to success is told only through the songs he writes to achieve it. Oh, and the Jewish writer with all the chips on his shoulder. A calculating lawyer marries a rich girl from the South who pays him out by sleeping with the black activist. The academic high-flyer with a mysterious, unbroken relationship with the ex-Marine redneck for whom he once 'doubled' in his exams (Master's thesis?) and to whom he is more in thrall than the other is to him. A Dick Cavett-style TV interviewer, *pas comme les autres*, who recovers his self-esteem only as he begins to slide down the ratings. An Updikish New Englander who has the way to distinction so sweetly paved for him that his happiness becomes unendurable and he is obliged to wreck it in order to save it. His success is like that of Polycrates, whose good fortune is so inextricable that he realises that there is no hope for him. A photographer as the link-man in the chain? Perhaps gay, for Herb Ross's sympathetic attention. One of them has to have a haemorrhoid operation and holds a face-down reception in hospital. A wife who repays all infidelity with fidelity, as Elizabeth Ayrton did (or Michael said she did). A Teddy Axelrod who sends inventive postcard montages to the artistic wife of a failed artist who has become an advertising man. Being gay, 'Teddy' is above suspicion. One day the ad-man burns the whole collection. 'Know what? I wish he *was* fucking you.'

Instead of a photographer, Teddy could be a cartoonist. *Great* idea. OK, he's a photographer. The screenwriter working with a Yale man like Alan Pakula, the *goyische* Jew whose enviable movie-star wife keeps falling asleep all the time. The interviewer could resemble the unspeakable David Susskind who asked me, enthusiastically, did I 'believe in visceral reactions?' I did; he made me feel sick.

Richard's Things. Mark Shivas telephoned. It seems that we shall close with Liv Ullman at $350,000 for six weeks' work; rather steep, but it ain't my money. They talk of shooting on March 17th, which means starting production soon after the Greek Orthodox festivities. Tony Harvey is scarcely the hottest director in town (actually he is in NY), but he has done some good work and at least he has a good script.

18.12.79. My father had been a passionate man, but passion betrayed and then embarrassed him. He settled for a beautiful, young and apprehensive wife whom he venerated and intimidated. After Molly, he told his parents – more in anger, one guesses, than with filial piety – that he would marry the first Jewess he met with good legs and a straight nose. Irene had an insecure childhood, the only daughter of a father both glad-handing and gullible, with little finesse when it came to women. Max Mauser 'adored' Fanny; she did not adore him: Irene was a honeymoon baby, but Fanny was determined to have no more, as was Cedric's mother. Max lived with my parents for most of the time from their marriage till they escaped to London in 1938. He seems to have had no idea that he might have been unwelcome. I have no memory of his weekday residence in 30 W. 70th St, but I do recall reading the 'Funnies' with him, in bed, on Sunday morning. He wore striped flannel pyjamas and pince-nez spectacles. Like many immigrants, he was a regular American: he believed in a sock on the jaw and a firm grip and the land of opportunity. An opportunist *manqué*, he invented things which did not sell or, if they did, he was robbed of the proceeds. He was once offered a job by the Prendergast Gang in Kansas City as a municipal hygiene inspector. All he had to do was collect graft from restaurants in return for a certificate of cleanliness. He wouldn't do it. My father tolerated him in those early years, as he did Fanny in his later ones.

Cedric never rebelled and seemed to feel no resentment, but he did have a very thin mouth. If irritated, he was never exasperated. Fanny was there because Irene wanted her to be. Cedric demanded only fidelity in return and without fail. He would have divorced Irene (she told me) if he had ever found her with another man. His last years, in that damned hospital room, were haunted by the fear that she had a lover, or had had one. He was found weeping by his visitor at the hospital and told him that his wife had left him for a younger man. Irene laughed at the idea. Yet he might well believe it; evicted from his own home, he had to live in a place he hated so that she might have four and a half days in the week free of him. Did she need all that time to recover from the effort of a weekend during which he was, for the most part, attended by nurses?

Irene said that Fanny despised Max above all because he was a failure. If she never accused Cedric of failing, he regretted his own lack of success. Not until he declared his disappointment did I realise that it was justified. He had schooled me in the virtues of modesty, but he himself had had immodest hopes. He would have loved to own a race-horse or a Rolls-Royce. Never interested in politics that went beyond efficient management, he criticised the government's 'P.R.', never its policies. If he remembered one thing from reading Greats, it was *mēden agan*. At St Paul's, although a natural mathematician, he had been compelled to switch to Classics. It had not occurred to him to resist.

In his lounge-lizard days, Cedric was a good athlete and a brilliant dancer. Phyllis Haylor, with whom he tangoed all those years ago, lightened his last days with renewed attention. He had written her love letters even when he was first keeping company with Irene, until she protested. He assumed that he could get away with anything; but he never did. Phyllis now lives with a lady novelist, *très femme-femme*, who is very friendly to my mother, who despises her. Unlike his friend Victor 'Ginger' Sylvester, Cedric was not tempted by the glamour of clap nor by that of show business. Ginger invited him to manage the Strict Tempo dance band which he formed after the Great War; Cedric preferred to join ICI. He was both a strong character and easily led; he took a lot of advice, nearly all of it bad. He had little foresight, even in so banal a matter as the acquisition of a house. He paid a high rent when he could no longer rely on the government to restrict it. He never realised that he might have lowered his own outgoings and secured his future by buying a freehold. Supporting a system from which he failed to benefit, he invested his Shell gratuity in shares which he was advised to buy and which then slumped. He played favourite nephew even after he ran out of uncles: as with Jessel, so generally, he hoped for tips.

Irene has found solidarity with Jewish ladies of a certain age. I recall her shame when, during the war, I was counting Flag Day takings at the WVS 'shop' in Putney High St and said 'Vell...' and spread my hands in a Jewish gesture, copied from what my father had recently done, mockingly, in private. Accurate mimicry of what had amused her in private mortified her when I repeated it, guilelessly, in public. 'Never do that again,' she said, 'ever.'

19.12.79. I have been putting off replying to Harry's letter. Finally I did respond, last night. Every word is justified; none is kind. And here we are with less than a week till Christmas. I shall not send the letter; but I do not withdraw a phrase. I shall greet them, should they ever come here, with politeness. I seldom declare my motives or spell out what really moves me. I have learnt a sardonic amiability which seems to speak for an unsuspecting temper; yet I always expect treachery. Harry affects to be some kind of a 'revolutionary'; his Guevaran moustache is cut out to prove it; yet he has no shame in hitching his wagon to a passing millionaire. He imagines that he has followed some errant star along an unbeaten path. Man Friday on Brighton Beach, he has enviable talents: his carpentry, his design, his drawing, his masonry; none is sufficiently extraordinary to procure success. He is not an intellectual, but he reads many newspapers and articles. He believes something to be true as long as it makes him unhappy.

When we were in New York in June, Lee Friedlander saw them as heedless riders on the easy wave of the times, lotus-eaters whose idle way of life was compounded of sloth and opportunism; nothing like the luckless artists which I had taken them to be. My despatch of money, however nice of me, was also an assault. Harry had told me, in Fuengirola, in 1961, when I was flat broke, that he was going back to New York to a job that would pay him $18,000 a year. After nineteen years, I threw his complacency back at him. Is there something there which I fear I cannot equal? I envy the music, the capacity to play and the knowledge to enjoy; what else? I have always imagined that I shall welcome their company more than I actually do. Having lapped him on the silly track on which we have for too long competed, I can do without his friendship.

1980

1.1.80. Brave new decade! What else is new but what is old? A 'researcher' came to see me yesterday to recruit me into a programme concerning the Seven Ages of Man. I was to impersonate Maturity. The director was a six-foot-four Oxonian, in his early thirties, with enough personality for someone of five-foot-ten. He asked intelligent questions, provoked me to a mature denial of maturity, ate lunch, drank coffee and took his polite leave. It is not clear to me why I have decided not to participate; perhaps I have had enough of myself.

Had I not spent four cold days filming in Cambridge before Christmas, I might have been seduced. The director was David Turnbull, who came down from St John's only three years ago; a tall, rather curved young man with a full mouth, the jaw slack, calm enough to mask a want of decisive authority. He allowed David Shaw, the cameraman, to take elaborate time over the set-ups, perhaps to prolong the shoot into Christmas Eve, when overtime was payable. Shaw's lean and handsome confidence promised that he knew his business. He referred to a time when he had been married, though he looked too young to have a past tense. The crew was sparse, but class distinctions were observed. The sparks drank and consorted together. Turnbull was correct and efficient. His First in Psychology made him neither bookish nor entertaining. The Blunt scandal disposed the mechanicals to be conscious of the Cambridge climate. When we were shooting in Hall, under the cathedral ceiling and the varnished eyes of the dignitaries hanging on the walls, one of the sparks came up to me: 'All Communists up there then, are they?' I was patiently explanatory, never guessing that he was pulling my leg.

On the first two days, they stood me a taxi from Langham and back (on the third, I drove myself). One of my drivers, a young man with a golden crucifix dangling from his left ear, had been taught riding by a gypsy. He was mad about horses and owned a mare and a gelding. Of the other drivers one had been a marine engineer from Newcastle who had, he told me, been chief engineer on super-tankers; another was a TV engineer who had been sacked by the Co-op for repairing an old lady's telly for 'a cup of tea and a biscuit', in the firm's time; the third, an ex-regular soldier in Army Transport. All seemed to be making more money driving a cab than they had before, though the two engineers may have been exaggerating their previous seniority.

The Geordie had left after a divorce and had two children on Tyneside whom he had not seen for two and a half years. He had a second marriage in Colchester, but he did not get on with his wife. She had had a baby after fourteen months and had two boys by a previous marriage. He seemed capable and mature, but he had an idle streak. On a very cold morning, he missed a warning sign and drove hard into a crossing where we should have stopped. He had served on all kinds of ships, including cruise liners. The engineers always fancied their chances with female passengers. The sea did something to women, no question. What really worked on them was coming down to the engine room and seeing them all 'stripped to the waist, muscles rippling' and then later meeting the same man 'covered with scrambled egg' at the Purser's table. 'It was a great knicker-dropper.' He was a dark-eyed, tall, sallow man who told his happy stories with an air of rueful disillusion. If he had had a lot of ladies, he did not think much of them or of himself. Can he have abandoned the sea only because cab-driving was more lucrative or had he never had the rank to which memory promoted him? He told me that engines were basically simple. His shiftiness made me sympathise with the two captains – one a Dutch-Australian, the other a Scot – with whom he said he would never sail again. One trip, he was at sea for thirteen weeks, out of Liverpool, without setting foot on shore. They left with a cargo of crude oil and couldn't find a market for it either in the Americas or at South African ports. Finally, they brought it all the way home again. That was in the early Sixties. They spent their time at sea playing cards, drinking and listening to music on the stereo.

The horseman was young, probably Irish; he looked like Joe Lyde, who used to play the piano in Jordan's Yard. He was too heavy for a jockey. His family had been in the cavalry; he learned to ride 'the army way', mounting from the facing backwards position. He had no fear of the horse; it was a stupid animal, though he respected its cunning. He knew patience: if a horse bolts, you have to go with it, though it can be stopped by a sharp blow on the shoulder. It is senseless to strike it on the haunches, as frightened people do, because that causes it to accelerate.

My driver home from Cambridge the first, freezing evening was an ex-boy soldier; eleven years in the army, all over the world, including Aden and Ireland. He regretted only that he had not learned a trade. In Aden, he had been in a section responsible for recovering equipment, and bodies, from the battlefield. They had to be armed to do that and were often under fire from inaccurate tribesmen. Sometimes they encountered booby-traps. He was a light fellow and had actually leaned on a sandbagged trap which exploded under the weight of the next man to lean on it and blew his hands off. He was now a 'semi-pacifist' and a member of the Labour Party. He had mourned Shirley's defeat in the general election. One quickly became hardened by battle or accident. In Kenya he had flown with a team to recover bodies after an army plane, carrying aero-engines, had crashed into a mountain. The engines were behind the crew in the baggage compartment and crushed them to pieces when the impact flung them forward. Callousness led to gruesome jokes. One of the rescuers picked up a skull fragment, with an ear attached to it, and said, "'Ere, 'ere, what 'ave we, ear?' He quoted the remark with appalled indifference, knowing how terrible it was to laugh at such things, and knowing that he had. He was slightly dismayed at the life he had chosen to lead. Having been a willing boy soldier, from a poor background, he was now possessed of a sensitiveness which made his heedless past a mine of anxiety. He had a pool of koi carp, a Japanese fish that came as long as three feet. He took them to competitions and won prizes with them. He used to go regularly to Diss, where there was a noted stockist. He drove skilfully. Ahead of us, a Cortina slid and turned twice on the black ice. We followed it without the slightest skate.

The TV engineer was plaintive with the injustice of things. He could not get another job as a result of his kindness to that old lady. I suspect that he had refashioned the story so often that he was now convinced of his innocence and generosity, although it was obvious that he had been defrauding his employers. He claimed to be bringing suit against them for wrongful dismissal, but he lost faith in his own cause when he talked about it.

The marine engineer did suggest that men of his rank did much better today; but he seemed scarcely too old for the sea. He may have had some specific blot, or blots, on his copybook; but his marital problems seemed to account for his dolefulness. He had had good times and now had nothing to look forward to. There seemed little in his nautical past of which he was actually proud.

He remembered even his pleasures in a sour way. He was a man to avoid, whereas the ex-soldier was lively and eager to learn, without prejudice or malice, due perhaps to the political conscience which liberated him from his colleague's glum selfishness. He told me that they used to collect the debris of battle – arms literal and metaphorical – in big nets. When they had put the metal and the plastic bags full of meat into the net, they sat down in the middle of the nets themselves and waited to be hooked into the air by the returning choppers.

Guy and Helen Lee live in a modest terrace house in Carlyle Road, opposite the footbridge in Chesterton Road, and have two adopted sons, whose manners and morals they tolerate. Guy drives a VW, but is otherwise patriotic. Helen has recently become interested in the ancient world and would like to go to Greece. Guy would not; he has all of the Mediterranean he wants in his head. His donnish mildness of speech and dress renders comic the reactionary fervour of his conversation. He might not believe in Marxist categories, but he holds Wedgwood Benn 'a traitor to his class'. He is also an advocate of capital punishment. Without vanity, he holds himself lucky to be a Fellow of St John's; yet he is merciless towards the failings of other scholars. When I told him of a howler I had detected in Christopher Hill, he was ready to consign all of that historian's work to the dustbin, Master of Balliol or no. Guy makes the Classics both dry and amusing. We were hunting in concordances the moment we met on the first evening of my shoot, looking for the source of the tragic taboo on blood on stage. I misread a passage – reading *ouk* for *oun* ('not' for 'therefore') – and Guy immediately applauded my 'emendation', observing that the passage made no sense as it stood. He insisted that that sort of thing often happened when one looked at a text which had remained unquestioned for years, although it lacked rudimentary coherence. He regarded both Latin and Greek as immeasurably remote; even now he dared not approach either ancient language without suitable crutches.[7]

Guy now plays a good deal of golf and he watches TV in the evening, as many intellectuals may well do, but few academics confess. He makes me laugh, like some artisanal *eau de vie* which seems clear and bland and leaves no hangover. He opposes the entry of girls into the college, while confessing, with open

---

7 No doubt Guy meant dictionaries, not cribs.

roguishness, that female pupils are very much to his taste. If he has an idea of himself as a character, he is decidedly not a *great* character. His edition of *The Eclogues* is to be published by the Liverpool UP. He thinks himself fortunate to have a publisher at all. Yet he is not quite modest and not in the least deferential. He considered Christopher Ricks' view that Housman was not intelligent 'extremely odd'. He also rejected the opinion that Cowper was a bad poet. Ricks backed the Leavisite valuation regarding the line 'poplars falling in the avenue'; C.R. said that the trees were actually elms and that Cowper did not know the difference. Guy demanded what evidence he had and argued, not foolishly, that his text was no sort of evidence against the poet: 'He may simply have preferred to say poplars'. Certainly these trees are more apt to 'topple' and so suit the imagery better than sedate elms. Backing away from confrontation with the little known classicist, Ricks promised to let Guy have further information on the matter, 'which has not been forthcoming'. Henceforth, no doubt, all C.R.'s valuations will be regarded by Guy as sceptically as C. Hill's historiography.

Ricks writes and speaks to me amiably. He neglected to shake hands with Ken McLeish when they met at a performance of *From the Greek*. When K. was Ricks' pupil, twenty years ago, he challenged C.R.'s unwise, or provocative, remark that Milton did not know any Latin and could not write Latin verses. Or was it (surely) Greek that Milton didn't know? Either view seems so silly that I cannot believe that 'our' foremost Miltonian can have advanced it. Ken quit his classes and claims to have an accurate recollection of the circumstances.

At Hilary Rubinstein's brunch, Bob Wyatt, a turnip-headed, bespectacled young man who is in charge of the BBC's 'odd hours', which include *The Book Programme*, informed me that they had taken up an idea I had suggested of a series of discussions along the lines of Pivot's *Apostrophes*, but shorter, and that they had been very successful. He seemed to be paying me verbal royalties.

The Milstein marriage is in a state of *stasis*. Carol has found a flat she would like, for £125,000. Dick is willing to give her half the money from the sale of their house, but refuses to underwrite the flat until Hereford Square is sold; and then will the flat still be available? He fears the property market will fall again. Meanwhile he has no home life. The children show no signs of suffering, he says, but – like Maisie – they must be marked by what they cannot fail to know. Carol is a girl with wishes but not desires; ambition but no charm. Claire Tomalin told me that she and Nick had the Milsteins to dinner years ago; she thought Carol the most disagreeable guest they had ever had. She began to tap her foot with boredom halfway through the meal and announced that they had better be going before they had left the table. How can such gracelessness be reconciled with that pale suburban girl so eager to make it that she married Milstein? Most unforced marriages begin at least with *deception*, but the wedding was a sorry affair, more enjoyable for the guests than for the bride. Milstein seemed content; he had mounted a spectacle sufficiently primed with celebrities to put Carol's Surbiton parents in the deep shade. Present discontents have softened his voice and made him belatedly aware of other people. He said how wonderful Paul and Sarah had been at Patrick Sergeant's party and how he wished that he had been nicer to them when they were small. They told us that they had sent him up shamelessly.

I advised John Peter that if he wanted to stay on the paper, he should on no account threaten resignation, lest the offer be accepted. He has rejected the job on the colour comic, less because it was a sinecure than because the editor, Ron Hall, had not given his assent nor even been informed. J.P. remains in the crowded Arts Department, John Whitley perched above him, though they were once fellow lieutenants. Meanwhile Fenton is making a name for himself by the practice of trenchant asyndeton. Theatrical London is loud with the bleating of sacred lambs as they go to the weekly slaughter. Claire Tomalin has offended Jack Lambert – who cleaves to his empty title of Chief Reviewer like an impotent *seigneur* to his *droits* – by allotting books to her *coterie* before he has taken his. While deluging me with commissions, she omitted me from the panel chosen to select Books of the Year. Steiner, similarly axed, predicts his own eviction from her pages: when not blessed with egregious favours, he will have it that he is being cudgelled with singular affronts.

5.1.80. Contrast the reaction of Achilles over the death of Patroklos with that of Perikles over the Athenian dead. Bristling with threats of revenge, Achilles omits to praise the courage of his lover. His reconciliation with the Achaeans has nothing to do with common purpose. He cares only to match death with death. The progress in attitudes to the dead, from the Heroic Age to that of Perikles, marks the politicising of mortality. In the Heroic Age, death was never an aspect of public service. Self-assertive violence was the epic hero's way of life. The anti-heroic ethos of tragedy is declared in the deprecation of *hubris.* Violent pride was less an accidental 'flaw' than a defining characteristic of the leading player. If his mortification purged the audience through pity and terror, it also instructed and reassured them. During the archaic period, the gods were the arbiters of the fate of great men. In the age of the hoplite, to step out of the ranks was to endanger your fellow-soldiers; self-advancement was a crime. With the coming of the *polis,* the Athenian *demos* alone decided when a citizen had behaved outrageously; trial by jury and ostracism were the instruments of mundane sanctions. Jurors in the dramatic competition assumed the divine office of adjudication. The sovereignty of the people was doubly established.

The notion that success lies in the acclaim of the largest number is the vulgar consequence of democratic power. The counter-vailing view, that merit is proved by the absence of popular endorsement, comes of Platonic disdain for popularity. The pursuit of accurate taste sublimates an oligarchic principle of judgment. The convergence of literary punditry and elitist politics stems from a common revulsion from masscult. Eliot's notion of the 'Age of Criticism', like his Christian society, proposes the self-righteous rule of the lettered few: in art and in morals, the majority cannot be suffered to have the last word. Censorship betokens distrust of the citizens' right to determine their own pleasures and regulate their own morality.

The playwright's direct access to public attention is an affront to the oligarchic mind, whoever garners the prize. As a reactionary innovator, Aristophanes comes between the two sides and plagues them both. Insolently theatrical, he mocks the grandiloquence of tragedy. At the same time he derides the self-importance impersonated by his up-in-the-clouds caricature of Socrates. Aristophanes has qualities typical of the satirist: unable to resist the parade of his own mimetic vanity, his comic disposition ridicules the fucking, farting creature who presumes to transcendence. He reminds the audience of the things which Authority seeks to deny or discount. Remarking the surging nakedness under all the uniforms we care to borrow or parade, he advertises the natural man. Since war is the enemy of life, he will not allow that any cause can justify it. He belongs with the anarchists whose precise political affiliations can never be defined. The comic writer is loyal only to the absurd.

Socrates was condemned and executed on much the same charges as Aristophanes plays for laughs in *The Clouds*. The question of whether Aristophanes 'really' hated Socrates cannot be equated with whether Juvenal really hated women. Aristophanes was playing politics; Old Comedy solicited the votes of the audience. Juvenal was a *rentier*. In the Sixth Satire, whether seriously or stylishly, he had no motive other than to revel in his scatological gifts. Attempts to excuse Ezra Pound from complicity with the Final Solution depend on making the conclusive verdict on him depend on aesthetics. His defenders first make a separate domain of poetry and then grant its denizens the benefit of clergy. If Plato is more indulgent to Aristophanes than to Aeschylus, is it because (as Nabokov with Kingsley Amis) their shared reactionary attitudes disposed Plato to excuse his friend's anti-Socratic jibes? Could it even be that, as an off-duty pontiff, Plato enjoyed a secret giggle at the expense of the man he honoured above all others?

6.1.80. Hilary asked me, as we were eating Stilton at his delicious brunch, whether I knew that the two great love affairs of Olivier's life were with Ken Tynan and Danny Kaye. I did not. Should I?

13.1.80. The reactions of a man released from unjust imprisonment, after the crusading efforts of friends and supporters, and – in parallel – the attitudes of (for instance) an academic's family after he has been passed over, as Lipson was, for a Chair he plainly merited. The two men might become 'lovers', of a kind; each unmanned by the support he has been given. If, by chance, they were members of the same sports club, they could find 'release' in furious fraternity on the squash court or bloody buddydom in the boxing ring. Solitary and together, they take pleasure in the exclusivity of their antagonism.

15.1.80. *A Modern Master.* A parody of the Fontana series about a fictional *maître* whose public life is devoted to pacific generosity and cultural elevation but whose secret life has no such qualities. Imagine a memoir of Alfred (the *My Secret Life* man) which deals exclusively with his public services. What a Gladstone his official biographer might make him! Does this offer a way in to my review of that volume of *The Times* obituaries? These are rendered the more amusing since they carry an introduction by W. Rees-Mogg, who was Head of the School when I first went to Charterhouse. He pronounces as if on some sublime Old Boys' Day, reviewing the generations and congratulating those who have hunted the right pots. Paying small tribute to the nameless ones, he concentrates his praise on those whom others have praised already. To those that have (or had) shall a *Times* obit be added. It is regrettable that the text does not indicate those who were given the grace of an inset photograph, the KCB of tributes. Each OB's *curriculum vitae* is complacently rehearsed as he passes into the university of death. They all go into the dark. And how few of them will be missed! Only the cricketers excite a vivid wish for their retrieval. I should prefer to see Gilbert Jessop play one great innings than to quiz any number of Regius professors. Failures can be more fascinating than successes: what peculiar fault made Oxford pass over Lipson for the Chichele Chair and in what precise form was his 'taking it hard' expressed? In what beery obscurity did Stoop, the implausibly named rugger player, pass the years of retirement from the game which earned him more than a column of print? Why have I never heard of 'perhaps the greatest motor-racing driver of all time' and why have I already all but forgotten his name? Nuvolski, can it have been?

Children can be more angered than distressed when people die. They think of dying as something decided upon by the dead.

17.1.80. It is tempting to base Catullus's Clodia on Antonia Fraser. Her sister, Rachel Billington, was at Richard Gregson's Christmas party. She now has four children, the youngest five months, and has become a wider woman than the one who, some years ago, said how much she liked John Russell Taylor when I was driving her and Kevin, Clive Donner and Penelope Mortimer back from Oxford in the blue Mercedes which had a puncture on the way. How patiently they waited for chauffeur Freddie to change the tyre! Kevin had been recently hailed by J.R.T. as 'the best director in England', so one could scarcely blame Rachel for her mutuality, though I certainly did. Kevin has since slipped into oblivion's ante-chamber. Aged and matured, rumpled by humour and by disappointment bravely worn, he directs only commercials and the odd play.

Rachel is erect and unlined. She was the only person, a fellow-author, to whom I spoke at any length. I remember her accusing me once of 'liking the money'. The question may have

been intended to pull the old novelist's trick of 'showing knowledge', a professional wink, but it had a whiff of Catholic prejudice.
She feels that her latest novel has been condescendingly reviewed,
and so it has. I have no notion of whether it deserves as much. Does
she all the time suspect that you wish she was Antonia? She may;
but I don't. How did Clodia Metelli's sisters regard her flagrant
beauty? In aristocratic families, with their apparent abundance of
personalities, everyone is a facet of the group identity. A *Sunday
Times* piece on the Kennedys remarks that Joe K.'s daughters were
somehow more married to their father than to their husbands.

Byron's affinity with Augusta licensed him to combine narcissism
with regression to the infantile state in which the mother is
sister, sister mother. Augusta was as close as he could come to
home. How could Annabella or Claire hope to compete? Byron's
emotional and sexual life was hooked on the lure of the forbidden.
Fidelity might be an admirable pose; it was a practical bore. His bi-
sexuality suggests that there was no avenue he would not explore;
all, he was sure, led to damnation. He was the emblematic stranger
in a familiar land. What other literary figure was ever so damnably
fortunate? At once the very instance of the intolerable and the
voice of tolerance, he transgressed every moral law, yet made
fools of those for whom laws were excuses for cant and brutality.
However wilfully scandalous, his verse can be so facile that it exemplifies literary convention. Single-minded in embodying double
standards, he was an actor for whom there was always sly space
between himself and the way he was behaving. His part never
fitted him exactly; his dandyism always had a crease in it. When he
sought to be smart, he overdid it, as his travelling coach signalled.
What he regarded as perfectly judged cast doubt on his judgment.
Never quite the genuine article, he played the lord in too lordly a
style. Mutable to the point of Protean, he could never arrive at a
settled form. For such a man, death is the only inescapable destination; he ran away from everything else. He knew that his repertoire
of contradictions could be reconciled in a bag of bones thrown in
a corner, the actor's wardrobe discarded after the performance. He
brought his own curtain down with 'È finita la commedia'.

Once expectation of uplift is removed, B. becomes a living text:
his work and his life cannot be read in distinct parts. Wee Georgie
happened on Lord Byron as an actor discovers a role. The great
performer inhabits the part he plays; but there is always present,
by way of a standard, the performance that would be being given

if a great performance were not. Byron's life as lord, as lover and even as debauchee is always acted in the light of another way of doing things. He makes love best when he is not the husband; when he is the husband he has to find an illicit way of coming to his bride. Scandal is part of what he gives her for her pleasure no less than for his own. The forbidden act which (if he did) he forced on Annabella was the only surprising evidence of desire that he could bring her; what was licensed in matrimony was unworthy of him. He had to make marriage an outrage before he could find it endurable. The lure of the forbidden sparked his sense of being alive; he was impotent in the face of what was conceded to him, hence his 'sparing' of Frances Wedderburn-Webster.

18.1.80. New snow crepitates underfoot with the same packing sound as a filling pushed home by a dentist. The walnut tree has a crepe bandage on its crooked knee.

19.1.80. His mother died on Christmas Eve. I did speak to him several times afterwards but thought it correct to write a note of formal condolence. Since his success, he has been introduced to the pleasures of secretarial help. Headed paper lent tone to his correspondence. I received a well-typed acknowledgment of my letter, with the secretary's signature at the bottom.

Having fixed her price, Ms Ullman is proving squeamish about what she does to honour it. She does not now wish to be asked to embrace another woman, although she can hardly not have known that *Richard's Things* is a love story between a dead man's wife and his mistress.

Liv, about a repetition: 'It's butter on butter'.

24.1.80. Sarah telephoned, little more than a week ago, to announce the end of the world. I hinted that she was exaggerating. On Tuesday, her announcement that she was about to go into her art history exam was more properly nervous. Today the world news is so ominous that we need no Pythian to augur an imminent Armageddon. Does art history matter when the USA and Russia come closer and closer to being further and further apart? What a time for the heads of the English Catholic church to launch a campaign against abortion, as if 'the rights of the unborn' were the most pressing matter! Oh but of course the decision to 'speak out' was taken some time ago; morality cannot be timed to keep step with the news. On the same morning that the world goes up in smoke, draft planning permission will be granted, in principle, for constructing dwelling houses on hitherto green ground. At every moment when men are faced with annihilation, they deny the menace by legislating over whatever remains within their scope. The helplessness of the present is confused by the uncertainty of just how serious the situation is and how seriously the Russians will react to our reactions. Who will be the luckier, those who die in the early stages or those who live a little longer, with the knowledge of what has befallen the others? If men are given time to pursue their inquiries into the state of the Labour Party, swing votes and cut corners, perhaps the triviality of most human enterprise will save us from our doom. Who passes sentence of death on those whose gravest sin is cooking the books?

The treason of the clerk lies in demanding a privileged style of life in return for his probity.

The humane side of medicine has yielded to procedures in which technicians do the work: care is replaced by tests. It follows that when everything mechanical has been done, there is nothing more to do.

I went into the kitchen and found Beetle with all last year's bills spread in front of her, diligently and loyally preparing the accounts for the US tax people. If she were not there to do them, I should become a fugitive rather than undertake the task myself.

The efficiency of the Nazis and their functionaries in recording their actions is often regarded as incomprehensible. How can it not have occurred to them that they were filing the evidence for their future damnation? Easily: in their eyes, the accurate tabulation of iniquity entitled them to put it behind them with a feeling of absolution. The fulfilment of one's duty and the completion of formalities are identical when all that matters is that one's accounts be in order.

How shall we react when the first shots are actually fired and then when the first 'tactical' missiles are launched? At what point shall we all become like the European Jews whom we claim not to understand, and allow ourselves to be annihilated, too late to resist and too sheepish to protest, for fear that we may bring on something worse than mere extermination?

As an architecture student in California, T. had lived with two good-looking girls. He returned to England and married a woman who would, he thought, lend him prestige. Fat, snobbish, mean-eyed, thick-ankled, shrill-voiced, she had been to a classy school and secured him entry to County society. They would now sooner remove their children from fancy schools than be unable to pour another vodka for the Joneses. They economise only on essentials. Intimidated by hope, T. hopes that the society he serves will remain strong enough to bless his tasteful parasitism with the security he craves.

28.1.80. *Oxbridge Blues.* Two couples have been in the habit of renting a house somewhere in Europe for the summer holidays. The two men (one now a professor?) were at Cambridge together, the two women at Oxford. Both couples make a virtue of being intelligent *and* happily married. When one pair announces that they are breaking up, the other can hardly believe it; that is their standard form of belief. The house in Tuscany has already been booked, and paid for. The errant husband arrives with his new lady, who is not a lady, but has other attributes, which she has no hesitation in revealing at the pool. The straight couple are bent out of shape. They feel the need to talk about things before it's too late, which makes at least one of them realise how late it is.

Ken McLeish claims to feel imprisoned in 'Thatcherland'. His de-pression may have more to do with envy of the success of P. Hall's *The Greeks* at the Aldwych than with the state of the world; but he laments that we are pitched between two immensely powerful, alien antagonists, neither of them with any single sincerely held belief. Both are armed with a vocabulary derived from ideological slogans; neither honours the ideals on their escutcheons. Yet what free man has honest doubts about where he would prefer to live? Graham Greene affects to prefer the idea of life in Gorki to that in California; meanwhile he maintains his flat in Antibes. Ken has the anguish of a clever man who cannot achieve originality. An adept parodist, as good classicists learn to be, he finds comfort in the view advanced by the music critic of *The Listener* that the emphasis put on Schoenberg and Stockhausen has been an error. As Bob Hughes said in the *Sunday Times* end-of-the-decade report, the avant-garde has been diluted and diverted; eclecticism is the people's choice, including the best people's. Ken bemoans the purposelessness of life, by which he means his dependence on the stimulus of being hired, which is followed by self-contempt at being for hire at all. I made light of his dismay; the *angst* of others excites levity. He is worrying about what to say to a committee deliberating on conscientious objection, quite as if he were in danger of being obliged to take the Queen's shilling. His dismay concerning today's world is more likely to be due to the lifting of his Marxist father's comforting, because threatening, shadow.

29.1.80. According to Julia, Richard Gregson's latest lady, John Updike had an affair with a Jewish girl in Melbourne, Australia, when he was a visiting celebrity. For her, it was an idyllic few days. Later, she read an Updike story in which she was depicted as hairy and depressive. She wrote to reproach him for such a cruel and unfair caricature of herself and of their affair. He replied that he had made what use of it he chose and that she could console herself with the knowledge that he had alienated the whole of his family and that no one he knew thought of him as anything but a shit. How typical of a writer to respond to deserved abuse by appealing for his victim's sympathy!

I dreamed of a savage battle in the Great War. I was among those retreating in disarray from a Turkish attack. One of our men, attempting to flee, received a knife in the back. Turning to surrender, he was robbed of his watch by a pursuer. We reached a steep redoubt and were scrambling to a defensive position when a Turkish general scaled the slope and announced his desire to surrender, just as we were preparing to do the same. We kept a straight face as he proposed to hand over his entire army, although we dreaded his seeing how few we actually were. It was as if I received a misaddressed dream and opened it in error.

I dreamed also that I was playing squash with my father at Queen's Club. He was a member and I was not. He was not young, but quite fit. He had booked the court from 5 till 6. At 5.30 a bumptious young man and a choir of white-kilted singers arrived, in the middle of a rally, to claim the court. We were playing with a standard ball but we were hitting it with a sort of wire with a ring attached to the end. As soon as people arrived, I lost the ability to make contact. The young man insisted that we clear the court, although I verified the booking on the sheet on the back wall. I was torn between righteous rage (for my father's sake) and the fear that, if I made an undue fuss, my small right to speak at all, since I was not yet a member, would be made public.

I suppose that the club, being Queen's, represented England and that my lack of qualification to speak out related to my American citizenship. But why were we playing squash and who was the cocky intruder and why did he have a chorus with him? There was a plastic cage lying on the floor of the court, in which bottles were stored. When the ball fell into the cage (*squash* bottles, were they?), I was obliged, unfairly I thought, to concede the point, even though I had earlier offered a generous let. Excess of scruple as a symptom of masochistic aggression? My father would have won the match, if it had continued, but I was conscious that he had no wish to assert his rights, even though the law should have been on our side. He was indeed always wary of undue excess. I dream of him quite frequently now, without embarrassing hostility or traumatic regret. He behaves much as he did in his prime: he says nothing memorable or abusive, remains aloof and devoted to his own purposes and disappears without recrimination.

30.1.80. A man leaves England, after living there most of his forty-something years, because of a broken marriage and a financial fall. He goes to California and, after some precarious months, retrieves his fortunes in the movies. He is made vice-president in charge of worldwide production. His duties include supervision of the London operation of the company. He returns in first-class comfort to the scene of his humiliation. He stays at the Savoy; his diary is filled with meetings with men who now crave his attention where once they denied him an appointment. Some of the dates have been made by his secretary, others he inscribed himself. He has kept the Thursday lunch free because he is sure that he arranged to have it with someone. He becomes more and more uneasy as the day approaches. Tempted to make another arrangement (everyone wants to see him), he has this feeling that the Thursday thing is important; he must keep the time free. How can he have failed to make a note of where he is to see whoever it is? He has to hope that he or she will call to confirm the rendezvous. At noon on Thursday, he has a car waiting in case he remembers where he is supposed to go, whom it is so important that he see. He sits in anguish in the suite for the summons that fails to come. He is convinced that someone, oh surely a woman – but what woman? – is waiting somewhere for him. He can imagine how well-dressed she is, how carefully she has prepared herself to appeal to him. No, it can't be the woman who left him and, as it turned out, gave him his opportunity for a new life. Is it someone whom he scarcely knows, whom he once approached, perhaps, with schoolboyish gaucherie? She never guessed that he was nervous, the girl he is thinking of, or that he hardly dared to ask for what she hardly dared to think he might want. She sits alone in some narrow, shiny bar, picking at the nuts and olives, an untouched glass in front of her. She looks at the slim watch (who gave her that?) on her slim wrist. She composes an expression of eager indifference, shaping the phrase 'It doesn't matter a bit', as what she hopes is his late shadow falls across her shining knees. Will she get up soon and ask the barman where she can telephone? 'I've been trying to get you,' he will say, won't he? Will he be able to bundle himself into the waiting Jaguar (or can she be sitting downstairs in this very hotel?). He waits in the suite. No one calls. He does a lot of important business that week and impresses all sorts of people. He goes back to California wondering only who it can have been that he was supposed to see in London.

The collapse of morality does not mean that we cannot recognise what is good, but that we can no longer convince ourselves that it is good for us.

The philosopher. He hardens candour into frigidity, the whited sepulchre of the imagination he dare not use. He has fewer feelings than ambitions. His public precision makes argument a moral exercise without moral consequence. Once he has proved himself not to be wrong, he loses interest. Neutrality has become his form of bigotry. He cannot allow the possibility that another mode of discourse might have any reputable quality. He will teach but he will never learn. While seeming to stand for independence of mind, he relies on the kudos of the academic preferment. Able to recognise genius only when it arouses his envious apprehension, he can perceive, but never admit, the rareness of whatever might give him the lie. An intellectual policeman, he can detect but never defer. Without him, genius might pass unrecognised; with him, it cannot succeed. He is driven to destroy what he alone has the rank to foster. His animus is reserved for those with the qualities he most wishes he could possess. The exceptional draws attention to the limits of his own achievements. He sees in a genius someone who should instruct him and whose friendship might fulfil him; but he is too clever and too well-placed ever to concede mastery to a natural master. Unable to deny genius his secret recognition, he must seek by all means to impede its possessor's social and professional progress.

Call him Anthony. Imagine him married to a nice woman, May, with whom he has had no children. They are both members of the Labour Party. Already active on the town council, she intends to stand for Parliament. They have an adopted adolescent son, whom they treat with exemplary affection. If Anthony is secretly repelled by the boy's loutishness, he also envies his sexual assurance. Anthony has a PhD student, Ben Sachs, an American, whose nervous brilliance he was quick to encourage. When first in Oxford, Ben is often invited to the house. He is grateful and unassuming. Anthony is at his nicest with him until Ben's return from a semester at MIT, with a beard and a startlingly attractive wife.

Miriam approaches Anthony in a bookshop where she has found a temporary job. He takes it that she is attracted to him, until she explains who she is. Anthony has cherished Ben's brilliance as long as he supposed him a lame solitary. The advent of Miriam arouses a vindictive envy which it is a sweet pleasure to conceal except from himself. Fidelity to May becomes a tax, wished on him by her Catholicism. He has always argued against population increase and has disagreed, politely, with her church's attitude to birth control. Now he craves a child of his own.

Ben is not thinking of having any children, yet. Without reliable income, he contributes to the conjugal budget by supervising undergraduates and by teaching English to foreign students. He might also be a capable musician, a flautist maybe. Anthony is a trustee of the National Opera, but can neither sing nor play an instrument. While obsessed by his pupil's wife, Anthony shows no outward sign of having turned against him. He does all he can to advance Ben's academic prospects. At the same time, he attempts to enchant Miriam with his wit and to entice her with his social connections. He urges Ben not to allow himself to be degraded by hack work. Ben admires Anthony so much that he is happy, very, for Miriam to benefit from the professor's generous sophistication. And so, with seeming complaisance, Ben begins to concede his wife to Anthony. Anthony can even persuade himself that he is being manoeuvred into doing something both Ben and Miriam will be grateful for. Before going back to the States, Ben has expressed doubts about being ready to get married and to undertake responsibility for someone else's happiness. Anthony confesses that he does worry whether the purity of Ben's work might not be affected by conjugal obligations. Now, seeing himself as the victim of desires excited against his better judgment, Anthony convinces himself that he is not responsible for them. He is rather a victim, isn't he? So much is expected of him.

After he has succeeded in doing down his main rival, and one-time close friend, in getting appointed to a provincial Chair, Anthony proves that he is capable of unselfish rectitude by persuading his College council to give Ben a junior fellowship. As if by chance, Ben is nicely locked into Oxford when Anthony leaves for Bristol, with Miriam. In an honest talk with May, now a Member of Parliament, Anthony explains that he feels guilt, of *course*; but that is a symptom of residual immaturity, doesn't she agree? Their marriage has run its course, 'except perhaps in some metaphysical sense which I know you would never expect me to honour'. May's faith has been proof all these years against Anthony's intellectual objections; it cannot survive the disillusionment of his defection. 'I've seen reason,' she says.

Ben must not be too pallid; at once more passive and somehow more virile than Anthony. A Jew, of an ascetic, febrile kind, perhaps with Italian blood. There is telling contrast between Anthony's championship of his protégé and his decided hostility towards another alien arrival, an ex-MIT hot-shot whose presumption of equality, at least, with the Oxford *gratin* excites his animosity. Ben's rejection of Samuel M.'s philosophical *prises de position* gains him Anthony's intellectual approval; but when genius lacks the force to be unreasonably loyal, Anthony guesses that he need not fear to take Ben's wife from him. He thinks less well of his pupil for endorsing his point of view. It leads him to helpful condescension: 'Oh, and may I say...? You'd probably be wise to lose the beard.'

When we first meet him, Anthony is the man who has been immediately and unquestioningly diagnosed as being first-class, the most brilliant of his brilliant generation. Dominating his peers, he harbours honourable doubt whether he can do work of high importance. Every academic achievement comes easily to him, but he is dogged by the lure of a life infinitely more daring than the one now open to him. Prisoner of his own advancement, he makes the best of being the best, but dreams of something better. Applauded and prized, he is less often pleased with himself than other people are. Modesty is his secret vice. Aware of a lack of passionate conviction, he craves meeting someone with the capacity to see through him. He gives Ben the opportunity to be that man. When his pupil fails to take it, Anthony is charged with vindictive geniality. He is tired of being good and honest and true. The shape of his own obituary grows clear to him: he is in danger of being the man who never put a foot wrong. Not a breath of ill wind has blown up the skirts of his reputation. He and May have been living proof that tolerant coexistence is possible in a marriage where self-deception and humbug have no place. They have an unspoken agreement that it is better to love than to be in love with each other. Sex may express something; it is nothing much in itself. The intellectual must be able to concentrate on abstract thought, detach mind from body. The politician, being more sociable, seems a less plausible ascetic; but May's public deployment of charm dilutes the intensity which she might otherwise have brought to her marriage. Her decision to be a public figure implies yielding precedence to what lies in the open.

It was easy for Anthony to live a life of rewarded, pacific propriety. To behave well was no problem; he was a man who always finished his exams ahead of time. The consequences of facility doubled with those of idleness: he had time on his hands. He could busy himself, in early middle-life, with all the dutiful offices which Chairs and chairmanships entailed. He had done everything he could to do everything he could. Was it his fault that even the most difficult things were found to be easy? He saw the essence of a problem with solvent speed. He was accessible to objections – of *course* he was! – and would never have sought to prove himself right, had he ever been shown to be wrong. He had the tolerance of those who never *have* to tolerate anyone. Bad behaviour would be a new, more dangerous test. What he missed, when all of a sudden he missed it, was having done something terrible, something unreasonable, something bloody and unconscionable. He had done everything he could, but nothing had been done to him. The more he admitted to himself that he had everything he had any right to hope for, the more he wanted something else. Call no man happy until he is given the chance to be unhappy!

The *cursus honorum*, mounted two steps at a time, mistranslated itself, for Anthony, as the curse of honours. Ripe for a lapse, he was still a professional philosopher; if he was going to behave badly, he had to do it *well*. Only love could serve to turn that particular trick. Once he had feared that a sexual scandal would damage his prospects for some eminence; early marriage took care of the danger. Now, in the late Sixties, one colleague after another was involved in amorous by-play. The great world was no longer boxed by the barbed hedges of propriety. The new frankness depicted what had once been illicit as creditable. Any life worth writing, or living, had to be spiced with erotic secrets. Anthony now saw his own intellectual asceticism to be the result of a misreading of the runes. He could not change his intellectual principles, which were, he hardly needed to tell himself, independent of their psychological motivation; but he was licensed to shuck the desiccating *mores* on which he had been raised. He had always argued that morals could not logically be proved to be true, although there could, of course, be logical discussion of them.

The most unendurable aspect of his marriage was the serenity of his wife. May never imagined that anything was, or could be, wrong between them. If she could accept her barrenness as God's will, how could anyone as reasonable as Anthony be distressed by living a life in line with reason? She had the extra dimension of the 'mumbo-jumbo' which he accepted so sportingly. If she respected him for exempting her from scorn, she esteemed him for the generosity which he might have withdrawn had it not allowed him, secretly, to despise her; her foolish faith was always the ground for a metaphysical divorce which, in due time, became a practical proposition. Enter Miriam!

Anthony and May have renounced so much of their privacy, have agreed to such an extent to regularise their lives, that an emotional crisis finds them strangers to each other. But then why would such a man have lived for so long with a woman, however clever and comely, whose Catholicism was so alien to his intelligence? Can it be that he suffered, and knew it, from a kind of psychic impotence and always craved a good reason to be unreasonable? Or might it be that he feared that he had married the wrong woman, and that was why he married her? He might have occasion truthfully to say to himself that it had been a 'mistake'; and are mistakes not defined as things which can be rectified? His tolerance (of her metaphysical faith) was always the nicest kind of intolerance. Had he really wanted to *possess* her, he could never have endured her allegiance to an absurd creed. Her faith was a noble infidelity which he could not, in honour, call on her to renounce. In due time, however, it confirmed to him how unimpressive he must always have been to her. Until he meets Miriam, he has been buoyed by his own broadmindedness. Now he dares to realise the degree to which May has had the better of him. Graced by his own magnanimity, he had conceded that logic could never refute her religious convictions. Adultery makes him an honest man: now he can acknowledge to himself that throughout his marriage he was implacably of the view that May's faith, albeit exempt from logical refutation, was every bit as nonsensical as it was held to be by the old, exploded positivism which, as a lecturer, he held to be untenable. May had made him untrue to himself before he was ever untrue to her. Trammelled in civility, he could not get to the heart of what was maddening him except by confessing, to himself – and perhaps, eventually, angrily, to the naked Miriam – that he needed a passion and a war. 'Death,' she says. 'Death?' 'I think so.' He looks at her. 'I love you, damn you.'

Another element: the envy of the straight for the bent, the heterosexual's dread that he is missing something, if only because he never wanted it. Anthony could be *excited* by the sudden exe-cration of a Blunt-like scholar of international renown (imagine being a scapegoat!) and, at the same time, he could play a righteous part in the defenestration of a Samuel Marcus figure. Anthony's virtuous motives (a man must tell the truth) cannot quite excuse enjoying the thumping fall of a too brilliant *parvenu*. I recall the animus with which Bernard Williams discussed the Middle East that evening at 'the Rubies', as Shirley calls the Rubin-steins. He mentioned his Arab students with bragging casualness. There again one could imagine how a sexual opportunity, un-dramatically presented, might remind Anthony of options he has failed to exercise.

S.M.C. never fully understood what he so clearly observed, the element of allusive camp at home in Oxbridge. He discounted its practical deposit: the English really mean what they like to declare they do not. They draw the line at excessive enthusiasm, unabridged sincerity, and serious seriousness. S.M.C. did not ap-preciate that conceits tolerated in scientists are less acceptable in arts men; what art is essential to the national interest? He took his high intelligence to be unquestionable. However many hackles might be raised against him, he could not conceive that practical barriers would not have to be lifted. If he barked against local customs, he brought rare gifts. If academic tastes were as refined as he chose to believe, was he not bound to find a post of capital significance? In short, he believed in a world which would believe in him. He knew that many of his kind had been rejected in the best places; but then he would have rejected most of them himself. He favoured discrimination, in the loftiest sense, but imagined that he had been convoked to England because he was both needed and wanted. He could not conceive that he himself was on trial; nor did he appreciate how keen those who lacked an outsider's versatility might be to convict him of something, perhaps as trivial as his tone of voice, which might confirm the irrelevance of whatever he knew and they did not. Even his exaltation of what he took to be their values and culture was distasteful to them. His presumption of their good faith was evidence of how little he deserved their company; his appetite for advancement, like the relish with which he spoke English with more syllables than the natives, less flattered than deterred them. His rejection afforded them the double pleasure of disappointing the postulant and embarrassing his sponsor.

How many people in Cambridge regarded Wittgenstein's alien provenance to be a reason to deny him a Chair? Not enough to keep him out of an appointment which he had to be pushed into accepting. Forbiddingly foreign, he was never socially assertive. He hoarded his contradictions. His homosexuality, latent or not, was nobody's business. His guilts doubled for virtues: they kept him discreet. Steiner, *par contre*, drew attention to the parochialism of literary Cambridge, its want of continental shelves. The English faculty acknowledged the justice of the charge by ostracising its advocate. As an 'inter-disciplinary' figure, S. was not central to any specific academic line. He could be rejected without being likely to prove the selectors wrong by some signal achievement.

Anthony takes proper pleasure in proposing, and with sincerity, the academic advancement of the man he means to do down sexually. Why should integrity not have two faces? At a sublime level, his judgment would be *en jeu* in assessing Ben Sachs's intellectual qualities; he was, in all conscience, bound to press for their due recognition. He would, nevertheless, have no compunction in conspiring to abort the ascent of a G.S. figure as long as the latter had no specific excellence. He could, with justice of a kind, deny that he was any kind of anti-Semite: look what he had done for Benjamin Sachs, for Christ's sake!

5.2.80. We were invited to Château Loudenne for the 'weekend'. The company was not *grand cru*. We had missed Paddy Campbell in September and were treated to the reserve team. Our host, Martin Bamford, recently fell off a horse in Burgundy and was bent out of shape. It needed several flutes of Dom Pérignon to tune up the occasion. The first couple we met, the Kuhs, live in Segovia. Michael Kuh had spent time in Fuengirola in the late 1950s. He was offered a partnership by Aubrey David, but fell out with him because he disapproved of the 'development' of Mijas; that is, its de-spoiling by Aubrey's speculative villa-building. Now over fifty, with long-at-the-sides grey hair, he has the modified dewlaps of a man who has decided, too late, to be careful about his diet. He was a poet in Fuengirola, but there is little room for rhyme in his present life. His lady was a 'researcher' no more than thirty-six or -seven; formless body, styled brown hair, yellow shirt, brown skirt. Kuh wore an air of controlled desolation which reminded me somewhat of Harry Gordon. And what do you know? He had wanted to buy San Anton in 1960, just before the Gordons bought it, but he had not got the necessary 60,000 pesetas (two thousand pounds). He now has a place in Segovia and a fisherman's cottage in Galicia. He always regretted missing out on San Anton; he even remembered the date of the *feria* when the locals come and re-dedicate the little hermitage. I was conscious of how much sooner I should have been talking to Harry and Charlotte, to whom I resolved recently never to speak again. Kuh is now a 'photo-journalist'; he does PR for Domecq and also for IDV. I quizzed him on T.S. Eliot's 'Pipit'. The reminder of his literary past brought on a depression which kept him silent for the rest of the evening.

We met them the next morning, walking up the long pot-holed drive in their loden cloaks. I accused them of looking like Guardia Civil. Kuh smiled a wan smile and called us *contrabandistas*. He and his lady rarely spend more than six weeks at a time in their Segovian home. They are forever travelling in search of 'stories'. Is he CIA? He has been bumming around Europe for more than twenty years without any stable occupation. PR provides plausible cover. He has the weary, secretive air of someone who wishes he had something to hide. If they were spies, one cannot be sure for whom; though certainly for the money. He comes originally from Austria, or his name does; a Jew, probably analysed into neutrality, he has no warmth but is not abrasive. He could never tempt you to look him up. He seems to live in a state of resigned intimacy with a woman, possibly English, who neither loves nor desires him, but is otherwise devoted. They live childless lives of industrious parasitism. He has known a lot of people a long time and no one has known him equally long. He has no discernible opinions; if he was once angry, he has no anger left. He may be cunning; he is unlikely to be clever.

Among the other guests were a French couple from Ducru-Beaucaillou, the wife in silk trousers with a haughty profile that might have been pirated from a high-denomination bank-note.

She and her spectacled, charming husband own about eighty hectares, ten miles from Bordeaux, which cost £25,000 in 1952. In addition, he owns a château in St Emilion; her sister is also loaded. They have a lot of *soucis*, Martin told us, with a smile. The husband performed elaborate bows over the ladies' hands, coming and going. Monsieur Hulot could not have made anything more inelegant than the swooping lurch which left his lips nowhere near the hand he was honouring. He told us about a rugger match between the French and the English in North Africa in 1943. The first English XV were very fair play and wore shorts which the French tugged shamelessly. The return match brought out the British thugs who thoroughly brutalised the Frogs.

Bernard Williams. How one-sided his impartiality is! It is a stringent exercise to try to inhabit the narrow mind of someone who has never had anything to complain about. Nothing has been denied him; yet his face is sharp with the piqued vigilance which is regularly read as alertness to the opinions of others. He dreads any idea which is not susceptible to benevolent condescension. He was alarmed, unless it was embarrassed, by my defence of John Wisdom. Wisdom lacked the masterful genius of Wittgenstein; his publications were idiosyncratic; his charisma could not be conveyed in paperback form: it required his presence, which was itself instructive. One sensed Bernard's apprehension of whatever fell outside the formal lines of his discipline. He is the very type of the functionary who would ask Socrates, should he apply for a teaching post, what he had published, and then smile. As if it really mattered! And then it would. His refusal to confess to envy is as honest as his lack of imagination. Resisting the opposites that work in the creative personality, he dismisses as woolly whatever cannot be woven into the lissom monotone of his own vestments. Bernard needs someone to whom he can safely confess his inadequacies and have them forgiven, someone both shrewd and ruthless enough to tell him what he knows already: that he has everything except what he wants. But then he would never forgive her.

11.2.80. I fly on March 5th to New York on Concorde to see Redford. In April, Paramount is giving us two first-class fares for us to go to Santa Barbara. A company called Marble Arch appears to be about to buy my Diana Ross idea. Only last week I announced to the desert ether that I was going to quit the movies.

25.2.80. Godfrey Smith told me that he had gulled the *News of the World* into not picking up a key phrase in Barbara Castle's memoirs about Jim Callaghan's 'total untrustworthiness', which Babs had indeed written and which had been quoted in pre-publicity. She insisted on excising it when the critical moment came, for fear of what her friends, and enemies, might think. On the eve of the *Sunday Times*'s serialisation of the memoirs, the *N.O.W.* had picked up the news from Capital Radio and were all set to make something of it. Godfrey called, referred to a 'failure of communications', and coaxed the *N.O.W.* editor into being a gentleman. Afterwards, Godfrey said that if an editor could be per-suaded that easily to spike a scoop, he wasn't really up to the job.

The *Observer* is seeking readers with an extra on cooking. Pretty soon the English will be able to wrap their fish and chips in the best recipes in the world.

I lunched with a man called Antony Rouse. He wants me to do a documentary about Willie Maugham. He warned me that he killed the people he worked with. He had odd eyes. I almost believed him. They almost certainly died of boredom.

26.2.80. Lunch with Claire Tomalin at *L'Epicure*. There are gas jets outside, in case a giant wants to stoop and light his cigar. She was wearing a suede suit; she favours brown. Her teeth seemed somewhat less ill-aligned, and a better grey. Her hair has been abandoned like a garden she has no time to trim. It might be the only symptom of distress she cares to allow herself. C.'s spina bifida son Tom is now twelve, I think. She is loyal and forthright about him. He had a speech impediment which prevented him pronoun-cing the sound 'k'. As we were talking, C. realised that his recent conquest of this disability could be the reason that he has ceased to call her 'mummy' and begun to call her 'Claire'.

C. and I talked as if we were very old friends, meaning that we are not. I discovered that George Steiner's apprehensions about his own place on the literary pages were largely justified. Harry Evans thinks him a bore, forever prattling about books no one cares to read. There is a measure of xenophobia in the editor's decisiveness. C. claims to be bewildered by George's aggressivity and does not know how to please him, just as he makes no effort to please her, observing that he cannot 'match the kind of higher gossip at which Martin Amis is pre-eminent'. C. took this personally as an allusion to her own 'famous' affair with M.A., about which I had heard, but had forgotten. Her air of baffled uneasiness will convert, opportunely, to open hostility if/when Harry Evans's attitude hardens. George's way of responding to such a situation is to confirm whatever it is that other people have against him. C. said of me that I was 'very fierce but very kind'. As Shorter Notices go, it is not a bad summary. I wonder if she has ever guessed how many of my *données* derive from her and her life. Determined to shine in all available examinations and to be an examiner too, she is vain enough to include such feline attention among my kindnesses.

Unlike showbiz, journalism does not make people more handsome. Harry Evans looks to have been photographed with an unkind lens. Face stretched with strain and devoid of colour, he might have removed his glasses under the shower and been unable to find them again. Authority in a waning society makes the newly powerful fear that they will be asked for a hand-out which someone in their position might once have been able to afford. The 'new' *Sunday Times* is like a convalescent whom everyone congratulates by saying that you would never guess that anything had ever been wrong.

Claire complains that she has no secretary, John Peter that he has James Fenton as a colleague. Fenton lives alone in a rented room and uses the *S.T.* as a club of which he is at pains to be the most famous member. Exulting in notoriety, he is particularly flattered by abusive mail. John P. watches him leaping up and down. The abrasive newcomer is unaware that within the company he summons to laugh at his impotent enemies he has an impotent enemy already. Fenton has decided to be 'honest'. He has done so, no doubt, in response to incitement from the editor, which makes tactlessness a commissioned virtue. The London theatre scarcely deserves anything better, if we are to judge by the Peter Nichols play we saw the other night. It required an evening at the Festival Hall (even though Janet Baker was said to have a cold) to purge the tepid sludge we endured at the Globe. It was my mother's first outing to the theatre since my father died. We hoped for something light and amusing. The curtain rose on a flower-covered coffin. As for lightness, Beryl Reid, cheap as birdseed, turned a drab text into a music-hall turn. Her mugging saved the evening from disaster. The play's humour depended on the presence of invisible 'mites', seconded by a trinity of Tampax, Durex and bullshit. The level of wit and culture in London leaves a grimy rim like that on a childhood bath.

In the Colchester train on Wednesday, burdened with an assignment from the *S.T.* which I was too cowardly or too vain to
refuse, I shared a first-class compartment with a grey-white man,
plump and benign, and a big-spectacled rather grand woman in
a woollen suit with a roll neck, browns and russet becomingly
woven together. I went to the loo and left my briefcase in her care.
When I returned, I put to them the questions which had been
put in the poll on morals from which I had been commissioned to
compose a Review Front article. Their opinions, willingly offered,
were unremarkably in line with those of the polled majority.
The lady, coming to life in her look-at-me spectacles, declared
herself in a markedly northern accent. It dawned on me that I had
chanced on the company of Mary Whitehouse, the moralist, who
lives in Ardleigh. She had put on her best suit to go and see the
Home Secretary, a rendezvous which she was proud to advertise.
She was amazed, and all but affronted, that I persisted in claiming
not to know her identity. Her companion was amused both by
my ignorance and, even more, by her incredulity that I had not
been immediately alert to her importance. She had been reticent
in the face of my sarcasms at the expense of moral crusaders who
sought, like ayatollahs, to impose their 'truths' on others. Perhaps
her vanity saw me as a 'plant', suborned by the *S.T.* to trail her to
her lair and extract a telling quote. Less strident but much more
conceited than I expected, she believes herself a national figure,
the unelected Minister of Virtue, burdened by a schedule of public
service (she was off to Bristol in the morning), her stern voice
primed by principle rather than by self-importance.

After the War. Mickey Marsden is a scholarship boy who has grown
up safely in an unsafe world. He has been in the army but endured
no baptism of fire. He has neither confronted nor evaded the
savage side of things. He has worked so hard at the Classics that sex
has no place in his curriculum. Yet his reading of ancient texts has
made him seem precociously eroticised. At school he had an affair
with a younger boy, Julian 'Flipper' Robson, who is serving with
the BAOR before going up to Cambridge to take up his Exhibi-
tion. Mickey was neither an ambitious member of the school nor
a rebel. What he desired in the beardless Flipper was his transient
femininity. The scandal of their affair (or rather of its discovery)
fixed in him the belief that he had loved the other; it was the only
excuse, in his mind, for what they did. Flipper has freckled charm,
but he is Mickey's intellectual inferior, someone whom he can

always patronise. While they were in the same house at school, there was a 'Jew-bait' at the expense of Karl Reiff, who had been in England since only just before the war. Neither Flipper nor Marsden took any active part in the 'one-man pogrom', but their amorous ardour was somewhat heated in the light of Reiff's ordeal.

After Marsden has done his National Service and has already finished two years at Cambridge, Reiff comes up to read Classics. A year later, he becomes (by chance, by choice?) Marsden's precocious pupil in ancient history. Reiff is now an articulate, assertive scholar. Marsden remembers his pupil's solitary schoolboy anguish with ambiguous tenderness; something at once for and against him. Reiff becomes an ADC actor and plays Antonio in *The Merchant of Venice*. The vehemence of his scorn for Shylock is greeted with loud applause, which he enjoys. Marsden hardly knows how to congratulate him afterwards; and Reiff knows it. That is what he enjoys.

Marsden is working too hard on his thesis to have time for Cambridge women. His paper on Caelius Rufus in the *Journal of Roman Studies* attracts attention from a female classicist in Oxford, Gillian Crisp, who initiates a scholarly correspondence. Their exchange of letters begins with doctoral decorum but becomes seriously uninhibited. Marsden's expertise *in malis partibus* serves him well. Although he never says as much, he is slightly shocked by Gillian's clear account of the meaning of '*glubit*' in Catullus's scabrous poem about Lesbia. They attribute to each other a sophistication neither would claim individually. Literary lovers, their courtship is at a distance and so much the bolder for that. They are more intimate for not having met. Since it seems that both want the same things and the same life, they come to believe that they want each other. When finally they meet, at some conference, Gillian is not quite as Mickey imagined her. She is pale and freckled and virginal. Forthright without being aggressive, she is honest but by no means as brave as her footnotes. He has imagined that they would soon be lovers, but he also expected that she would take charge of the timing (as Pierrette did when Marsden was a nineteen-year-old second lieutenant, on leave in Paris). Gillian and he choose to be amused by the easy uneasiness between them. He quotes the line, 'I've got those Oxford and Cambridge blues / Afraid to win and hate to lose', from a Footlights number written, as it happens, by Karl Reiff. They plan to go to Italy (Sirmione first!) during the next Long Vac. But they have to postpone the date when Gillian's parents announce that they are coming home from India.

It is then that Mickey goes to Paris to see Flipper Robson (now a theatrical agent?) and meets Karl on the Dieppe ferry. Karl is about to have his first play produced and treats Marsden with condescension, quite as if he merited some kind of retaliation. In Paris, Marsden is capable even of betraying the prostitute he chooses in the environs of Les Halles: he goes to his hotel and masturbates before he goes back to find her talking to a *képi*'d French officer, who taps his swagger stick against his boot as he negotiates with her. Marsden watches them together and feels the odd pleasure of being betrayed.

After the death of Euripides in 406 BC, the great period of tragedy came to an end. It is entertaining to muse, in Borgesian fashion, over the possibility that transcendent works of the imagination, now lost to the mice, were composed under the Seleucids, or during the Roman occupation, but what straight-faced Cavafy is likely to persuade us of their existence?

George Cawkwell suggests that Demosthenes was foolish in provoking confrontation with Philip of Macedon when a mundane compromise was available. Cawkwell reckons without the education which Athenians had received from the tragic theatre. It taught them to live at a high pitch of moral awareness and also to honour their particularism: to preserve, for the sake of their own pride, the identity of the city. Tragedy as an aesthetic had its counterpart in the ethics of the city and its institutions. Demosthenes miscalculated the odds, but he acted in the light of Athenian glory, as Churchill did in that of the Marlboroughs in 1940. How much less foolish it would have been to go along with Halifax and crave terms from Hitler!

Who now quite understands why, faced with the stake, the heretic ever chose to endure an agonising death rather than opt for tactful concession? Our leaders find it difficult to claim that any principle whatever can excuse a decision to incinerate millions of people. The West is at the end of a tradition of cultural vanity (to put it disparagingly) or of cultural pride (to put it vainly) and of cultural significance (to put it depressingly and defiantly). Who will deny that the defence of 'values' implies the defence of material interests?[8] Demosthenes' policy of independence required Athenian

---

8 The singular status of the Jews in the Diaspora, when all realistic assessment

control of the Thracian Chersonese and access to the mines on which her wealth largely relied. The genius of Athens had always been subsidised by affluence, however crass it may be to derive the former from the latter.[9] Demosthenes was right to insist that, from an ethical standpoint, there was nothing to choose between the Persians under Xerxes and the Macedonians under Philip II, except that the Macedonians, being nearer and better led, were the bigger menace. The Athenians (and Spartans) had good cause to regard them as marginal Greeks, not to say barbarians. As so often, what was said to be happening had actually already happened, just as the present state of Britain is not a situation which is occurring but the result of what has already taken place. British despair is aesthetic and ethical: the values and vanities we have lost, like (and somewhat unlike) those of ancient Athens, are associated with successful adventure. In *Henry the Fifth*, Shakespeare licenses the violent vanity on which Greek dramatists looked with suspicion, if not abhorrence.[10] The heroes of British imperialism were spared a critical literature. As Churchill proved, until 1943 or so British rhetoric was incautiously self-assertive. Morale took precedence over morality, except on Sundays; and even then the head of the British state was also the head of the Church. Before proceeding to the business of aggrandisement, both Athens and Britain generated an empowering and exceptionalising metaphysic.

Shakespeare provided an upholstered rationale for order. Having witnessed civil war, he saw monarchy, in the Tudor style, as its desirable antidote.[11] The eloquence of his historical plays is slashed with gory interruptions; bodies fall with slapstick rapidity. The comedy depends on the audience not identifying too closely with

---

argued for the renunciation of their spiritual values, suggests that the human capacity for unrealistic piety, whatever its humiliating consequences, should never be discounted.

9 Democracy itself was, to a great degree, a pragmatic agreement to abate internal dissent in favour of the common pursuit of wealth and power.

10 With the rise of Puritanism, Cromwell's attitude to Spain (and Catholicism) was wilfully implacable: they were *the* enemy. This contrasts with that of Aeschylus with regard to the Persians. In the *Persae*, their enemies' common humanity was represented to the victorious Athenians as a warning against the 'sin' of overweening pride.

11 Prosaically similar to Shakespeare, Thomas Hobbes, born in the year of the Spanish Armada, posited monarchy as the cure for social mayhem. He was also the first translator into English of Thucydides' *Peloponnesian War*, which dwelt at some length on the horrors of *stasis* (class war).

any of the parties on stage. If Shakespeare's revisionism warranted his audience to regard the past as full of absurdities, he never asked them to see themselves as laughable or defective. His texts digest the church and the erotic: sacred and profane are reconciled in marriage (the standard comic culmination). Only in his tragedies, where outsiders such as Cleopatra and Othello rupture routine social practice, does marriage take on the lineaments of passion, bringing hot confusion in its train. Medea is the Euripidean example of the dangers of miscegenation. That something is dangerous does not fail to be part of its enchantment. Jealousy is not Othello's incidental misfortune; it is the consequence of his unbridgeable apartness. So too one of the mythical *attractions* of Medea was that she was a witch and a barbarian. There was nothing she might not do. The forbidden stands for everything we would like to do. Why else do the Ten Commandments take the form of negations?

Shakespeare spoke for an England newly independent, as a result of the double thrust of the Reformation and the defeat of the Spanish armada. He provided a just version of a chronicle-cum-pageant that, as if incidentally, legitimised Tudor autocracy. Aeschylus sprang from a literary tradition based on Homer and the values of an arcane chivalric order in which the Olympian gods, unlike the Christian God of the sixteenth century, played an intrusive part. The action of the Trojan War, as depicted by Homer, was masterminded by the gods. Mortal motives were inexplicable without them. Homer's gods were envious of human mutability. Attic intelligence realised, in dramatic form, that it is possible to be both powerful and pitiable. The tragic hero (always an obsolete figure) testifies to the fragility of tyrannical power. Tragic drama goes further: it announces the frustration of gods who have characteristics but are incapable of humane changes of mind, of the kind which democratic Athens showed when it rescinded the death penalty on the rebels in Mytilene. Aeschylus presages this in the *Eumenides* when Athene contrives to make the furies defer to the decision of an Athenian jury. The ambivalence of attitudes to the gods is an element of the Greek sense of intellectual sovereignty. Hence Protagoras; hence Thucydides' account of the Peloponnesian war dared to be essentially godless.

3.3.80. C. told me that her sister, who is fifty, is living in the Lot and having a Lawrencian affair with a married *agriculteur* whose wife is unsophisticatedly angry. C. cannot imagine her senior in the arms of an unwashed peasant. I suspect she has less difficulty imagining herself in the same pose.

10.3.80. I saw Bob Redford for three hours at his office in the Warner Communication Building, high up. He has a desk in front of a dark cork wall. The side wall is covered with pictures of himself. There is the usual 'conference' nook at the bottom of the room: narrow couch, two wide armchairs. The place has a brownish, studious tone. The 'artist' prides himself, it seems, on being business-like, and liking business. He wore a brown roll-neck sweater and has the hint of a hump, outward sign of a back problem which has been with him since *Gatsby*, a movie of which he speaks with puzzled fondness, still not sure what went wrong, though he is fairly sure that it should be pronounced Yablons.[12] The latter shouted the odds loudly and incessantly and drove his star into a reclusive rage, which displeased the press corps and soured the already turning publicity. As promised, Redford is fair-haired and boyish, though it needs cosmetic care to enable him to keep his promise. He is about to have prolonged 'parodontic' surgery which entails his gums being split and curetted. He was told that it is one of those things that come with age. He grins with dismay as he repeats the story and says he doesn't want to hear any of that. Who does? He is slim and full of handsome enthusiasms, for skiing and for new ideas, especially his own, although he deprecates them with actorish modesty.

He started by showing us the latest copy of *The Rocky Mountain Magazine*, a publication founded by an old client of his, which is now a big success. Its founder is after money to expand it. Redford flapped the boring, soft issue as if to assay the gold which he already suspects is dross. He was timid in propounding his Big Idea, for which I had been fetched across the Atlantic. I could soon see why: it amounted to very little. He wants to do a 'political' film without real politics, a man-meets-woman story with opportunities for boyishness and girlishness; he and Jane maybe, because they are good friends. As to what makes the pair friendly enemies and then lovers, he had no special notion: that was where I came in.

---

12 Frank Yablons was president of Paramount Pictures when *The Great Gatsby* was released. He was later, briefly, the head of 20th Century Fox. After he was fired from the latter post and replaced by a troika headed by Alan 'Laddie' Ladd Jr, people asked what a troika meant. He put it about that it meant that if you made a call to Fox and asked for an asshole, 'three guys run to pick up the phone'.

The vice-president from Universal was the pretty Mary Anne Maloney, who might have been no more than the PA on the project if we had been sitting at the BBC, which happily we were not. She was nicely dressed in a brown silk blouse and skirt and substantial boots, as if she had advance notice of impending blizzards. Her young-executive hair-do got older during the long day. She had worked for Tom Guinzburg (who published me at Viking) and then for Evarts Ziegler, who was briefly my agent, a man who could talk non-stop for an hour, especially when he had nothing to tell you. Her presence reminded me of Guinzburg's office, full of silly toys. I recalled going out to dinner, in May 1967, with him and his new young wife Rusty, a girl not so much slim as *narrow.* We must have gone to a smart restaurant because the Windsors were at an adjacent table. He looked very thin, the Duke, as if his famous face had been printed on tissue paper. There were at least two dozen long-stem roses on their table.

Mary Anne was discreetly silent. It was more important to remember what others had said than to contribute anything herself. She did not propose to foul the deal or to promote it; she observed. While as poised and amusing as a man can be expected to be when he is six hours older than anyone else in the room, I was wary of endorsing a project scarcely taller than the surrounding bullshit. If not jet-lagged, thanks to Concorde, I had certainly been transplanted. My flowers threatened to droop. I was sitting with the most bankable star in the world, but apart from that, what was I doing there?

I went from the meeting to the Gotham Book Mart on 47th Street, where I happened on a bilingual edition of Odysseus Elytis' *Axion Esti* and failed to procure *Underground with the Oriole*, which the well-informed staff said did not exist. I bought *The Fiery Hunt* instead. It sounded more suitable for the purposes of *Richard's Things* than the unavailable or non-existent volume.[13] Back at the Sherry-Netherland (where we once ate a lotta lotta caviar with Richard and Natalie), Burt Weissbourd and Mary Anne agreed with each other that, thanks to me, the meeting had been a big, big success. I am not sure why. Perhaps I should be paid for just meeting people, if I am that good at it.

I dined with Peter Gethers and an editor from Lasset, who have set up a New York operation, at a restaurant on the Upper East

---

13 *Underground with the Oriole* by Frank Lima was in fact published by Dutton in 1971.

Side, in the 80s on 3rd Avenue. The place had been a butcher's shop. The steaks were said to be excellent, though none of us had one. If you have a reservation, the wait is only three quarters of an hour. The food was the familiar Italian, the waiter merely familiar. He thought to add to our pleasure by mimicking my British accent. I was very tired and lacked the will to be sparky. He walked all over me for a twelve-buck tip. The place sported a well-known 'Singles Bar'. The front was crowded with anxious-eyed ladies in little dresses and less hope. As we went in, I heard a greying, vulpine man saying 'The great thing about being single is that great things can happen to you any minute'.

American women really do look different from European. Is it only a matter of how they do their eyes or is that appetitive gleam the reflection of their predatory caution? They may give men their bodies but they will not give anything else without talking to their lawyers. Near us were three female couples; they may have been romancing lesbians but they were more likely to be discussing business, always more rewarding than pleasure in the American scale of things. Gethers has no fixed relationship and lives happily alone. He works Tuesdays and Wednesdays on his novel; weekends, he rests or amuses himself.

The following morning, I went book-shopping and then had a pastrami sandwich at Kaplan's deli. It was too early for the lunch crowd so the fat-gutted boss was making off-jokes with his female staff, like 'What weighs only half a pound and you rub it up and down and it spits at you?' I can't say how much liberated pleasure the girls got out of this. They indulged him, like a dirty father. I sat next to an art dealer, Alan Brandt, who dealt in African stuff and knew Bill Wright, rather patronisingly. Brandt was fifty-four, bearded with rectangular metal-rimmed glasses. Having taken up acting only recently, he has a part in a Jewish Theatre production due to open Saturday. The cast is non-denominational: Brandt has an Italian kid as his son; the producer, a 23-year-old girl, is a WASP. He won the part in an Equity open audition, against a hundred and thirty other contestants; he is the only licensed member of the cast without a union card. His wife is a failed actress from whom he had been parted. She has now resumed living with him, but feels threatened by his new career. Brandt had seen *The Glittering Prizes* and was extremely affable: I should come to his house next time I was in NYC. By that time, he might be a star but he would, he said, still be unspoiled. He does all his art-dealing from home and made himself out to be a golden-hearted toughie.

Concorde. On my first trip, we were courted with its unlimited caviar and *foie gras frais*, presents and promises. Now the flights are quite full and they still lose money. The speed is marvellous; but the magic carpet has been rolled up. I had a double to myself on the way out, but on the return (with the same crew), I sat next to a plump Italian lady who had been on holiday in Miami. She spoke affectionately of her *marito* who manufactured dental equipment in Torino. She was a pleasant, bespectacled, russet lady of placid humour. She had three children, one an engineer who had chosen not to go to the USA, despite the leaden situation in Italy. '*Siamo Italiani*,' she said. Torino was a frightening place to live. She never went out with a handbag or with rings on her fingers. Women no longer wore jewellery. The fear was not limited to the conspicuous: middle managers at Fiat had been attacked. You never knew who was next. She was a complacent, contented *bourgeoise* and no sort of a fool. The Red Brigades knew very well what they were doing and what they wanted. She was both alarmed and quite sane in her appraisal. Italians were used to such things; the frightfulness need not necessarily have frightful consequences. She ate what was set in front of her without greed or comment. With her pride in husband and family and her slight aversion from lobster, she might have been a fair Jewess.

How little one blames one's friends for their treachery until they make the mistake of apologising for it!

24.3.80. Phil said that what he had particularly admired about Orson Welles was that he always criticised his own early films and repudiated the praise lavished on them. It proved that he hoped still to do better. Recently he has begun to say how good they were.

27.3.80. *Richard's Things.* I went to see Liv Ullman and the pretty, but not too pretty, girl whom they have found to play opposite her, Amanda Redman, the great-niece of Joyce, whom she has never met. Paul said of Liv, when I asked him on the telephone what she was like, 'She's a star, Fred.' His description proved accurate; she has no striking feature, but radiates unmistakable quality. May she never know how badly (and how justly) I treated her tiresome feminist book! We read the script together with Amanda, whose youth has unsettled the beautiful, forty-something Norwegian, or so she says, perhaps the better to be sure of winning their contest. Liv has the slyness of vanity, fearful that you may not be aware of who she is. In New York, she had a mystery virus, which prevented her from meeting me as planned; in London, she was suffering from its treatment: she had to go to the doctor because she had come out in lumps. She was in sour humour because she had been in the receiving line at the Royal Film Performance and had been ignored by Prince Philip, who can be assumed not to be an Ingmar Bergman fan. She was wearing a high Norwegian order, but the passing Duke proved not to be an expert on Nordic chivalry either.

We had had Tony Harvey foisted on us as director, since he had got the script to Liv. There were rumours of his unreliable temperament. As happens, a reliable script had a calming effect. The atmosphere at the Southern Pictures offices, 58, Frith St, was luxuriously businesslike. Paul brought us excellent salads for lunch, but restricted himself to a sardine sandwich. He revelled in privileged access but never abused it. He seems to be the darling of both Liv and Tony. He is easier with the famous than I am after all these years on the fringes of the business.

On the ground floor of the same building, Richard Broke is working on the Churchill project with his director, one of those friendly, pasty people whose names I can never recall. They spent their day reading books on W.S.C. and his contemporaries. After the disaster of the *Oresteia* (only now do I perceive the treacheries and the incompetence), we shall never recapture our friendship. We settle for seeming unchanged, which shows how much has changed. I remain vexed by the failure of Bill Hays to give due weight to my scripted ideas and by Richard's unwillingness (or inability) to argue my case. It is not worth doing TV without a good measure of creative control. The best safeguard is a foolproof script, but then one must avoid allowing a fool the chance to prove himself on it.

Saturn Three, which I agreed to rewrite for Stanley Donen, under a veil of anonymity, has proved to be a hit. Today the *Evening Standard*, in the person of someone called Anwer Bati, who sounded like an Oxford aesthete of the 1920s, called to discover why I had declined to have my name on the thing and cast provocative aspersions on my motives. I consigned solo credit to Martin Amis who must, for whatever reason, have informed Bati of my contributions. The success of the movie has led Marble Arch to pay for me to go to LA. They propose to pay $145,000 for a first draft screenplay of *Songbird*. The smartly twisty plot would have the Marble Archers cut me off, in due time, and hire Martin Amis to do the rewrite.[14]

We took Paul, Sarah, Liv, Mandy Redman, Mark Shivas and Tony H. to a celebration dinner at the White Elephant. I suggested to Liv that, to avoid too many people seeing her, she might like to sit with her back to the door. She chose to sit with her face to it. I had ordered hot *hors d'oeuvres* to be ready at the table. We drank a lot of champagne. The bill came to about £270. That same night my little film about Cambridge was being transmitted. In it, I told some stories about Leslie Bricusse, although I never mentioned his name. While we were at dinner, a note was passed to me. It carried an address and a telephone number and was signed 'Leslie B.' He was dining at a table in the other section of the restaurant. I went over and was diplomatic.

A propos Kent State. A faculty member, John Konrad, promises his wife that during the whole course of the Sexual Revolution he has not enjoyed so much as a minor uprising. John has always been on the side of 'the kids', but that's as far as he goes. His wife, Kelly, should think so too: she has put up with their intrusions into their house, the broken glasses, the cigarette burns, the spilt coffee, the semen-soiled couch, all the evidence of the ungrateful presumption of 'revolutionary' youth. The same kids went and burnt the Stars and Stripes outside a downtown bar. When the shooting takes place on campus, John brings a wounded student to the house. Suddenly he wants his mother. Kelly takes care of him, holds him as he shakes in shock. John is outraged at the shoot-to-kill behaviour of the National Guard, several of whose members he recognises as citizens of the local town. 'No wonder those kids are increasingly radicalised, don't you agree, darly?' Kelly says nothing. A few days later, a student deputation comes to thank the Konrads for what they did. John brings out some beers and they all drink, quite quietly as a matter of fact. At the door, they again thank Kelly in particular. Any time they can do anything for her... 'You can do something right now as a matter of fact,' she says, 'and that is none of you or your friends ever come back to this house again.' John is embarrassed in front of the kids and again, even

---

14 Martin Amis's *Money*, generally considered his best novel, is said to have been composed in the wake of his experience on *Saturn Three*.

more so, when he is alone with Kelly. 'What was that about?' She tells him that the kids were responsible for what happened. 'Five of them died, Kell! Did anyone fire so much as a shot at the National Guard?' Kelly looks at him. 'They burned the flag, they despised the townspeople for being patriotic, for not reading the Little Red Book and... They asked for it and then they didn't want it. Incidentally, I'm leaving you.'

31.3.80. The Kahns' daughter, Liz, seemed to have a permanent relationship with a judge's son, Peter, an amiable and gentlemanly young man with pleasant manners and confident good looks. She was rather lucky to have him, since she was chubby and had small eyes. Her parents were flattered to be about to have a judge in the family. Their unspoken fear was that Peter might weary of Liz. The opposite appears to have happened: though she still liked him, she broke the engagement. He was shaken by the breach, perhaps because he loved her, perhaps because he had opted for a less than strikingly attractive girl in the expectation that he could command her fidelity (or hedge his own). They stayed friends and may well have continued to sleep together, but the official romance was over. Was Liz dismayed by the rather too manifest relish of her parents at her having landed so eminent a prize? She may simply have enjoyed being the twist in the tale. Imagine a story in which a girl such as Liz lives on a different time-scale from that of her lover. She takes revenge on him for a betrayal which has yet to take place. She can see what is going to happen and hates him for thoughts he does not yet have the intelligence or maturity to entertain. He loves her for what she is; she hates him for what he will be.

Call him Plakeotis. A Chicago Greek family man, suddenly driven to walk out on his wife and children, perhaps 'because' he has fallen in love, after a long heterosexual life, with a younger man, Alex, who at first uses him shamelessly. Soon Plakeotis declares against Alex the war which he never dared to wage against his wife. He is thus not 'taught a lesson', certainly not the lesson which his wife hoped, by his fugue. Rather than go back to his family, he becomes a nude dancer in a male strip club to which he invites his wife. Shamelessness gives him a new lease of virility. He takes up with several young girls, perhaps through 'working' in a porno movie. He then discovers that he has cancer and finds in himself the strength to die alone, music playing, loud. But *what* music exactly?

Harlem 1963. We went down to Lenox Avenue, sight-seeing, and happened on a big meeting at which Malcolm X was speaking, to a black audience. We were not molested. After a while, the Gordons said we should maybe go back to the car before the meeting broke up. So we did; and made our getaway; but while we were waiting at a stop light, a car with a bunch of black guys drove into the back of the station wagon. Harry said 'Don't turn round, don't get out, don't do anything'. The light changed, we drove on downtown.[15]

A famous writer who has always prided himself on the foibles and failings of the human species, for whom every cupboard has its skeleton, takes great care to deprive posterity of any material which a publishing scoundrel might find profitable. Conscious of the prying thoroughness of enterprising biographers, he destroys whatever might serve to cast light on his darker places. He incites his friends to destroy his letters and makes no effort to deserve the gratitude of researchers by depositing his papers at the usual American university. Prouder of his art than of his life, he proposes to leave the world only with the fruits of his pen. In fact, his self-effacement creates a morbid interest in the minutiae of his personal conduct: after his death, his works are regularly disparaged, but his private life becomes a subject of captious curiosity. Had he taken no pains to cover his tracks, who would have chosen to follow them? If he had been selective in what he left to be discovered, he might have prompted the sedulous sycophancy which allowed E.M. Forster's dreary life to receive deferential two-decker treatment from P.N. Furbank.[16]

Santa Barbara. Doctor Mastoff came to the hotel Miramar, on his motorbike, to minister to me. A doleful Dutchman, he examined me thoroughly and slowly and concluded that nothing was wrong except a petty virus which might or might not yield to the antibiotic he prescribed. In the event, he cured me promptly enough,

---

15 Harry related that in the 1950s, black drivers habitually expected to be blamed by whites for any accident, even in Harlem. One white man, bumped by a black driver, got out and began the usual litany of abuse. Then he looked again at the black driver, who had said nothing. The white man said, 'Hey, wait a minute! Don't I know you?' The black man said, 'You don't talk like you know me.' It was Archie Moore, the light-heavyweight champion of the world.

16 David Garnett told me, when I went to see him in the Lot not long before he died, that Furbank had misunderstood Forster and that his biography was wide of the mark. It has become a classic.

though the symptoms of the cure were as depressing as the disease. Mastoff had several fingers missing from his right hand. He held his pen like a cartoon pig. He had himself been to his doctor that morning, suffering from back pains which were of greater concern to him than my transient malaise. He appeared at once touched and suspicious that I showed interest in him. A fellow-European wary of, and longing for, confidences, he had a reticent curiosity about what we were doing in Santa Barbara.

On the one day we were in LA, I raced out to the Valley with Burt Weissbourd to see Sydney Pollack, in an effort to secure a director for *A New Wife*, though none of us had him on our original list. He had just had a hit with *Electric Horseman* and was desirable again. His office in Burbank Studios was in a block that looked like low-price housing. Inside it was personalised with happy stills from his various productions. A biggish man, with large hands and a moon-face, enlarged by round spectacles, energetic but not strong, his cordiality did not come from the heart. I did my best to lure him into coming in with us, but the prospect did not excite me, nor him apparently, although he was effusive about the script. He said it was 'further along' than anything he had ever been offered. He had read bits of the dialogue aloud to his wife. He quoted it to us. He asked to be given till after the weekend before he made his decision. Burt refused, which meant that we knew on Friday rather than Monday that we still had no director.

We drove from Burbank to Burt's office for another meeting with Bob Redford, who is said to be a Mormon and has notice-ably slim hips. It was the same *galère*: the pretty producer-executive from Universal and Bob's lady from NY, both with blank legal pads in front of them. The meeting again went very well; everyone was reported to be even more excited than before, though we seem still to be a long way from any specific story. The generalities proceed splendidly; we are in agreement about the dramatic construction, though we have nothing that resembles a drama. I sympathised with Redford over his treatment by Jilly Cooper, who recently had a go at him in the *Sunday Times*. I assured him that he had been less ill-used than he thought; the English press has little use for foreign celebrities save to put them through the wringer. He is the kind of charmer who so palpably admires himself, without the smallest blemish of irony or self-deprecation; bland, agreeable, bleached and smug, blond hair blowing like a tethered, tawny cloud about his pretty face and even teeth. Blessed by good fortune and perhaps by sane judgment, he appeals to those who like it tepid. There is no devil in him. He knows the score, but it will always be a low one. He did tell one fairly amusing story, of going to a fancy apartment house for a political dinner with people he did not know. He and his wife took the elevator to the appropriate floor, they thought, and got out in the lobby of a fancy spread where they were greeted by an elegant lady and escorted into a magnificent room and seated in the best possible position to admire and be admired by their hostess. Everyone was poised and full of sophisticated gush. After some minutes, the Redfords realised that they had come to the wrong floor.

A cow on its knees,
Praying in the grass;
Tame Hera in its eyes,
Goddess stalled in hide.

At UC in Santa Barbara, after my lecture on Plato and Aeschylus, I was buttonholed by a blond, determined, unsmiling man who had also been at the meeting of screenwriters to which I was convoked by Paul Lazarus Sr, a big-handed ex-executive at Columbia who now teaches screenwriting. The blond guy was less interested in ancient Greece than in success. Twenty-three years in the military, he now wanted to break into movies. He was a West Point man and had the ring to prove it, quoting the motto, something to do with honour. He had been shot at all around the world. I stood talking to him in the parking lot where I had left the Oldsmobile I had hired in LA and which contained the sticky typewriter that I was due to return to Judy Godfrey. She was waiting in her dull Buick. I said that I had no access to the secret of success. If I had, I should certainly regard it as classified. The best thing he could do was to tell me something I didn't know. After all that time in the army, there had to be a lot. He declared that honour forbade him to disclose what he knew of the US military mentality. I urged him not to underestimate civilian curiosity about the mundane aspects of army life. He was not convinced that a new story told in a new way was his likeliest entrée into the biz. He had, he disclosed, 'an ace in the hole'. He opened his wallet and pulled out a cellophane-faced deck of photographs. Wife and children were folded away to reveal a buddy picture, two young men with cigars, leaning their puppyish faces together. 'Do you know who that is? Do you recognise him?' One of the two was clearly the speaker, the face of an unimaginative man who had done things which I did not care to imagine. The other guy was pudgier and darker, with a look of virile slyness and confidence. 'That's the face of a man who gets five million dollars for twenty-one days' work. My old buddy Burt Reynolds.' They used to double-date in the old days and knocked around together quite a lot. All that my conversant had to do was write the right script and he could call up his old pal and have him read it, pretty well while he waited. A guy like Burt Reynolds would never forget an old pal, would he? They had been real close; Burt was a regular guy. So all he had to do – was I beginning to see his point? – was get a bundle of pages together and he would be in there, ahead of the pack, and old Burt would be sure he got a fair shake. He put the photographs back in his pocket and gave me the firm hand-clasp and the look in the eye. He'd see me around. Burt would take care of that.

29.4.80. Frank Frost, a professor colleague of John Sullivan's at UCSB, had a hot tub in the garden of the house he designed high on the hill behind Santa Barbara. The hot tub, covered by a piece of three-ply, was like a big cauldron, plastered, with a seat all around. It has no evident purpose, since no exercise can be obtained in it. Presumably it excuses the decorous nudity which precedes Californian overtures. Frost gave his annual bake-out, lamb in the Greek style, at noon on the Sunday after our arrival, on the same day as Sullivan cooked a curry dinner, to which none of the same guests were invited. Frost was married to a youngish woman, his second wife, dark, sexy and silent, as if intent on establishing her *sérieux* after the scandalous collapse of Frank's first marriage. He wore khaki shorts and a blue shirt and Greek sandals. The *arnaki* party was habitually held on the Greek Easter. Does it ever occur to him that hardly anyone from Santa B., except for fossils, lives by the Greek calendar? He had an apprehensive gentleness. As if fearful of being accused of a misdemeanour which he would be too honest to deny, he looked you in the eye, but not in both eyes. His house was tall and white, the front door so high that Gulliver would have walked in upright. He had planned it himself. The living room was the whole height of the house, its triad of tall narrow windows capped with semi-circular fans. Frost pointed out that the windows had not been finished with perfect semi-circles. The reason was that the builder had not known of the use of *pi* in calculations and did not therefore know how to impose a semi-circle on a rectangle. He made much of this deficiency, but what relevance did it have? To impose a semi-circle above an upturned rectangle, it is necessary only to find the centre of the side of the rectangle and then apply a pair of compasses.

Frost has a Steinway grand piano in the corner of the room, under the tall windows. He plays in a restaurant to meet the payments. It was plucky and admirably unEnglish to be playing piano at the Chanticleer (imagine Hugh Lloyd-Jones in a pop group), but it also suggested a modest re-make of *The Blue Angel*. Frost had ruptured his dignity. There was watery shamelessness in the grey-blue eyes, vigilant for reproaches which he feared he deserved. He was polite and hospitable, but had no notion of who we were (but then who were we, after all?) and showed no interest even after his sister, recently returned to S.B., her home-town, after years in San Francisco, had gushed like a bobbysoxer after hearing that I was the author of that TV series, etc. Perhaps she was no great credit to him, a woman in her mid-thirties, with a figure shaped by despair, a complicated youth behind her, sorry prospects ahead.

Jim Wiseman, who was to lecture next day on the archaeology of Corinth, was also shown the hot tub. He seemed little im-pressed. He teaches at Boston University and was at Texas with Sullivan. His lecturing manner is largely inquisitive: he interjects little calls of 'hmp?', tactical hiccups which give the class oppor-tunities to respond or disagree, though they have to be quick about it: the lecture proceeds as if the speaker has a meter running. He wore a creamy suit and a brown moustache and has genuine enthusiasm for digging. He displayed the sites with transparen-cies that were rendered pale by inconclusive curtains across the lecture-room windows. His small audience did not dismay him as much as my larger one had me. He took his money and ran, almost literally, after giving me a hint as to where he thought the ancient agora of Corinth actually was, *not* under the Roman city as tradition recounts.[17]

30.4.80. They have been married for seven years, if indeed they are married, although Dinah still calls herself by her maiden name, perhaps to distinguish herself from the previous, prettier Mrs G., who has the same first name and discovered Women's Lib (and

---

17 Wiseman's paper on the excavations at Corinth argues, with precise evidence, that the alleged destruction of the city by the Romans, under Lucius Mummius, in 146 BC was not as extensive as is usually alleged.

another woman) in the early Seventies. Stee and Sarah disliked and despised Dinah, sentiments I do not share, although young judgments, being uninhibited by hypocritical politeness, are often just. I recall how dismal I thought my parents' friends were and how insupportable their opinions. Dinah never addressed a word to either Stee or Sarah, who is scarcely a child (she telephoned the other night because the *Daily Mail* had got hold of the story about her and Warren and had sent a photographer to Camberwell to root her out for the delectation of Nigel Dempster's readers). Dinah, not yet forty, suffers from the pinchedness of sterility; she does not seem quite to be a woman, although she is no longer a girl. She has opened a small school, which does not yet break even. Neither maternal nor idealistic, she relieves the parents of children, guilt and money. Her admiring aggression reminded me of Charlotte Gordon: Dinah picked up my reference to 'Bob Redford' in the same mocking manner in which, more than twenty years ago, in the Calle Tostón, Charlotte pulled at my blue (Colin Wilson-style) sweater: 'What's this? What's this?'

They live in a bungalow which cost $105,000, at the end of a cul-de-sac, Taormina Drive. The back garden faces onto a ravine. They have peaches, lemons and avocados. Gilbert talks of installing a hot tub. The place looks clean, but does not smell clean. Dinah used a lot of make-up quite as if intent on making her small eyes smaller. Gilbert sports a mat of grey-black greasy hair and a grizzled beard. Affecting the Californian vocabulary, he speaks of being laid back and heavily into things. He prides himself on his spontaneity but appears merely unprepared. He must be a good scholar; he told us that they are making him a 'professor seven', a new rank for Field Marshals who warrant promotion. 'Professor six' was previously the highest available rank. Whatever his merits, G. cannot be there for the quality of his jokes nor for his skill in introducing visiting lecturers. He referred to me as 'F.M. Raphael' and not one of his sallies provoked the smallest titter or *cachinnus*. He wore cumbrous sun-belt clothes, favouring a sallow mustard-coloured cotton suit which made him look like a plucked duck. His skin did not seem to be his size: he is as generously pouched as airline luggage. In the two years since we last saw him, on Ios, he has become the dwarf image of tenured self-indulgence. He works eighteen hours a day quite often, but he also drinks, a lot; it's the Irish blood, he says, and he smokes both cigarettes and 'grass' as well as having his cocaine connections. He has nothing between his studious virtues and his toxic vices. He is proud of making nearly $40,000 a year and refuses to entertain the idea of returning even to Regius eminence. He is an industrious lotus-eater with an unenviable Circe.

5.5.80. A short-story plot delivered by a dream starring Norman Rodway. A man and a woman have been living together for some years when she decides that she must have a child. The man fears she is closing the trap on him. She tells him that she doesn't mind if he leaves her once she has had the child. On those terms, he agrees. Her pregnancy releases unexpected feelings in him; he becomes increasingly interested in his baby. All the same, his suspicions and the hard things he has said remain vivid to her. When he proposes marriage, she takes the baby and leaves the house. (I guess that I dreamed about N.R. because I was reading Norman Podhoretz, converted 'Pod' into 'Rod' and the rest followed.)

Redford has the blond grace of those who have come up the soft way. He would like to pass for a thinking man, if only he could think of something. Ever since he began to be a star, he has wanted to take a hand in production; he does not like being a mere actor. He now treats himself like a smart vintage car, not as old and never as slow as some people would prefer to think. He takes delight in his office and the accoutrements (not at all grandiose) of the star as institution; he loves being the head of himself. He is prepared to be modest about his abilities, so long as nobody chooses to share his opinion. He is already older than Alexander the Great ever was. For all his charm, one can imagine him being as suddenly irascible, if criticised, as the man who killed Black Cleitus. Ronnie Reagan has probably excited political ambitions. His electoral success has made it manifest that you need not be a great actor to play the great president. R.R. may yet be succeeded by R.R.

6.5.80. After Dudy's pathetic, sharp letter comes the reply to my reply, clever and faintly crazed in its Jean Rhys-like acknowledgment that she must seem bad news to those who are good enough Friends to tolerate her. It is ten years since she and John visited us at the Wick. She wore a cartwheel straw hat and her mouth reminded me of an arse-hole: a hoop of pinched inward-pointing wrinkles. She was always a strange-looking party who needed a myth. It was supplied by Mark Boxer's *Granta* caricature of her, captioned 'the Well-Known Animal Lover'. There was an energy about her, when young, that was misleadingly romantic; all her tastes were classic (Henry James above all). Now she speaks of John having acquired her because he took her to be the first prize. Like her daughters, whom she has driven from gymkhana to gymkhana, she has won no prizes at all. She now threatens to become her mother, a Quaker girl who has long abandoned her oats. Dudy's calvary has been long and lonely; it is unlikely to abate. Jane M. has not a tenth of her brains, but she has a lectureship at UCL and, living in London, enjoys a wide acquaintance. Dudy, stuck in the sticks, is likely to retire even further beyond the metropolitan horizon, to Yealand Conyers, after her mother goes to her last Meeting. Has there ever been a perkier despair? One's heart, or at least one's next letter, goes out to her. She is an attractive correspondent, though one would dread her as a neighbour and run, over the sticks if necessary, to avoid her embrace.

It is twenty-five years since the four of us formed a weekly club in London and played happy couples at alternate dinner parties. We were neither candid nor amorous. Our disequilibrium was not helped by Dudy's affectations of intellectual superiority. After my small initiation in showbiz, I advised her, despite her amateur stardom at Cambridge, to go to drama school, which she did, the Webber Douglas. She learnt a lot, but not enough to save her from calamity. Cast in the lead of *The Duchess and the Smugs*, in which she played a sassy teenager, she was fired before the production reached the West End. She continued to be as conceited as ever and dropped names as though her hands were full. She patronised Beetle so exquisitely that one never remarked how much she lacked in comparison. Her legs were so short it was a wonder she had room for knees. She concentrated all her attention, and yours, on her strongest feature, her brains. She was one of those girls, like her friend Anne, whose clothes even one's crudest imagination never dreamed of stripping. Nevertheless, she advertised her adventures on the tube, where countless gents pinched her bottom (a part of her that was difficult to miss).

After that terrible first night in Brighton in 1954 (which Beetle attended, while I was on my travels), John did not chide her, but he decided to abandon buying books (I remember him lending us Patrick White's *Voss*) and become a businessman. I never saw another new book in their house, except on marketing (Dudy read only old books). John proved as devoted to business as he had once been to pleasure, and found it a pleasure to be so. He has become well-off and, like most of those who do, he has hoped that money would buy him something worth having, for instance a happy wife. Dudy has lost interest in buying things. She cannot even be tempted by sweetmeats. She prefers to buy seeds than expensive groceries. She has become a nut nut. She does not care about clothes; she has always been an eager nudist, although her naked-ness would be unlikely to attract visitors. John lost patience and again found someone else. Dudy may hate him, but he has merely wearied of her. He wrote us a letter in which he boasted (after all, he need not have told us) that he had had an affair with Dorothy W. back in the Sixties, but that he had renounced it and gone back to Dudy and that they were more in love than ever. The letter, sincere and touching, seemed to presage a middle age of learned lessons. They had another child, of Stee's age, who is now the most pained by John's departure. Dudy had liked Geneva ('In Geneva, I had my friend'), but who could like Peterborough, to which they returned when John changed jobs? Dudy reverted to the Quakers. John, she said, resented her Friends and the slightly cracked society which so comforted her. He worked alongside hard men – one of them an accountant who rejected Murray when he so badly needed a job – and he wanted a wife who would impress them and do him credit. Dudy refused to wear falsies in a false society. Her assets were all mental. Her academic measurements less seduced than alarmed the marketing men and the cost-efficiency experts. John went to work in Holland and came home only at weekends. He turned the family into an allotment which he worked in his spare time. He preferred work. He again found someone else; he had always relished straight-faced secrecy; he liked to touch knees below the decorous table. I do not blame him. He left his pain, discreetly, under his napkin, like a tip.

There was a sorry couple in Fuengirola in 1961, John and Pauline M. He wrote unpublishable stories, after having tried to be a painter. She was scrawny and had been a schoolteacher. She had a corncrake voice and a chapped complexion. When John tried to grow a beard, he looked like a eunuch who had failed to put on weight. They lived on the meagre proceeds of some Mutual Funds. Charlie Reiter was married at the time to a very beautiful opera singer. They had a little boy called Jason. Charlie was handsome, and knew it. He was about to have a short book published by the Grove Press. It was well enough done for Tom Maschler, down there on a visit, to be tempted to publish it in England. Charlie's story concerned a white man who goes out with a black call-girl in NYC. Their evening ends with the client being ashamed at

using the girl as a sexual toy and, although (and because) they
have achieved a certain rapport, he decides he will not take her
to bed. He imagines she will be gratified by his finesse in saying
that he doesn't feel the way he did before, so their deal need not
be honoured. The girl says, 'And what about me? What if I want
it to be?' The writing was wilfully 'experimental', but the twist
was nicely contrived, even if one did not quite believe it, more
through prudery than cynicism (but is it likely that a black – or
white – hooker would be disappointed at having to take the fare
without giving the ride?).

Some years later, we heard that Charlie had been to bed with
Pauline. It seemed a degradation; he was so handsome and she was
a wreck. Harry said Charlie had fucked Pauline because he felt
sorry for her; it meant nothing to him. There still seemed to be
something displeasing in a man of Charlie's elegant virility finding
pleasure in fucking so dry a husk as Pauline. D.H. Lawrence would
never have licensed it. It occurred to me only recently that there
was unpriggish generosity in his action. His gesture of affection
(attention at least) to a woman whom no one was likely to desire
was of a piece with the story he had written so many years before.
There was something gracious in that 'love' so casually bestowed
by a man who did not take himself, or his actions, too seriously.

Charlie later became fat. The last I heard he was editing a Union
magazine in Oakland and had pretty well lost interest in women.
He had the strangely vacuous smile of a man who could switch
himself on. He seemed to regard the loss of his wife as a foregone
conclusion. He was not especially sorry to have Anne go, however
beautiful she was. I suspect that he found her vanity tedious,
perhaps vulgar. He was not prepared to pay the price in admiration
which her wide, white smile solicited. He took pride in his complaisance; although beautiful, she was not worth the trouble.

I was in a deserted street, with railway tracks down the middle.
A button was pressed and a panel – the whole façade of a dingy
shop – slid back. An antiquarian of sinister, sullen aspect was
revealed in a room full of dusty valuables. Here as elsewhere, my
dream landscape has little to do with my present or recent life. It
is above all urban. Often there are railway or streetcar tracks down
the middle of the road. Antiques and bookshops abound. There
is always a good deal of dialogue. I often tell stories in the midst
of unlikely companions, stories repeated, more or less word for
word, without amusing or embarrassing textual variation, from

my waking repertoire. I am also capable of spontaneous repartee, sometimes quite witty, but it seldom has any effect on my conversants. I go in fear, above all, of being found out. I used to believe that I had buried the corpse of my father in a trunk and was about to be unmasked. I often dream that I am a Member of Parliament who has not yet made a maiden speech and who, after years of membership, has to confess that he is (no twist here!) an American citizen. His constituency, in East Anglia, has been remarkably patient about his neglecting to speak, but it cannot continue like this. I suppose that my decision, in 1953, not to be British weighs on me like a crime I have never committed (cf. Kierkegaard's putative bastard!). I have succeeded neither in becoming my grandfather's 100% American nor in staying British.[18]

9.5.80. They finished shooting *Richard's Things* last week. It was a wrap without a party. Liv had become venomously hostile towards Amanda Redman. Her relationship with Tony Harvey was not in much better case. He told her to fuck off ('Not something I'm in the habit of saying to ladies') the day before they finished. She paid him out by leaving without a goodbye. He (and everyone else) put the blame on Liv's make-up man and hairdresser whom she had insisted on bringing over from New York. Ray was tall and slim and bleached. He wore a grey baize apron with front patch-pockets for pins and powder. Homosexual without opportunity to practise his game, he persuaded Liv to dump Paul, at the last minute, when she was due to spend the weekend with him at the Wick (we were in France at the time). She never recovered her early amiability. Ray's jokes about Liv's resemblance to Miss Piggy became unfunny; they served to undermine her confidence (she hates being 43) and at the same time became the means, through self-mockery, by which she pretended to repair it. Ray made trouble throughout, but the real trouble was Liv herself. She is a star who lives in a hazed halo. Doubting the durability of her looks, she takes the worst possible measures to preserve them:

---

18 Since I was born in the US of a British father, I enjoyed dual citizenship until I was twenty-one, when a choice was forced upon me by the fact that I was eligible for conscription in both countries and could not join the armed forces of either without abandoning the other. In due time, I received a note from President Eisenhower telling me that my services would not be required. The war in Korea had recently ended and so had the draft.

hair girlishly long and loose, pixie dresses. She seems irremediably morose. They all say that the picture is wonderful. Tony has kept his nerve pretty well and is generous about Mark, although he did not do all he might have to jolly the cast. I hope that *Richard's Things* will get an American release, but neither Liv nor Tony Harvey has any recent success with which to attract a distributor. What concerns me more is how good the picture is.

George Steiner, in a *Sunday Times* review, writes that sex is 'humourless, coercive and banal'. The friendship which is the fruit of a good marriage works against sex, for the adjectival reasons stated. Is he trying to tell us something? He is certainly succeeding. George's paranoia comes less from Jewishness than from want of narcissism and its reflective reticence. He relies on his brains and has a suspicion that he will never be on easy terms with the world. With a Sartrean tendency to verbalise everything, he cannot see that there is a humour of the flesh, a wordless comprehension, a smile (or straight face) that is comment enough. Nature herself makes the paranoid feel superfluous. Bernard Levin's prose style, with its ironic keel, its reliance on the long sentence (typical of those who are forever saying 'Let me finish') suggests the reasonable man haunted by irrational dread. Might G.'s misfortunes, like his misreading – what else? – of the secret joys of marriage, derive from never having been on confident and confidential terms with a beautiful woman? With such a wife, there is constant play between the physical and the mental, the said and the unsaid; when she is clever as well, allusive reflection is at the heart of the meum-tuum sense. G. is a polysyllabic overdresser. He can cloak any idea in a tailored suit of more words than it needs. What a shame when his arms fail to reach the ends of the sleeves!

Hilbert, the Miramar tennis professional. Stocky, short-legged, both slow-talking and garrulous, Sarah imitated him to perfection. Between rallies, being older than he was, he leaned over the net and dropped names. He could not ask you how you were without telling you how some famous person was, Armand Hammer a frequent instance. Hilbert was, he said, a close friend of Ziggy, who was my agent for a short period in 1970, during which Sharon Tate, the pregnant wife of his best client, Roman Polanski, was murdered on Cielo Drive. Did I know that the 'Baron de Mouton-Rothschild' had dined recently at the very best French restaurant in town? Hilbert gave fair measure to his pupils: the ball came back to them fast, but within reach. He had a basket with a trap in the bottom so that he could collect balls without bending down. A weathered Frenchman, a Breton without his onions, pedalled around the place, knees out, checking that there were no interlopers. He ran the gym and was happy to speak French to Stee.

We had been promised a 'rare human being' in Ray Byram who was in charge of the lecturing rota. He was a heavily bearded young man of the kind that is nice to elderly ladies, if they have the money. Ingratiating, but with small grace, he was efficient, but at the last moment. He came into his own when he came into other people's: he played the host at the cocktail party on the terrace of a rich lady where we were privileged to meet Judith Anderson, George Cukor, Virginia Cherryl and Eleanor Boardman. One felt that select inhabitants of Forest Lawn had been given ticket of leave. Miss Cherryl had been the blind girl in *City Lights* and was once married to Cary Grant. George Cukor, over eighty, was chipper enough to lift a courteous cane chair from here to there. He was attended by Paul Morrissey, who is writing his biography. When Cukor saw us walk onto the terrace, he called out, nicely, 'Here come the haughty Raphaels!' Morrissey directed several of Andy Warhol's deliberately trashy movies. A rusty person in a tall tweed suit, with long wrists and a snub nose, he gave the impression of being cleverer and more decent than it had been prudent to reveal. He seemed to have been slumming intellectually for many years. He said that he wanted to direct more conventional movies, but now that he had been typecast as way-out, it wasn't that easy. His residual glamour gave him an air of confident desperation. He was like a man who had appealed against an unjust sentence which he expected to be rescinded but which, meanwhile, he continued to serve.

The rich lady's house had a big parking circle in front of it. Her guests were likely to come in vehicles which needed ample acreage. We arrived last and there were indeed several Rolls-Royces, surveyed by a cigarette-smoking heavy who would have said something sarcastic about our rental car if only Raymond Chandler had been there to supply the line. The house dated from the end of the last century; rosy brick, sliced thin. The terrace, also brick, offered long shots of the Pacific. The pearly post-sunset lustre reminded those who had the purse for it of Japan. The palm trees seemed printed on the silky, unreflecting sky.

Dame J. Anderson remembered the 1960 movie[19] on which Dennis Cannan and I shared credit and which was produced by Fritz Gotfurt, that wince-eyed, cigar-smoking nice old voyeur. Anderson puts away a lot of sauce. She received her dameship because, in her day, the Australians had the right to confer a limited number of honours and someone persuaded Menzies that she deserved it. She was a star in New York. I recall her doing *Medea*, though it was hard to imagine it on the terrace, and at that weight.

Our hostess, who had never married, was a benefactress of the arts, not above plucking a painting from her well-covered walls in order to finance a worthwhile project. Her generosity was as legendary as the parsimony of the lady (Mrs Knapp?) who sat on my right at the country club to which she had afforded the entrée but nothing else, although uncountably rich. We helped ourselves to the round table of *hors d'oeuvres* around which there was so tight a huddle of *goyim* that one could scarcely reach the pickled herring. They defended the dishes with the tenacity of a circle of pioneers wheeling the wagons around their loved ones. The main course was sole or prime rib.

The Birnam Wood Country Club, cavernous with overstatement, was built on the site of an old ranch. It was just the sort of place from which Jews used to be (and may still be) excluded. It was easy to imagine a local Julian English throwing his highball in the face of some implacable politico at a Republican fund-raiser on the premises. One of the academics, who had sunk several large martinis, looked hectically burdened by the alcohol. My genial neighbour assured me that it wasn't the alcohol, but the proximity of his wife which caused him to adopt a pose of glazed torpor.

John Sullivan had recently been to Mexico City to take part in a conference of international sexologists. Xaviera Hollander[20] was the star turn. When she gave John a copy of her guide to sex, she inscribed it 'To John – once a John always a John'. He found her bright and tough. Although retired from professional practice, she was offering blow-jobs to selected panellists in the bathroom of his suite. J.P.S. proposes to co-author a history of prostitution, his favourite sideshow, with her and another academic who is

---

19 *Don't Bother to Knock*, starring Dickie Todd as some kind of suburban Don Juan. He loved the script.

20 Her book, *The Happy Hooker* (1971), was a phenomenal bestseller.

keen on cash. They will do the work and Xaviera will play the madam and rack up the advance. He has not told Judy, but he had a 'neat experience' with another panellist who became extremely amorous. 'She was all over me,' he said (in John's case, not a very large territory). He suggested that they go back to his room where he had a bottle of Johnny Walker. 'I'd love to,' she said, 'but I really mustn't. You see, I'm a Lesbian.'

14.5.80. We drove down to LA and had breakfast in Westwood before I went to see Stanley Donen in Stone Canyon. We were due to meet Marty Starger out at Malibu. He rents a house owned by Lee Marvin. Yvette was in Thailand. Stanley had not heard from her for a week. He was alone in the house, although the Hickeys, his English chauffeur and his wife, were somewhere around. Stanley now carries a big block of stomach before him. He had a new BMW adjacent to Yvette's Mercedes 450SL. She cannot find work at the moment. We drove down to the coast and had lunch at the Chart House, a big unplanned plank building right on the water: smoked fish, scrambled eggs, fruit salad. A big motor cruiser, crammed with people, rode in the swell. Fishermen pay by the hour for the pleasure of lining the sides. Stanley said that the local restaurants made most of their money servicing alcoholics who come and sit in the long bars, morning till night, watching the swimmers and the tariffed fishermen.

Recently, they had serious mud-slides on the Pacific Coast Highway. Malibu was cut off. Stanley had sent Joshie in the Jeep, which has four-wheel drive, to try to rescue Marty, but he never got through. The road was clear now. They had constructed a screen of steel girders and heavy timber to hold back the next charge of mud. If the rains are really heavy again, the barrier will become an addition to the debris on the highway.

Starger, in his fifties, was slim and grizzled and sported a blue jogging outfit. He had just jogged in from New York, where his company had a musical in rehearsal. Burt Shovelove was directing, from his own book and Kern/Berlin songs, when he had a heart attack and had to go into intensive care. 'He did that before,' Stanley said. 'He always does it,' Starger said, as if it were a party trick. He regarded the likely fiasco ('The show isn't really right and it never will be') with intrepid fatalism. He might have been the shore-based operator of the *Titanic*, about which Lew Grade's Marble Arch company has just made a $30m movie, of dubious quality, very much against S.D.'s advice. The model shots alone cost three million bucks. Starger was amiable, even deferential, although Stanley says that he is tight; he doesn't even have his own place. He has never been married ('Oh maybe once'). Stanley pointed out that he asked us to come to the house at 2 p.m.: funny time. Starger has been president of ABC television and knew Phil Barry Jr, on whose father's play the film *Philadelphia Story* was based. Phil no longer calls himself 'junior', but he still doesn't have a chin. We sat on the deck above the beach which was bony with flotsam. On the night of the worst storm, the electricity and the telephones were out. Police helicopters clattered all night, surveying the benighted houses with their searchlights, intimidating reassurance.

Stanley offered to go to New York and take over direction of the tottering musical ('I'll gladly give you a week for nothing'[21]). He seemed to like Starger well enough, which did not prevent him from marvelling, as we drove back to Bel Air, that Lew Grade had trusted his empire to such a man. He might not have given us lunch, but he could not resist hiring people and now had a payroll which set the company back a million dollars a week. Lew had complete faith in Marty, whose taste was unreliable. If the *Titanic* movie fails, Starger – who retains good relations with ABC – may find himself less admired as a pilot. Meanwhile, he is 'excited' (what else?) by the *Songbird* project and seems to be spilling cash into its development. Can he then be all bad? He has a girlfriend in LA and lives in her modest apartment during the week. He went to college and everything, Stanley said, probably Columbia.

The men came to Lagardelle to repair the leaking roof. Some of the tiles had become porous because of the frost. In the fibreglass lining underneath, one of the men found a nest from which – wearing a bulbous protective glove – he extracted two small, snarling beasts with dogged eyes and sharp claws, pups of a family of *fouines*, as the French call martens. They were covered in silvery black fur coats and had plump bellies. The book promises that the usual litter is from three to eight pups. The bumps we have been hearing on certain nights were caused by the homecoming of their agile, but never light-footed, parents. The *couvreurs* said that *fouines* prey on chickens and eat their eggs. They were vermin, but they were cuddly. We bedded them in some of the yellow fibre-glass and

---

21 I once offered to do a week's anonymous work for nothing on a script with which Jo Janni was having problems. Jo said, 'Fred, nothing is too much.'

ensconced them above the access to the septic tank, where they would be safe from marauders and Pushkin the cat. We presumed that their mother would come looking for them. She didn't; so we moved them to the far barn which a litter of eggshells suggested could be the family refectory. I put them in a cardboard box, lined with more *laine de verre*. They seemed to prosper for a couple of days. We hoped they might disappear into the wild. They did not. One of them found its voice and shrieked at our approach, biting at my gloved finger. Big flies began to circle vulturously. The pups lay across each other; one raised blistered eyes, little raisins in the crew-cut heads. On Friday, it was clear that they had been abandoned. On Saturday, the smaller pup was moribund. I became their executioner. I took a supermarket potato net and a bucket of water to the barn, plucked them from their box, one by one, stowed them in the net and thrust them into the bucket. The little one went down without a struggle. The other fought the sack, fish-like mouth – I thought of a pike – opened wide in the hope of air. The beany eyes glared through the orange netting and the dull water as my boot thrust the squirming pup down to its death. The killing, however merciful, gave me a long headache, uncured by West Ham's unlikely victory in the FA Cup. I swam in the pool on Sunday for the first time this year. I circled it with trepidation, fearful of the *erinyes* of those little pups from a species I had never seen before and could only kill.

A gracious letter from Deborah Kerr, who had hoped to revive the idea of doing *Richard's Things*, until she saw, in the *International Herald Tribune*, that Liv was doing it. She wished us well all the same. When I told Tony Harvey about her geniality, he said that she was a charming woman and that she and Peter Viertel, who had been in the US Marines, used the most filthy language he had ever heard between a married couple. They had done nothing of the kind when we went to their house on the Costa del Sol for a barbecue dinner cooked by Peter. Imagine if they went out of their nicely spoken way only to scandalise poor Tony.

15.5.80. I have been recruited into a syndicate seeking the ITV franchise for East Anglia. If successful, we shall replace John Woolf's gang in 1982. When first contacted, by an anachronistic-ally polite Scot called Forbes Taylor, I did not take it seriously, least of all when he spoke of bestowing grand titles such as 'Head of Drama'. I became involved not least because it would afford me a privileged seat from which to observe a particularly British *valse d'hypocrites*. How sincere were the protestations of desire to 'serve the region', how regretfully contemptuous of the current outfit's performance, how keenly selfless the plans for a 'more appropriate' programme in the future! No one would ever suppose that one clutch of businessmen was seeking to displace another in the collection of easy pickings. I soon declared to Forbes that I could never, in reality, become an administrator. I had not dreamed of seeking to become Head of Plays at the BBC; why would I want a similar post in the Fens? Since I could not even promise to attend board meetings, I had better figure only as a consultant. Meanwhile, Peter Hall and John-Julius Norwich had also been found places on the modest bandwagon as 'non-executive directors'. Unwilling to cede to P. and J.-J. a position I could as well share, I agreed to join them on their bench. To be serviceable for publicity purposes, I had to become a full member of the syndicate which, they tell me, is more likely than not to displace the incumbents. The formal application has now been 'printed up' and I discover that I am to be eligible for 3% of the voting shares. At my scarcely youthful age, I find that I am not taking part in some childish charade but in a grown-up version, with the prospect of a stake in the so-called real world. It still seems probable that the forces of inertia will prevail. The English have long preferred what they know to what might be better.

How gravely, on the day when I did attend a board meeting, did they mull over the precise terms of the clichés with which they proposed to beguile the examiners! The application was a sort of test paper; a series of questions demanded unsmiling answers. At the least sign of frivolity, our cause would be lost. 'No hope for them as laughs' remains an indelible rubric. To succeed in public life, it is essential to have no sense of its absurdity. I do rather hope that we win the franchise, if only because I am curious to see how the plot develops. Can there really be a TV station which shows imagination and intelligence? Might P.H., John-Julius and I enrapture East Anglia? J.-J. has written on several topics that interest me, especially Sicily. Peter Hall and I have the comic comradeship of long parallel lines that began in Cambridge and have met only at parents' days at Bedales. I suspect that he will be too busy to make any practical contributions and that John-Julius and I will find it impossible to be in the same places at the same times. I invited him, several years ago, to contribute to *Bookmarks*. When he sent in his amiable piece, it proved that he had totally failed to read the question.[22] I was obliged to omit it. I have to hope that he has forgotten all about it. The idea is proposed in the brochure that we collaborate on a drama series about Byzantium. It implies a budget which I cannot believe will ever be forthcoming.

The assembly of *Richard's Things* runs for three hours. Tony Harvey is apprehensive of cutting anything, for fear of damaging the piece. His anxiety proves how badly he wants to direct *A New Wife*. He regrets the loss of Liv's friendship (he sent her flowers and love to New York). I have little doubt that he lost it through no fault of his or that it will be restored if the film is a success.

Even as they sip his champagne, a writer's friends are likely to suggest either that it is too good for him or that he has not chosen a particularly good year, or both. If they are in the same trade, they will declare that he has sold out; if socialites, they will wonder at the ease with which he allows himself to be duped by climbers and freeloaders.

It is assumed that Willie Maugham liked Bert Alanson because he made money for him. I suspect that he liked honesty and found it more conspicuous in the distant San Franciscan Jew, who could so easily have fiddled his books, than in the smart guests who were content to feed off his table and snipe behind his back. One of the routine errors of novelists, from Balzac onwards, has been to assume that businessmen are either scoundrels or wish that they were not in business. The artistic life has been taken to be superior to that of commerce. The often questionable moral record of artists, to which modern biography has testified, in salacious detail, suggests that they are not better men because they do something better, supposedly, than make enterprising money. It seems inconceivable to canting biographers that the company of a banker or an agent, let alone an accountant, might be a relief after long exposure to literary critics or publishing scoundrels. Vulgar Freudians would have us think that details of someone's sexual habits will be more true than the truth about other relationships. Maugham, who did not connive at the notion that one must live on terms of social equality with bedfellows, was never likely to consider that his sexual conduct had much to do with his public reputation. If he reserved his bedtime for those who chose, or were

---

22 'If you were a shelf of books, what would they be?'

paid, to indulge him, if only for the *foie gras* and the caviar (being used is also a form of independence), what did that have to do with the merits of his work?

In the last twenty years, society has become indulgent to com-mercialisation of sex to a degree that might have scandalised even the Regency (leaving only the Romans to be unfazed). The pursuit of money has been raised to the level of venery, in both senses. Yet we are expected to remain sentimental in our expectations of the famous. Was Victorian high society's dread of having to meet 'trade' socially to some degree displacement upwards of the fear of being presented socially with someone with whom a man might have had commercial sexual dealings? Gide's cry of '*familles, je vous haïs*' suggests homosexual irritation with the intrusive machinery of legitimate procreation. Flaubert and Sainte-Beuve, and who all else, found it convenient to use prostitutes. Available without preamble or the need for any more money than one happened to have on one, *les putes* were less demanding than mistresses, wives and children; they never encroached on a man's working arrangements. The promotion of sex to a definitive place in biography is the last consequence of the romantic tradition which insists, no less than Dada, that when an artist spits (or shits), that's art. Maugham's disparagement, by both Bloomsbury and D.H. Lawrence, leads to his shit losing the savour it might have had if it came from Virginia or from James Joyce (whose genius licensed him to relish the brown stain in Nora's pants). If there are no stains on your sheets, do not expect the attentions of a modern biographer. An unbuggered Lawrence of Arabia would be long covered in the sands of time.

We found one of the Lacombes' cows among the roses. She (or was it he?) had come over the electric wire during a *coupure* on the *journée d'action*. Several buds had already been chomped before I appeared with a hoe and sent the beast skipping, plunging awkwardly, hurdling the wire, into its proper pasture. As I glared at it, I realised that I had dreamed the previous night of confronting a vacuous-eyed bull, dun-coloured like our trespasser, and of my effort to face it down, despite its pawing threats.

When we went to Fuengirola in 1959, I had no notion of being an American, despite carrying a green passport (today it is blue, but the eagle remains golden). I gave the impression of being an educated Englishman. In truth, I could still be intimidated by Paul

Hecht's being a 'poet'. I set Wittgenstein's *Philosophical Investigations* prominently on the table, little imagining that the son of a New York taxi-driver could have any trouble playing his poetic part. Now the American elements in my origins seem louder. Meanwhile the Englishness of the English, at one time seemingly deep-rooted and immutable, now appears to be flaking away. To be American always used to seem rather a provisional identity. Today, the diversity of Americanism confers a kind of freedom on those who sport its badge. The English cannot change, yet are not what they were. To be English is now to be limited without being dominant. I tried for forty years to become an authentic antique, only to discover that the thing I was striving to reproduce was itself a reproduction. Americans are people of decision. One may join their club by the vigour of one's desire to do so. To be English is a matter of birth; once it was to be a member of a mundane aristocracy; now it is simply mundane. What modern Henry James would want to make the transition to the land of dukes and moats? The old institutions are still there, but it was their now vanished power rather than their antiquity which lured the New Englanders to old England. There is now a reverse Jamesian theme, the lure of the transatlantic transfer. America offers opportunities for Protean innovation.

27.5.80. Ken McLeish came down to Lagardelle, laden with Mitchell Beazley material, to spend four nights sorting out our choice of books. Affectionate and industrious, he is indignant as he reports whatever slights have been offered to my reputation, though he is not slow to inform me of them. I am not certain about his purposes or even his appearance: when I went to meet him at Le Buisson station, I promised myself that I would recognise him when I saw him. How should I describe him if he were lost? He is of medium height, with brownish hair, too much flesh below the waist, and around it. He has the gaucherie of someone who has never been attractive. Beetle remarked that he moved the seat in the Mercedes as far back as it would go, luxuriating in the space, even though it cramped her in the back. He is not solicitous of women; perhaps because he has not had much luck in soliciting them. He speaks proudly and frequently of Valerie. Having taken decisive action to lose weight, she is said to have invented a pastry that requires neither fat nor flour (and tastes, one guesses, at least as good as cardboard). She is often ill-used. Ken recounted how, though shy and socially uncertain, she contrived to compliment Kate Slack on some pears in red wine which she had served on a somewhat formal dinner for the Bedales staff. 'Was it a special recipe, because they were absolutely delicious?' Kate said 'No, it wasn't' and walked away. The children are no less victimised. Ken speaks of 'open season'; they have been beaten up in Lincoln for no reason except that they are clever. They live among delinquents. While Ken was here, he telephoned home to discover that another local child had been assaulted. Its father, a South African refugee, called the police and is suing the assailants, something which Ken preferred not to do. He seems incapable of violence, even in self-defence. He was for a time a Quaker; he still has a measure of atheistic piety: if only he could believe, he would certainly be a believer.

Ken retains the Quaker aptitude for concern; he is least worried when worrying about others. He has a friend called Peters with whom he collaborated on a few anthologies. P. is clearly a man of some intellect. He had a very happy marriage (and two children) with a wonderful woman called Imogen. When P. was quite young, he was left a large sum of money by his father (£70,000, Ken said) which was to be held in trust until he was 'adult'. The trustees were his mother and grandmother. They were authorised to live off the interest until they should judge P. to be 'adult'. They never came to that conclusion. The boy-man never did come into his inheritance. Had he elected to bring suit, he surely could have, but at the cost of alienating his mother. He lacked the nerve, or had too much decency, to do so.

A freelance writer and a teacher, P. came to live on advances on books which he never wrote, although eminently qualified to do so. He sometimes taught at summer schools. At one such session, he met a young girl who became besotted with him, and he with her. He left his family and decamped with his young mistress. Ken became counsellor to the distraught lady in the once happy house in a beautiful spot some ten miles from March, a magic place where a witch is said to have lived. The rational and intelligent Imogen had felt a powerful urge to take the place as soon as she saw it, although it was in poor repair and had an overgrown garden. She had a mystic rapport with it and was able to divine where in the garden herbs would grow. It seems that she chose exactly where the witch had raised the ingredients for her potions. Since she told Ken that the same herbs had failed to grow elsewhere on the property, there seems to have been as much trial and error as mysterious guidance, but she had some sense of numinous attention. She then fell under the influence of an Irish priest of much charm and little erudition. She was greatly distressed by P.'s fugue and not wholly comforted by Ken's sensible advice to sit tight. After a short time, P. returned to the house, a broken man; he threw himself on Imogen's mercy. She forgave and comforted him. His penitence took the form of abject helplessness. He could not work; he became a child, and then a Catholic. He became dependent on the ministrations of Imogen's ignorant, but self-assured, priest. How pretty, if glib, it is to read P.'s escapade as an attempt to repossess the youth which, on a literal-minded interpretation of his trustees' attitude, he had yet to shed; then came his relapse into infantilism and credulous dependence on a spiritual second Father and the wife-mother who would minister to his endless immaturity. The belief in an eternal life might happily be predicated on the sense, aroused by that unredeemed inheritance, that his father is *toujours en vie* and overseeing, from afar, the long childhood of his son. P. and Imogen still live in the magic house. She has the reputation of being a wise woman. People come to get her advice and her herbs, which flourish by the well.

29.5.80. England is moving towards two million unemployed. At the same time, we are promised a fourth TV channel. Meanwhile, through ambitious docility, I hope (do I?) to acquire a piece of that ponderous machinery whereby, after prolonged lobbying, nearly everything is returned to the state it was in before. We are involved in a variant of musical chairs whereby, when the music stops, a chair is *added* to the number already there. Ionesco the musical! To those who have nearly everything, more is likely to be added. The rulers of the British – anyone, I mean, with a paid job in authority – will have more and more reason to play a double game: they will speak earnestly of the interests of the nation, but they will be more and more conscious of the need to placate the comatose masses in order to preserve their own well-being. I recall the contempt of my school-masters for the Rome of *panem et circenses.* How incredible it seemed that a great imperial power should have at its heart a parasitic and demandingly hedonistic urban mob, at once listless and politically central, mindless and dangerous! The growth of unemployment is leading to a situation in which the British, in growing numbers, are going to be fed and lodged in order that they may sit placidly and watch TV rather than take to the streets. It cannot be very long before the possession of any job at all will be a privilege which it will be awkward to conceal and impossible to repudiate: the employed will be the new bourgeoisie, never mind their ancient class. The proletariat will not supply a 'corrective' to the market price of labour; they will be increasingly uneducated and useless. In a short time, the unemployed will become the unemployable. The mental hospital will become a paradigm of all social institutions. Keeping people quiet will be a politically paying proposition, never mind which party is in power. When 'revolution' comes, it is almost certain to be either vandalistic or fundamentalist. Religious dogmatism is the only ideology which can outflank the collapse of the economy and impose optimism on decline.

When Kingsley Amis postulates a Russian invasion, he is – deliberately or not – bailing the British out by depicting them as no longer responsible for their own impotence (the theme of his recent novel[23]). It would have been far more true, and wittier, had he made 'Russians' the nickname given by the excluded – the unemployed and their 'leaders' – to the ruling class whose repressive Philistinism has given them the lineaments of an occupying force. Kingsley appears to be the kind of candid Tory who thinks that people should own up to their failings and accept responsibility for them. In fact, he has only the grumpy, accusatory habits of those who hold that time is flowing in the wrong direction and spend the sorry journey downstream facing backwards, admiring the mountains which they have quit and bemoaning the molehills on either bank. Kingsley is a grumbler in a moralist's rig, a gimcrack Man of Letters appropriate to an age too lazy to be reactionary. Such a writer, ponderously lightweight, requires scapegoats in order to explain to himself why so much success has brought him so little peace of mind. A Russian invasion, with the excusable defeatism it excites, is presented as a justifiable burden on the spirits. In truth, it is a consolation. The withering of Britain turns powerlessness into a motif at once so pathetic and so natural than no one can pass for brave by making light of it. The Leftism which, in its Fabian form, for so long regarded the Establishment as a conveniently strong scapegoat, is deprived of its traditional *bête noire*. Like Kingsley, it has had to move to the Right in order to be opposed by a spectre sufficiently forceful to reassure *and* unnerve the new mediocrity. The Russians in the new novel fulfil the baleful office previously held, in Kingsley's bestiary, by the rich and the professoriate. What he now advocates is less a commonwealth of free and mature

---

23 *Jake's Thing* (1978).

citizens than a nursery where the strong hand of nanny will be tempered to those capable of telling naughtily endearing bedtime stories. Amis's *nouveau* Toryism meshes, loosely, with Orwell's anti-Communist socialism. Both parade the clipped prose which the English, not caring for the effort required by anything abstruse, choose to see as the best flowers the national hedges can put out. Their aversion to intellectual fancy dancing is laced with mournful complacency: what is wrong with the world, they are happy to tell us, and the British are happy to agree, is due more to the cleverness of the clever-clever than to the stupidity of the stupid.

30.5.80. Ken can turn out the stuff according to almost any brief. Mimetic versatility is typical of old-style classicists. It is founded on the proses and verses which students no longer have to compose. Brilliance was based on mimesis and the selection of the right maquette. Novelty had no place in scholarship. A good composition was a collage of existing elements and tags. The walls of scholarly respectability were filled, like those of the ancient Piraeus, with the rubble of the past; the longer and fatter the walls, the more secure the tenancy. An old-style classical scholar has all the attributes which a well-run world requires for literary eminence: he has read everything, he recognises every allusion, he winces at originality; he does nothing out of line.

4.6.80. Beetle, this morning, passing me my 7.30 eggs and bacon: 'Here you are, have the charred remains of some pig!'

24.6.80. I am sitting again in the heat and the wind at the concrete table on the terrace on Ios. Everything and nothing has changed: the Greeks are a new generation, but the same old Greeks. You can now get everything you want in the village, and nearly everything in the bazaar at the far end of the beach where the bus comes and honks its regular, charmless call. What can be enjoyed above all is what they have yet to ruin: the hull of Sikinos, at one time hardly more than a hard, low cloud on the horizon, later an outline rigid enough to flash a border of white houses on its high hem. Mylopota carries a heavy new freight of gimcrack hotels. Rock music blares at night. The island has become a huge squeezer which presses youthful travellers into discharging their pennies. The money is quickly processed into bigger and grabbier machinery, fancier cafés, louder speakers, faster food. The Greeks can afford better doctors, better schools, and live longer, more comfortable lives. The vices with which rich sentimentalists reproach them are those which were once proper only to themselves. The tyranny of the peasants over their children no longer holds. Prosperity loosens the shackles, although it does not dissolve the family structure. It is exceptional to see any tourist families. We seem to be the only parents with children above the age of twelve. The symbol of the clash – as they always say – of cultures is nudism. Today's Greeks affect to be disgusted and shocked by the nakedness of the foreigners; the latter, having consented to be fleeced, resist attempts to persuade or coerce them into decency (they get enough of that at home). Neither Bohemians nor naturists, they do not strip to honour any programme, quirky or aggressive. Their nakedness saves washing and implies indifference towards a society which, dedicated to their nocturnal exploitation, has no claim on their respect during the day. The Greeks are mechanicals who supply amenities. The native of Victorian myth was a naked and ignorant savage, with no moral sense. Now the image is reversed: the tourists speak no Greek and have no shame. Nakedness proclaims their lack of evangelical assertiveness. They come only to do what they want under a reliable sun. What is Greece to them?

9.7.80. Flying to Geneva to rendezvous with the unit for the Byron film was like going to boarding school: the prospect of a single bed in a single room, the forced company of strangers, the fear of unpopularity, the hope of acceptance. I dined with George Steiner at the Chat Botté, the restaurant of the Hotel Beau Rivage on the Quai du Mont Blanc, a swank establishment, its staff at once condescending and glad of our custom. G. insisted on paying for the *Kirs*; I played the royal part when it came to the dinner. We drank a bottle of *Blanc de Blanc* and ate a rich meal, at once delicious and forgettable, a little too *measured* for one to be unaware of the accountant who audited the kitchen. We talked easily and without pause, fondly if never comfortably. He believes that England rejected me when I was refused citizenship, whereas I assume, almost certainly rightly, that I was treated as perfunctorily as anyone who, on the routine face of it, did not fulfil the essential requirement (five years' permanent uninterrupted residence). George suggested that if they had really wanted me they would have found a way. I doubt whether 'they' were ever alerted. The Capitoline geese neither cackled nor might they have been cajoled into silence. I was one more banal case. George sees me as a foreign legionary, like himself, but we do not measure for the same

style of *képi*. He is impressed, overawed even, by the success of
Jonathan Miller who, he is convinced, is destined for membership
of the British Academy and for the Order of Merit. G. has little
doubt, since Jonathan seems to have none, that Dr Miller is the
Isaiah Berlin of his generation. 'But he hasn't published anything,'
I said. And 'But nor has Isaiah' we both said together.

G. is more cheerful in Geneva than in England, and about
England, which he now believes Zara would be happy to leave. His
son David proposes to return to the US. He came to England as an
American; he goes back as a kind of Englishman. He telephoned
G. the night before his Finals and asked his father what 'moral
philosophy' was, apart from being the subject of his first paper. G.
sees him eating with a wooden spoon for the rest of his life, while
his peers waltz into the Foreign Office and the BBC. G. cannot
conceive of a felicity that is not urbane. He sees life as a matter not
of happiness or unhappiness, but of success and failure. He chides
me for getting to his point before he gets there himself, but he
listens carefully to my spontaneities. His intimidated contempt for
English ways excites his frequent amazement. He wonders how
Jonathan, who speaks so manifestly with his hands, can be acceptable to people who rarely even shake hands without reluctance. He
sees the power of the Establishment everywhere and yet marvels at
its impotence over such matters as the ownership of the *Observer*.
The French, he says, would never have suffered so signal an
institution to fall into the hands of a foreign financial organisation
which is utilising it as a tax write-off and may well soon write it
off instead. He boasts that Harvard wants both him and Zara as
professors, but says that he could never endure the institutional
second-rateness of the US, despite the intellectual glamour of
Cambridge, Mass.

George had been besotted with J.R. Oppenheimer. He met
him one day after O.'s 'disgrace'. He was still a famous man and
respected at Princeton above all. Oppenheimer told G. that he
had just been to Paris where he had seen his own story dramatised
under the title *In the Matter of J.R.O.* or something catchy like
that. He said what a scourging ordeal it had been to watch himself
being impersonated and having to endure again, in anguished
detachment, the whole of his calvary. G. looked closely at the man
he venerated and saw in him only pride and exultation. In that
moment, the long love died.

We were discussing Proust when G. became transfixed by the
face of a diner sitting directly behind me. He was, George said,

the very image of Marcel, that Armenian face to the second
life! I looked and it was true: there was a luminous similarity in
the pale darkness of the young and spoiled *gourmand*. I did not,
however, share the sense of Pentecostal epiphany which galvanised
my companion.

G. took me for coffee to some friends, a heart specialist and his
wife, the Bouviers, who belonged to the narrow Genevan *gratin*.
They lived in a walk-up apartment in the old town, an address
which could not be obtained through any currency but blood.
One could be forgiven for thinking that, in that particular city,
money could buy all the blood one needed. The couple were still
famous, after twenty-five years or more of marriage, for having
been lovers before they were married. It made them notorious,
even after years of distinguished propriety. G.'s heart condition
made him glad to have such friends, but he had not met them for
cardiological reasons. They had come to his public lectures on
Shakespeare and one day, when he still did not know who they
were, the specialist had pressed into George's hand a monograph
on medical imagery in, I think, *Hamlet*. G. recognised 'something
rarer than dilettantism'.

The heart-man was grizzled, about fifty, tall, self-assured and
without elegance or grace. His wife, the bold one, had promising
grey eyes. Like many doctors, he was prompt to offer whisky and
cigars. His affability was courteous with complacency. If he was
modest, he was immodestly pleased to seem so. He was researching
the weakness of the heart walls and announced his predilection
for female breasts. The flat was quite large and rather cold (a nice
contrast for the season), stuffy evidence that racy myths could
be housed in formal binding. Our hosts were *aficionados* of the
opera. Madame Bouvier sighed at my frank appetite for *bel canto*.
Doubtless, she seconded G.'s appetite for Wagner. The president of
the Genevan opera-house, an anaemic Baron of languid courtesy,
was one of the two men already there. The other was an Argen-
tinian who worked for UNESCO. He had been his country's
ambassador to the UN under one of the more respectable regimes.
He claimed that little could have been done in accordance with
the constitution in order to destroy or repress the *Montoneros*. He
acknowledged that the murder squads of the military junta had
made a return to democracy 'difficult', not least because of the
fear of 'vengeful' trials. Such proceedings might be 'just', but they
were bound to excite recurrences of terror, left and right. The
only hope was some kind of statute of limitations, an agreement

to forget. The Federal German Republic had more or less worked the trick, but could it be repeated in a Latin-American context?

The ex-ambassador was civilised and civil; he regretted the degradation of his country and was strongly patriotic, but he was content to be on a tax-free international salary and to spend his time in the counsels of the comfortable as they debated uncomfortable things. He might have been an old Scotsman, pale and wrinkled. Like a retired Jimmy the One, he knew where the power was generated but had never been on the bridge. An exile unlikely to be greatly missed, he had made his sensible, distant assessment of Argentina's condition and was waiting for the blood to be swabbed away so that he could be proved right without unpleasant remainder. He would, one guessed, never have been so reasonable had he had reason to think that he might have been able to be anything else.

The flat had the grand shabbiness of a place which had for so long been the home of the wealthy that they had ceased to notice just how old their antiques had become. Lack of anything new made it seem like a family vault. To warm things up, G. told the company of a haircut enjoyed near Kiev – no, a shave – which had been recommended to him by a Russian 'with a solicitous leer'. The *barbiera* rested G.'s head between her breasts, which cushioned his ears, thus exciting 'a new Eros'. I was glad to have the taxi arrive to take G. back to his *garçonnière*.

Waiting for the BBC people to arrive, I walked the hard streets of the old city, attempting to enjoy the dust-free dust of the bookshops. I went to a branch of the UBS to change some money into travellers' cheques and was told that I should collect them the following morning. When I woke up, I could not recall the address of the branch and had a comic treasure hunt before I found a cryptic stamp on my receipt, which had to be decoded, at the main office, by a disdainful clerk. He evidently took the view that anyone who could not remember where he had left his cash had small right to retrieve it. I was told that families who do not know the number of the account in which a dead relative deposited his money have no means of recovering it. The post-war wealth of the Swiss is partly funded on the unreclaimed wealth (very often of murdered Jews) which their banks righteously refused to the owners' heirs.

Frank, my director, is married to an actress he calls 'Bids', whom I must have seen in *The Norman Conquests* but did not remember.

He is very tall, bearded, and wears earnest square-cut glasses. His height and quiet voice remind me of John Nimmo. He and Bids had been together for about six months and each was, he told me, thinking about 'moving on' when she went for a routine cervical smear. It proved positive for cancer. She was kept in overnight. Frank, a kind man, went to see her, more out of courtesy than deep concern, and became involved in the anguish which followed. After long consultation, the Great Man (the Queen's gynaecologist) advised radium treatment. The cancer was destroyed, but there was a good deal of collateral damage. Bids felt very ill and depressed; she could not digest anything but vegetables, on which she now lives, nor could she ever have children. It was during this grim time that they fell in love. Frank felt less trapped by his own kindness than happy to have found a worthwhile destination for it. Six years later, they are now frequently apart, on account of their professions, but are very close indeed. They have considered adopting a child but they would have to find someone else to look after it. He is about forty, erect, ungreying, with a sort of unbowed resignation. As a director, he will never lack work, but has no expectation of fame. He has joined the ranks of TV officers, as others might be recruited into the police or the secret service. There is an official anonymity about him.

Having moved to a new house with the intention of making a fresh start to their marriage, she refused to curtain the windows.

15.7.80. Frank deals gently and cuttingly with the exuberant John Hooper. Bearded, brown, balding, Hooper plays the rascal with manly buoyancy. He never accepts the obvious and is always willing to change the set-up if it fails to deliver happy results. He talks of things being 'naff' (a variant with the same meaning is 'pony'). He is a great seducer *jusqu'au bord du lit*. One night, as we sat in the Piazza San Marco, he volunteered a foot-massage for a chinless, big-eyed American lady from Houston. I was assured that a few nights later he visited her and her girlfriend at the Gritti Palace. I doubt whether he got into bed with her, or them. He can make rejection seem an achievement of a kind. His only embarrassment was when a courtly sweep of his arm goosed an unamused Venetian woman with a scornful vocabulary in English and Italian. He swore that his cheek was unintentional. He has sustained energy and a capacity for swift decision. He rarely changes the position of the camera; then only with an air of being even more right than he had been before. He always advances and never retreats. He is as charming as a man can well be who is concerned above all to enchant himself; other people are his mirrors, a voyeur who likes to be looked at.

6.8.80. We took the Steiners to a fair meal at the Café Royal (he offered, diffidently, to go Dutch, which I refused) and then to Michael Frayn's *Make and Break*. Too long and too predictable, it was saved, if it was, by the one-man brilliance of Leonard Rossiter, who scarcely needed so cumbrous a crutch to perform his solo pirouettes. How could anyone read the piece for anything but an abject slice of lifelessness, as full of bloodless stereotypes as a waxwork show?

G. and Z. were gleeful in telling us that, against all predictions, David had not merely got his degree but had received a 'straight First' (no viva!). I wonder if it had occurred to either of them to wonder how great a service they had rendered him by advising him, in his last term, not to stand for President of the Union, lest he plough in his Finals. They will, I suspect, receive more credit for his academic achievement than he ever will. If he had been elected to the Presidency and got only a Second, he would have been the sole rider in the triumphal chariot. He has already procured himself a job on Wall St. His parents, gleaming with the lustre he has shone on them, take it for granted that he now thinks as well of them as they do of themselves. G. was in despair when he heard what David had said about Kant in his philosophy paper. 'If he had said what you would have had him say,' I said, 'he would probably have failed his degree.' Zara agreed, and so did G., not all that agreeably. He has finished his piece on Blunt and is still indignant at the cynically esoteric attitude of Hugh Sykes Davies, who ostentatiously refused to turn his back on the disgraced Apostle. I informed G. about the novel about rats which H.S.D. once wrote, in which the hero goes down into the sewers to join the rats, the future rulers of the world.

7.8.80. Malcolm Sinclair, speaking of the Queen Mother, who had been radiating at her eightieth birthday, 'And she does it all on a colostomy bag!' He had never been before the camera until I suggested him for Byron. He looks so like his lordship that we will be accused of having sought a lookalike. In fact, he played Adam Morris, in the theatrical version of *An Early Life*, in a convincingly virile style. He plays love scenes with a manly confidence which neither Dirk nor Alan Bates ever achieved. His frank levity (he declared that he had been suffering from 'a social disease') is matched by a pleasant voice. He is loyal to old friends and spoke up in defence of Robert Flemyng, who had been kind to him on tour. Flemyng (whom I saw in John Whiting's *Marching Song*) was sorry that Malcolm had not been young in the 1930s. He should have been in the war because he was a 'leader of men'.

Malcolm approached our producer, Eddie Mirzoeff, for re-assurance about the rushes, which none of us were shown. Mirzoeff made a sour face and said, 'Well, they're all *right*.' He did not refer to Malcolm's performance in particular, but the documentary shots of Venice which, he told everyone, he found disappointing. Mirzoeff has never learnt that when an actor asks a general question, the answer has always to be 'You were *wonderful*!'

Greek TV was represented by a woman of thirty, Mary, from a rich Athenian family. She was short and dark, with an olive complexion and a sprained ankle which grew pitifully worse whenever some promised item failed to appear. She wore her years like a white beard, lamenting the loss of a youth she would still have had, if she had not bewailed its loss. She was forever making telephone calls to the mayor (of Missolonghi, of Nafpactos, of Megara) to confirm or make arrangements which should have been settled weeks before. A spoiled rich girl delegated to work with foreigners who denied her the deference which her connections usually promised her, she had no push, though some pull. Supervising her was the mistress of Mr Charanis, the director-general, a blonde woman with voluble English whom I first heard at the airport ('Where is Mr Raffel?') and who telephoned my room in the appalling President Hotel, on the penultimate morning, to complain about the co-production deal, a matter which had nothing to do with me.

The Greeks bargained until the last moment, now surly, now placatory. They denied what had already been agreed and reopened what was already settled. The country is still run by the old boy network; only the old boys change. Everything could have been fixed very easily, since friends need only call friends, but the affectations of having proper channels meant that new obstacles could always be found. Mary must have been appointed as a decorative ambassadress. She was incapable of any practical work, despite having spent two years at the London Film School, where she was taught by Clive Donner. At Missolonghi, we came back to the hotel from shooting at 9.30 to find that the meal which she was supposed to have ordered was not forthcoming. All the edible food had been consumed. My fury took the form of leaving the table and going to watch the Olympics on the *teleorasis*, hardly a resounding slap. The evening ended with our all going to the *taverna* on the quay and having refreshers of kebab and retsina. Mary had thought the *taverna* too plebeian. We celebrated the appeasement of our hunger with time-trials on a borrowed bicycle. There was something happily spontaneous about our silly competition. Each of us in turn pedalled to the first, distant, lamp-post and back, fearful that the brakes wouldn't work, conscious of a dotty obligation to do our best. The event was won by Simon Wilson, the sound man, a withdrawn, gentle person who took the stake money, 500 drachmae or so, and settled the bill with it. We exemplified the democracy of sport, in nice contrast to the rancid formality of the Olympics.

We watched the Moscow 800 metres in a little café near Dodona, which I persuaded them all to visit while we were in Joannina. Even though the theatre, which is 'late' and grimly grey, has none of the grandeur of Epidauros, the loneliness of the green site, and the absence of tourists, gave Dodona a numinous aura. The feet of the unwashed priest, it was nice to suppose, lent no offensive odour to the shrine. We were eating cheese and tomatoes and drinking *sitsa*, as the patron called it, under the café's trellised vine when Tony Bragg, Hooper's assistant, called us to the TV and there was Steve Ovett beating the better liked Sebastian Coe in a race in which they had both been urged not to run by the moral Mrs Thatcher. One of the Greeks, who spoke good English, was studying at Bristol University, in Hooper's home town. I took Hooper and Dick Coles, the designer, to buy *flokati* carpets at a little shop in old Joannina. The young man who served us watched John Hooper warily during the long, white proceedings. When the sale was clinched, he asked, not discourteously, whether John was by any chance a Turk. He did indeed have the walnut complexion, domed head and dark-eyed fleshiness of a petty pasha.

The mosque at Joannina has been converted into a sad museum commemorating the war of 1912. The mementos are rumpled and unmemorable. How gladly one would accept a reconversion of that dull little outpost to Islam in return for the re-Christianisation of Hagia Sophia! The triumph of the Greeks seems unhappy recompense for what they were forced to abandon. Joannina is quite prosperous. There is a smart island in the lake, to which the comfortable repair in their motor-boats. Ferries take *tous pollous*. The waters are marked off in lanes. On the Sunday morning, eights, coxless fours and pairs worked up and down, hectored by a coach in a motor-boat that nagged the silence and made filming a matter of prompt timing.

The designer, Dick Coles, was a vegetarian, on a diet of salad or salad. He did not reproach us for our carnivorous habits but he did make one conscious of them. We all elected to have vegetarian meals on the flights. Coles is separated from his wife and two children and lives with a woman who has a four-year-old of her own. He is a 'Friend of the Earth' and a member of the Labour Party. He went to art school and remarked with surprise on the fact that he sells his skills. He paints at the weekend. I suspect that he likes the society available in the designing community at the BBC. He wears an oval-shaped, bushy beard and speaks with a gentleness charged with an aggressivity he does not dare or care to express. The beard muzzled a tongue which I suspected capable of violent opinions. He was a powder keg that never went off.

Frank has made a TV series called *Escape*. The first programme will concern Lord Lucan, but contains neither conjectures nor revelations. F. fears that it will be rather dull. The likelihood is that 'Lucky' is dead. How could a man with so few mental resources keep his head down for all this time? Even the most amiable old boy or girl in the Clermont set would surely have tired of his enforced company. He would have had to be passed on, like a hot book, or potato. A more interesting case was that of Jeremy Cartland, who was suspected of murdering his father and then setting fire to his caravan in a lay-by in a part of France where the loud-mouthed Cartland senior had been in SOE during the war. Jeremy's statement spoke of watching his father, on the night of his death, eating creamed rice out of a tin and described his revulsion as his father tucked into the 'execrable concoction'. (Nice, the hints of excrement and cock in the rather elaborate phrase!) The loathing and contempt in the 'introverted young man's' vocabulary gives his narrative a sinister ring, but a man cannot be convicted for his choice of words. The French police closed the case. A Scotland Yard man refused to make any comment on the programme, which struck Frank as significant: English policemen can usually be relied on to disparage the French for their intuitive methods. The inept procedures of the *Police Judiciaire* meant that the crime scene yielded none of the clues which a circumspect approach might have preserved. The heavy rain was no help either, especially since the *flics* had thoroughly trampled the area. All the same, the discovery of an axe, the murder weapon, nearby added to the suspicion that Jeremy was the killer. There remains the matter of Cartland senior's connection with the Resistance and all the political and financial complications in the background. Jeremy's sister told Frank, 'He could never do such a thing'.

Imagine a man who, over long years, gives sense to his life by adopting a deliberately false personality so that, when he does what he has been planning all that time to do, no one can believe him capable of it. Such a false character might be agreeable to impersonate, as generous and cheerful as anyone might choose to be. His charitable geniality would be sustained only by the dark purpose behind it. Without his murderous scheme, the man would not have had the patience to maintain his saintliness. If, for some reason, he renounced his secret motive for being so amiable (or if the intended victim died), he would cease to be likeable. Better, through the natural death of his victim, he comes honestly to inherit the fortune which he was scheming to acquire. People wonder why the wealth has made him so miserable.

8.7.80. Peter Sellers died. I remember an occasion in Simpson's when he greeted me with winking complicity, as if to acknowledge that we were in the same club of those whose slender hold on good fortune had not yet been broken. It was generous of him to make me feel that our talents were equally fragile. When I first met him he was one of the legendary Goons whose accents had marked our generation, but he was just beginning his individual career. In 1954, Roy Speer, the BBC radio producer who first allowed the Footlights access to a microphone, said that radio might have been invented for Peter, since he was too ugly ever to go in front of a camera. Pasty-faced and pudgy, with National Health glasses and a greasy skin liable to eruptions, he squeezed his face into nervous creases of amiability. There was nothing attractive about him, except for the subtle versatility of his voice. More embarrassed than liberated by his fame as Bluebottle or Grytpype-Thynne, he refrained from any kind of social stardom.

He came to dinner at the Deutsches' flat in Park Close, when *Lindmann* had just been published, and listened, with a generous show of amusement, to the stories of my uncle Jessel, which David insisted that I tell. I was fearful that he would cap my amateurishness with some virtuoso descant. He either refrained or felt no temptation. After a few drinks, I told him that he should play a real part for a change and urged him to consider doing *Lindmann*, which he would indeed have done brilliantly, in both his 'Jewish' and his clerkly personae. I had written a script for him some years before, when I was in the news. Peter Forster had given a whole page in the *Daily Express* to his rave review of *The Limits of Love*. Wolf Mankowitz hired me to add pepper and salt to a novel called *Memoirs of a Cross-Eyed Man*. I was callow enough to listen to Wolf's advice about the level of humour to be administered to the screenplay, which was unfinished by the time he and Peter fell out. It was in Wolf's first-floor Piccadilly office that I met Cyril, a dodgy accountant who later cost both of us a packet. Cyril told me how he recently fucked a girl who liked it from behind. That way she could smoke a cigarette *and* read a book while he was on the job.

9.8.80. On location, Wendy showed banal signs of falling in love with me: chiding familiarity, a tendency to touch, grooming attentiveness. She told me in Geneva that when she was eighteen she had always dreaded 'dates': men were always diving down, or up. She hated the onset of the inevitable, but never knew how to avoid it. She adored her stepfather, who was a good deal older than her mother, whom she does not much like. The best that can be said of Wendy is that she was more attractive than Lucy, the other thirty-something female on the trip. She has teeth that would be better if false, beige hair, blue eyes like boiled sweets and unhappy skin; the mention of mosquitoes brought her out in lumps. She carried large sums of Greek money in 1,000 drach notes in a sponge bag. Probably a virgin, she sports the showbiz camouflage of larky outspokenness. Wendy likes one to think that she has had a number of men, if not recently. She was once on the point of getting married, but remembered her stepfather's advice, to do what suited her, which was, she said, to remain independent. I said, 'I suppose you didn't love him enough'. She had not thought about that. She makes £8,000 a year at the BBC. She was pleased to be adding a verandah to her Chiswick home. She has one eye out of alignment with the other. She asked me to put sun oil on her back. The bony, sloping shoulders and leathered skin did not prompt enthusiastic massage. Although they had lived together for thirty years, her mother did not marry Wendy's stepfather until the quite recent death of her real father. Wendy arranged the proceedings, at Chelsea Town Hall. During the preliminaries, her mother did not like to tell the Registrar that it was her own, not her daughter's, wedding. During the ceremony she was unable to remember the formula and had to be taken through it word by word. Her paralysis caused Wendy to 'break up'. The whole congregation became helpless with laughter. After we had finished shooting, she was going to meet a lover in Paris. She had told a man with whom she was ending an affair that the shoot would last a week longer than it did. 'They make you do these things.'

11.8.80. Julia was commissioned to interview Shirley Conran after she wrote *Superwoman*, a huge bestseller, and had been advised to 'do the year out' to avoid tax. Julia found her living alone in her house in the Lot-et-Garonne, near Miramont. Julia went to call *sans rendezvous précis*. She saw *la* Conran through the window, walking about the house, very slowly, in a doubled-over posture, like a transvestite Groucho Marx. She announced that she was not hung-over, or drugged; she had been suffering from acute menstrual pains for which she had to take aspirin, although allergic to it. Julia's encounter with S.C. led the latter to say that she would like to come over and see us, which she did yesterday.

Stee and I have had a remarkable run in the Sarlat tennis tournament. I have been driving there and back twice a day with victorious consequences: Stee beat a sixteen-year-old 6-2, 6-3 this morning. We returned yesterday at 11, expecting the lady at noon plus, but a car with Monaco plates came up the hill at 11.30 and there she was, *tout de noir vêtue*, over-coated with make-up, saying hullo in a deep, dark voice, with not a flower in her hand. Although her life has apparently been a long – perhaps too long – success story, her demeanour demanded indulgence. She was egregiously anxious – and a little too precise? – about her age. She claims to have been in the same form at St Paul's as Shirley Catlin, who is fifty. She has a way of closing her right eye in a slow wink at odd moments. It then remains shut, like a shop-keeper's blind in a city threatened by riots. Once perhaps a very attractive girl, she is not an attractive woman. Her skin, tanned by the tax-free sun, clocks the years. She sunbathes naked in the picture window of her Monte Carlo flat. A model of helpfulness, she is the flesh-backed cheap edition of her own bestseller. Success has not banished panic; an authority on living, she is not sure how to live. She needs more help than she is capable of giving. There is something splendid and not entirely appetising about her husky beauty. Despite the endearing gap between her upper front teeth, her photogenic smile, like her candour, seems calculated.

Well-supplied with PR men, agents and lawyers, she has no doubt that she can give them good advice. Exalted by her own myth, she is glad that the world knows who she is, even if she does not.

She declares that she hates writing, yet sentences herself to a punishing schedule. She has come to her house in the Lot-et-Garonne in order to write a commissioned novel. She is larding it with the ingredients which she assumes her female readers will want, including blood. She achieved quick rapport with Beetle, based on common experience of St Paul's in the 1940s. She had asked Julia whether Beetle had had a 'white girdle' (the mark of athletic excellence). B. imagined that she was worried about her own lack of such a distinction. In fact, *la* Conran had indeed received the precious colourless colours herself and was preparing to pull rank on her hostess, who had (though she would never have mentioned it) been in almost every first team.

S. was gratified to have been invited. She liked the 1969 Meursault and she seemed to like the house, over which she threw an eye or two of consciously professional assessment. She did baulk at being given water in a (cheap) green glass. She envied only the pool, from which she emerged cleansed of all the ageing preparations which she had applied to make herself younger. She had told Julia that she was no longer attracted to men of her own age. She fancied only men of thirty or so. There seems to be a shortage of them in the Lot-et-Garonne, except for the horrible squatters she found in the house she had been persuaded by the *maire* to lend to a clutch of *stagiaires*, whom she described as '*étagères*'. I did not correct her; but when she cited 'Archimedes' as having said that 'everything is in a state of flux', I did propose Heracleitus. She alluded frequently to Anthony Burgess, a fellow-exile in the Principality where Björn Borg is a modest neighbour, always ready to pose for pictures in front of his sports boutique. Burgess seems happy to play the accessible guru and has put himself in charge of her education. He lent her my book on Willie Maugham, which she remembered effusively.

She is haunted by her marriage, although Terence is now on his third wife, Caroline, whom he is said not wholly to cherish. Shirley has two sons by him and has bought them the house which the *étagères* are said to have trashed. She told us that she had been forced to turn her back on her business in London in order to avoid the tax bill which had claimed 83% of her profits. She claims to have sold eight million copies of her book, though she has had to rewrite it for each major market, a treadmill for Midas. I asked what her London business had been. 'Textiles.' She had started it when she twenty-three and had designed and commissioned materials, as well as importing and re-exporting Finnish and other fabrics. Frustrated by ignorance of the technicalities, she decided to go to the Central School to learn how to weave. They made her wait a year before accepting her as a student. She was often there in the meanwhile (teaching?) and discovered that there were two unused looms on the premises to which, it seems, she helped herself.

She had scarcely started to take instruction than she was creating designs which were incorporated in 'the Canberra' (I am not sure if that was a bomber, a hotel or a luxury liner). Already a married woman and mother of two, she was not interested in playing the art student. She became so involved in the quality and calibre of cloth that, she told us, she was strongly tempted to feel men's suits in the Underground. I had gathered that it was on account of the tax on the textile business that she had quit London, but she now said that all the shares were in Terence's name; she had derived no profit from her endeavours.

Her profitable activity was buying and letting houses (she had five) and apartments (she had two). She furnishes them down to 'the last teaspoon' and supplies a maid as well, Mary, an Irish lady who takes *The Times* and whom she has promised to set up in business in a few years' time. Mary has many cousins and relatives and recruits a freelance army of odd-job men and women who take care of the houses. The properties are rented to IBM and Texaco executives in need of a roof. It became slowly, but then rapidly, clear that S. is hot for money. She had complete accounts of how much everything had cost her as far back, at least, as 1968. She advised us not to restore the ruined house next to our big barn; it was better, because cheaper, to rebuild it from scratch. She estimated it would cost us £25,000. She winced when we declared that we had never been much interested in being rich. She would have liked to be a banker.

Her smiles, as regular and as spontaneous as the chimes of Big Ben, are designed to be enchanting. She had had a 23-year-old secretary, with the face of a Botticelli angel, whom she enrolled in London and took to Monte Carlo. Sarah-Jane turned out to be a pusher; she bought 'uppers' for three a pound and sold them for a pound apiece. She had done good shorthand and typing in London, but never matched her audition speed and competence once she was living with S. She stayed out till all hours, not making love (as S. first imagined) but making connections. While her typing degenerated into gibberish, she was busy taking notes on Shirley's private life. In an unwise moment, S. boasted that articles about 'Superwoman' could be sold for a thousand pounds for syndication around the world. 'Her eyes,' Shirley said, 'filed this information with a blue shock of recognition' (not bad). The girl began to make up lurid stories of S.'s addiction and also claimed that she, the girl, had had to write all of S.'s book because she was helplessly drugged or drunk.

Shirley said that she found all these false confessions in 'the filing'; but she must have gone through the 'angel's' things when she was out on the town. S. was shaken enough to call her solicitor, Michael Rubinstein, who sent a threatening letter to Sarah-Jane, reminding her of the contract of confidentiality which she had signed before leaving London. The girl departed, without too much unpleasantness, and has not yet published any articles. She had confessed that she had already had 'cold turkey' treatment (Shirley used the expression several times, with an excited shiver). Shirley had described the process already in her novel and asked the angel to confirm the verisimilitude of the passage, which she did. Shirley emphasised that she herself had 'gleaned all the details from Pear's Encyclopaedia'.

There were a number of flies around the table at lunch. Shirley said that the French had a new gadget which you plug into the mains and which deters insects. She had bought one because her bedroom had been invaded by a sort of super-fly 'two inches long', which attacked at 1.30 a.m. and crawled all over her face and into her bed. She was terrified 'because there are so many places a woman can be penetrated'. It was impossible to get rid of the invaders until 3.30 a.m., by which time she was exhausted. A neighbour, when quizzed, said that they were '*bêtes*'. I wonder if she was shown any corpses.

The drama with the *stagiaires* also has its *bizarreries*. S. said that she had lent her spare house to these nice young people, from good Parisian homes, and that they wrecked everything (eight chairs were specified) and broke all the windows. They invited a dozen friends, including *Arabs*, and all kinds of orgies had taken place. She said that she had been keeping chickens in the gardens of the house. When the evicting party – S. herself in a hat and carrying a clipboard on which she made deliberately officious notes, her diminutive, big-nosed son Jasper and a couple of good girls with pitchforks even – started to get the squalid squatters out of the place, with a mixture (we were told) of terse politeness and pointed menace, the ringleader stripped off and slit the throats of the chickens and sprinkled their blood all over the hallway of the house. It must (if it really happened) have been terrifying, especially when the naked magus raised his arm in Hitlerian mode and cast curses on Shirley.

Threatened with the gendarmerie, the intruders were bluffed or shamed into decamping in several vehicles, taking most of the contents of the place with them. When the mayor and the cops arrived, they seem not to have been convinced that the young people had been present in the number alleged. Shirley was able to provide proof in the form of letters, addressed to sixteen different people, which were delivered to the house in a single bundle. The *stagiaires* played the innocent well enough to induce the mayor to find them another billet, which they also wrecked. The landlady is bringing suit.

Such things may well happen. The details had some plausibility: for instance, one of the girls had her scapula broken in a brawl and had to walk into town to have it treated. Yet the narrative concerning the dawn raid on the hippies seemed fantastic. If the kids were as numerous and dangerous as S. said, how did they come to accept eviction with such loud docility? She said that, by the time the forces of order had arrived, she and her helpers had cleaned up all the sanguinary signs of the chickens' execution so thoroughly that the mayor and his companions doubted whether it had ever taken place. Ms C. and her cohort may have been domestic Stakhanovites, but to remove *all* signs of so barbarous an outrage required something more than a dustpan and brush. And if she was that indignant, might it not have occurred to Superwoman to leave some evidence of the atrocity? The hurry to efface the damage suggests that she had exaggerated its extent. She said that she worked so furiously that she started at 5 a.m. and did not stop until ten that night.

There was something sad, and unappealing, about this lonely woman with her penchant for telling the beads of the famous people whom she knows, or knew. She had been 'in and out of Number Ten' during the Wilson premiership. She had been editor of *Femail* and one of her staff was having an affair with one of Wilson's. She affected to have been shocked at the facetious superficiality of the ruling set, but I suspect that she was keener to announce her intimacy with it than to denounce its morals. She has worn so many smart hats in so many brilliant careers that it seems perverse not to want her in one's life. We did not look forward to a return invitation; nor has she given us occasion to decline it. Did she presume herself so important that she thought she had brought enough colour into our drab lives by deigning to descend on us? She seemed appreciative and admired our Villeroy and Boch tableware, although she did say that she preferred wooden plates. When she was in Greece she had complained to Heleni Vlachou (who else?) because the *tavernas* served hot food on cold plates. Kiria Vlachou was sufficiently mortified to publish a leading article the following day denouncing the barbarian ineptitude of her compatriots.

Why did we welcome the Conran lady? Only because Julia had suggested it. Oh, there was also a certain interest in a personality who had struck it rich in the big world. It was unnerving, and reassuring, to find that success had crusted her with exemplary cheapness. Keeping one's finger on the pulse of the public does not leave one with particularly sweet hands. She had the marketable complacency of today's smart women (Penelope Mortimer was another) who advertise how happily they cope on their own and who carry an aura of unpurged powder and sour underwear. Determination to be female tough-guys turns them into evangelists with bad news. S.C. gave us a lot of advice, because it cost her nothing. Was she Jewish? She was not: her maiden name was Pearce. She hated her father and said she was glad he was dead. Her mother lives in Canada; so do S.'s three younger brothers, who were failures in England but are big in Canada. One is in heavy engineering ('He deals in nothing which has wheels smaller than the height of that door'); the others lease helicopters. Only five helicopters have licences to fly across (over?) Canada and they own two of them. She wrote a charming thank-you letter to Beetle and sent us the magic machine for deterring insects. If we get any two-inch flies, we shall make prompt use of it.

13.8.80. John Griffiths, the outgoing public orator at Oxford, told Ken McLeish that an essay on justice in the *Oresteia* had so impressed him that he showed it to Hugh Lloyd-Jones. After reading it, L.-J. declared glumly he would have to rewrite his book on the subject. He asked on what precise topic the essayist was composing his D.Phil. dissertation. 'Oh,' Griffiths said, 'he's a first-year undergraduate. He isn't writing a thesis yet.' 'And I shall make sure,' L.-J. said, 'that he never does.'

Ken was quick to tell us of the hospitable malice of George Watson and Renford Bambrough when he dined in St John's. An adjacent Oxonian asked Ken what he was doing these days. When advised, with due modesty, of the translations and the Penguin project, the young man said, 'Downhill all the way, I see.'

I called on Guy Lee when I was in Cambridge and had tea and Coffee-Mate with him, playing the person from Porlock as he interrupted footnoting his *Georgics*. He had remarked, in a specimen he showed me, on the current spat between objectivists (championed by George Watson) and subjectivists, whose banner John Carey has unfurled. Guy's note was terse and tart, but I suspected that he had misunderstood the point at issue between Dee and Dum. Guy presumed that Carey was claiming that there could be no decisive solution to *textual* problems in literary criticism, whereas I am pretty sure that he was saying only that there could be no conclusive judgments on questions of merit. White-haired when he was in his thirties, Guy is taking on the lineaments of the reclusive scholar, at once dry and sanguine.

14.8.80. John Summerskill has been made President of Athens College. The appointment has made Mimi much bigger; arms bangled with soggy flesh, she still prides herself on her knowledge of the Kama Sutra, although age and status have made her prudish. How long ago is it that the Summerskills spent much of their lazy time on the roof of their Mylopota house scanning the landscape for naked bodies, including our own? They often turned their binoculars on our terrace; and later their telescope. Now Mimi is exercised that the beautiful young people give offence to the Greeks by their brazen parade. She was quick to report Paul to us for naked frisbee-playing, a charge he denied. She told us that the Minister of Tourism was threatening to make an incognito inspection of the beaches. One suspects that only his disguise would make him recognisable. Mimi was scandalised by the sixty-year-old men 'with full erections' (nice going, 60-year-old men!) who had been seen standing between the legs of shameless young girls in the middle of the beach. A few days earlier, a party of one hundred and fifty Germans, who refused to put their clothes on, were set upon by indignant moralists, with a bishop at their head, and expelled from Hellas.

Irene, a Swiss woman in her late twenties, is marooned on the island. She had been married to an Egyptian Greek with whom she had two children. When he was sent to prison for drug-dealing, they were already divorced; but she cannot, by Greek law, take his children out of the country. When she had the second child, some of the villagers collected a bundle of money for her. Others call her a whore. She has a rich (?) brother in Brazil, who does not answer her letters; her mother, in Switzerland, has disowned her. She is beautiful and desperate; high cheekbones, grand eyes. Her hands are big and rough. She cleans out nightclubs for fifty drachs an hour. She has gypsy pride, wears poverty like an ornament; her amused despair makes no direct claim on your sympathy. She was, however, prompt to discover, and count, the notes I slipped into her bag. She had failed to notify the Swiss authorities of her marriage and, so she said, had therefore lost her right to a Swiss passport. Her dignity did not argue against going along with any sexual arrangement which might relieve her tight predicament. When Mimi said she was a whore, Paul was outraged and challenged her right to abuse his friends. As we went to catch our boat, she came down with a bunch of flowers and some beads on a string, capped with a small linen handkerchief to give to Beetle.

One morning a trail of blood was seen to be running through the centre of the village. The Greeks assumed that it had come from a knife fight between drunken tourists. It turned out to belong to the son of one of their worthies. He had been out at night, on the far side of the island, dynamiting fish. They shine a light into the sea and, when the fish come, throw a stick of dynamite into the water. The young man delayed too long or made the fuse too short and blew his hand off. He walked back to the village to seek help but bled to death as he arrived.

18.8.80. The self-important Fenton quotes Ken Tynan in this week's piece and adds 'I wish I had met him'. Ken had an extraordinary career, based on enthusiasm and cynicism, earnestness and flippancy, iconoclasm and snobbery. A relentless pursuer of the famous, amongst whom he flashed the jester's licence and the libertine's effrontery, he began as an admirer of the gorgeous. There was something suburban in his appetite for the grandiose. He dreamed of sumptuous stuffs and an arsenal of epigrams. A fluent stammerer, he was a blanched and saturnine harlequin who imagined himself superb. He had the shamelessness of those with lordly airs and a bastard's provenance. Never handsome, he had a remarkable face, gaunt and chalky; eyes like chips of slate. Cursed with knowledge beyond his age and tastes beyond his means, he knew it all and not much of it was nice.

I first heard of him dressed in a purple corduroy suit and a *torero's* tie in which he had given an Oxford party to which he had persuaded Orson Welles to come, if persuasion was needed. He charged the groundlings a pound a head to meet the great *mondain*. Irreverent toady, he had from the beginning a smart sense of the cash value of celebrities. He would trade his best friend for a by-line and yet gave the impression that he was above pecuniary purposes. Proclaiming himself a socialist, he expressed his political activism by showing blue movies to Princess Margaret. He lent himself to the smart world the better to make its cheeks smart. Sado-masochism gave cruel pleasures an ideology.

Ken could introduce you to all the right people, but he was never quite one of them. An intellectual pimp, was he ever convinced that he was wanted for himself rather than for the rare merchandise he could procure? He had Cyril Connolly's sloth, an inability to produce major work, or much work at all. Both were masters of the 'proposal', in several senses. Ken was converted to socialism by the Berliner Ensemble; if he could never be a theatrical innovator and seraglio commandant, as Brecht was, he could try to be as big a shit. Like a non-combatant Georges Bataille, he blessed sexual perversity with *avant-gardisme*.

A social astrologer, he remained star-struck all his life. He idolised the Algonquin set and made himself into a kind of *nouveau* New Yorker. He declared his allegiances best by betraying them: no sooner had he realised his dream of being hired by the *New Yorker* than he was taking part in anti-American demonstrations. He could not fail to run foul of anyone whose favours he enjoyed. What socialist society of the kind he affected to crave would have tolerated him? The stammer was an almost too neat symbol of defensive aggression. He was a parody of the elegance which he failed to possess. More scarecrow than dandy, he said a few things which were widely reported, but not many. His reviews were cutting, but they lacked a variety of strokes. Had he not persuaded himself that he had a cause – sexual liberation, socialism, the National Theatre – he would have found himself low on fuel. He had the insolence that craves a master. If he could never claim to be an artist, he could play at being a revolutionary.

He married first a glamorous older woman. When I visited them in the Mount Street flat, Elaine seemed the essence of American sophistication. Like many of his generation, Ken confused being a grown-up with being married to one. Elaine Dundy was a short, bulbous, pop-eyed little party in a little black dress and black slippers. She regarded me with beady indulgence. It may have masked her amusement at the fact that I took Ken so seriously. Their flat was by no means fancily furnished, but one wall was emblazoned with a spot-lit blow-up (in black and white) of Bosch's *Garden of Earthly Delights*.

I first met Ken in 1954, during the success of *Out of the Blue* which owed a lot, but not everything, to Jonathan Miller. For a few weeks we were the buttered toast of London. Leslie Bricusse took me to a big party at the Tynans' place (north of the park in those days). Frankie Howerd was there. Ken explained that I was one of the brightest of the whizzing kids who had taken London by storm. Howerd looked at me balefully. 'I hate talent,' he said.

When Leslie opened as the second string to Bea Lillie in *An Evening with Beatrice Lillie*, Ken did not temper the wind. He always had enough integrity to savage his friends. He and the other critics gave Leslie the worst notices which any debutant ever kept, proudly, for his scrapbook. They were the more barbed for being adjacent to the roses with which they pelted Lady Peel. Leslie endured critical hostility and reluctant applause with the stoicism of a man who knew where he was going. Ambition is a powerful anaesthetic: a man will endure having his vanity flayed as long the prospect of success continues to play before his mind's eye. Leslie's conceit was self-effacing; he never hoped to be mobbed in the streets. With no wish to be a performer, he made his nightly humiliation into a means to a happy end: it enabled him to become a familiar of the theatrical elite without being a threat to them. Without any wish to adhere to the cultural *gratin*, Leslie made no effort to maintain his acquaintance with Ken. The louche revels of Binkie Beaumont and his circle more alarmed than enticed him. He was simple enough to want only to be rich and successful.

In the 1960s, by announcing the bourgeois world to be in-defensible, Ken excused his opportunism as principled. To play both sides against the middle was his way of being uncompromis-ing. I recall his insisting (while eating *steak tartare* at the BBC's expense, at Overton's in St James's) that he was an irredeemable coward. I was naïve enough to insist that, in the crunch of reality, the ethos of the team spirit would impel him to do his duty in the eyes of the straight world. Tenacious in his lack of tenacity, he swore that he would be yellow no matter what. The hedonist can never happily envisage a world in which he would have to fight for his pleasures. Consent implies a lack of coercion, even when coercive rites are in prospect. For the bedroom philosopher, the elimination of property entails an embargo on jealousy; *that* kind of pain is no fun.

Ken might have been aware of a savage world beyond the gates of consent and complaisance, but he was not going to go through them. He was an improbable but dedicated *aficionado*. The bullring's combination of horned menace and subtle evasion fostered his dearest and darkest fantasies. He thrilled to think of the danger to which the *torero* exposed himself (especially the castrating thrust?) and he was relieved of guilt by the deftness of his evasions. The *torero* and the whore had something in common: the soliciting shimmer of their bodies – a challenge to the timidity of the punters – and that essential coldness of address. Professionals in physical ostentation, their livelihood depended on heating the audience to an excitement that they could never afford to share. The *torero*'s dexterity demands unblinking self-control. The audience's catharsis requires that they have the emotions which he must deny himself. If a role had to be found for him in the ring, Ken might, just possibly, have been a padded *picador*; he could never achieve the accurate poise of the soloist.

He was most at ease with actors, socialites and tarts. There he could play the paymaster and the pimp. *Oh! Calcutta!* procured him his own whorehouse-cum-bullring. He devised a way to entertain himself, by the abasement of others, and to make a fortune at the same time. Why not? In sexual fantasy, as in Auschwitz, there is no 'Why?'. If the bourgeoisie would not consent to be improved, let them be degraded. If the theatre was not to be the university of socialism, let it be the brothel from which, as Genet had gloated in *Le Balcon*, there was no escape. Ken was perfectly positioned to take advantage of a society rushing in all directions. He made himself infamous by the most banal of means: by saying 'fuck', for the first time on television, he shocked a public to which the word was a commonplace. The scandal came of insolence, not of daring; bullshit has no horns; his moment of truth was only a moment of publicity: he was awarded all ears, but no tail.

During the shoot in Venice, we took the motorboat along an alley of stakes, to San Lazzaro to visit the Armenian monastery. The island is not far from the Piazzetta. It was a calm, milky morning; high heat over the lagoon. We were met on the quay by the Father in charge of public relations. A handsome man with glistening hair and prune-dark eyes, he was no more than thirty-five with a slim, good-humoured virility; no hint of subjection. He spoke eagerly and charmingly to the females, including poor Lucy, who never did anything right or anything wrong. The persecution of Armenians in Turkey proceeds with renewed malice, it seems. Technically a Turkish citizen, the PR monk dared not appear on film lest he be barred from pastoral work in Armenia, which he still visited. The Turkish authorities encourage the desecration of its holy places.

There are only some fifteen monks and twenty-five seminarists. The main church was destroyed by fire in the nineteenth century. Its replacement is a Victorian pile, decked with icons and ornaments salvaged from the blaze. There is a pretty cloister, enclosing a garden. The empty refectory was laid for lunch. Its tall windows are set too high for the diners to see out of (to prevent day-dreaming?); tables along three sides of the room; high above the long table on the left a lectern from which a monk reads to the assembled diners. The abbot has an ornately sculpted chair, facing the door. On the seat, hidden by a discreet cushion, was a jar of Nescafé.

An older Italian monk, tall, grey and voluble, improvised eagerly as we walked away from the camera. He said that they still had Byron's Armenian dictionary in the library with his notes in his own hand on correct pronunciation. In the slow rush to complete the shoot, I never saw the texts. As his letters to Teresa Guiccioli prove, Byron was a quick study when it came to foreign languages. He was as much a parodist as a poet. The Italian Father agreed that there was a measure of theatre in religious ceremonial. His colleagues had not failed to put on their best costumes for our benefit. They paraded the seminarists under the sign of the cross and marched around the cloister and into the church, several times, before some rather patchy singing around a harmonium which had to be carried into the nave.

The monks were capable of humour, even skittishness, but they did indeed lack personal ambition. They loved each other in the light of a common belief which both commanded their allegiance and relieved them of the need to confect a world for themselves. The question of truth scarcely arose. Their sense of common identity, rather than any issue of creed, was the heart of the matter. The Armenians relied on these few priests, and on the boys whom they had captured or persuaded, for the continuity of their race and culture. The place was more than a museum: the monks lived the life of which they were the curators. It seems somehow comic (worth smiling about, at least) that these bearded, celibate men – isolated in the unlikely Venetian lagoon, only because the monastery has been endowed and is available – should incarnate the hope and the despair of their distant, persecuted people.

We were introduced to the oldest monk, a tiny, upright figure who declared that when he was a very young seminarist he knew a monk who had known Byron. He had quite big feet and a largish head. His body seemed out of drawing, a little columnar log of flesh and bone, no shoulders, no hips, the purplish cotton smock cinched with a leather belt. The security of the faithful seems at once courageous and noble. It may be that their renunciation of pleasure looks more enjoyable than it is, but there is something enviable (almost) in their abandonment of personal gratification. To agree to belong to an enduring establishment and to take one's life's meaning from that allegiance seems at once terrible and terribly seductive. The studious monk is at home in the knowledge of his predecessors; he knows his duty and his destiny. He may have moments of lust, doubt and despair, but – provided he remains within the discipline he has chosen – he has the recompense of being a link in the spiritual continuity of mankind, no matter how particular his sect. His consolation is that not everything is going to waste. At the centre of his life he preserves what cannot be touched, like the Holy of Holies that was at once a void and everything, absence as presence, in the inner sanctuary of the Temple.

The folly of the Jews in refusing a compromise with the Romans can be read as the origin of all their woes; yet without such obstinacy, what culture will survive? The persistence of religion, magnificent and illusory, teases and challenges the sceptic. The scholarly, self-denying monk, however naïve his credulity, mocks the egotistic nihilism of the sophisticate. Scepticism is based on assumptions about the validity of science and the omnipotence of technology which few can clearly elucidate. We depend on the prosperity of a society whose promises are no more reliable than those of the metaphysicians whom economic man is pleased to disregard.

The Armenian monks have their duties where we have our fears; while they are solitary, we are lonely. They dispose of no formidable intellectual reservoir and keep no arcane secret. Where the free-thinker of the twentieth century is obsessed with the need to make an original mark, to prove that it has made a difference that he has lived, the monks are fulfilled by maintaining what they have been given to maintain. We fear death like the invigilator's cry of 'Stop writing!' The doomed candidate races to get one more sentence written. Each exam is taken only for the purpose of success and in the fear of failure. It qualifies a man, when it does, for further inquisitions. He will never achieve the quietus to be found at San Lazzaro, where modesty is also a kind of success.

The bluffer takes greater pleasure in his triumph than the man who has all the cards.

Life offers only second prizes to those who play fair. Just deserts tend to be on the dry side.

Tom Maschler boasts that John Fowles retains complete control over the content of the film of *The French Lieutenant's Woman*. Does this mean that it is bound to be as dull as the book?

22.8.80. While we were away, old M. Barat at the farm up the road died. He was always referred to as the *pépé*. When we were first here, he used to lead his old cart-horse to pasture in the field below the house; a strong, stout chestnut, with bulging hips and a sagging, powerful back. The horse's tail was docked and the flies persecuted him while he whisked the futile stump. The old man usually wore an old black suit, once his best perhaps, and a striped shirt, no collar. He shuffled as he walked but he knew what had to be done about the place and did his share. He watched the sheep, he chopped wood, collected logs from the neat stack and under-took small errands. He was happy to stop, remove his cap, shake hands and discuss the weather. Sometimes he was abruptly tearful, compressed with anguish in the midst of the commonplace. He particularly liked Stee, who shook his hand and was French with him. He could sometimes predict the weather, indicating the direction of the wind; at other times, he disclaimed all certainty, shrugged and pointed with his stick at the sky and gave a modest laugh. He remembered when there had been eighty *feux* at Lagar-delle (each fire stood for a family). I saw him agitated only once on our account. We needed some hard core for the terrace and I helped myself to a barrowload of stones from below the wall of the ruined house opposite, which we had bought from M. Cabanne in Grives. The stones came from a wedge of land, two or three metres wide, between the house wall and the road. The old man came down to tell me that the narrow triangle of useless territory was, in fact, a continuation of his field. I apologised and he was promptly assuaged. I said that I would return the stones. '*Non, non, prenez tous que vous voulez.*' He did not mind that I was taking the stones, but he was at pains to establish his title to the land.

Locals recall the war with uneasy wariness. '*Ils étaient rudes, ces messieurs*', a local woman said to me about the Germans. Our neighbours had no cruel time in the war; they had more than enough to eat and could sell their surplus on the black market. But they were pinched from both sides: the *Maquis* demanded that they leave food for them; the Germans promised to shoot anyone who did so. Peasant simplicity became culpable. After the war came *réglements de comptes*, metalled roads, tractors, bureaucracy and then the common market. The old horse went out to pasture. The peasant life was still hard and unremitting. There were no holidays and little leisure. Yet the intrusion of modernity, which began when a German tank attempted the slope up the *côteau* to Lagardelle and failed to make it, was bound to come. Arcadia was breached; the post-war generation no longer learns its Occitan *argot*. Most of today's *jeunes agriculteurs* have been to technical colleges. The old man's son, Norbert (who is my age), is one of the few who acquired his expertise by working alongside his father. He also has to operate tractors and machinery which never existed in the old days. The old man had a sense of place which was almost magical. When our three ducklings matured into vigorous drakes and quite suddenly took off and disappeared, he pointed with his gnarled stick in the direction of the farms in the valley. He may have been alerted by a neighbour, but the Barats had no telephone in those days. I like to think that he had divined the flight track (it is more likely that he knew where the local scoundrels lived).

When we went to offer our condolences, the Barats said that the old man often asked whether we had returned yet. He was distressed by our absences in England and had to be assured that we would be back. They said that he had taken particular pride in looking after our post which was left at the farm when we were away. We took the old lady down to the cemetery where she put fresh water in the pot of gladioli at the foot of the grey granite family tomb. We added a bunch of our own dahlias.

A letter this morning from Julius Hogben, the film editor who plagued me with virulent attention soon after *The Glittering Prizes*. He desires encouragement, but lacks the assurance to play the equal of those to whom, as a practising nay-sayer, he disdains to defer. Insolence is the nearest he can come to intimacy; cadging stands in for comradeship. He has compiled a short film about an old lady and implies that I should care. He brags of his anarchist allegiance, but I notice that he still works for the BBC; the better to abuse it perhaps. He has a florid script and signs his name as if one should have heard of it. Aggressively eager to resume our correspondence, he enclosed a naïve essay on California.

Deadline. A Hollywood writer has always prided himself on punctual delivery. He may not be good but is he ever on time! He does, however, have an incurable tendency to leave things to the last minute. He and his wife Joanie have been warned that they should never swim in the pool when there is no one else there. Several people have drowned all alone, although excellent swimmers. The day before he is due to deliver his latest script, he comes home from tennis and finds his wife floating face down in the pool. They have always been a devoted couple. He goes in and finishes his script before calling the ambulance. At the funeral, everyone is moved by how shattered he is by Joanie's death. How will he ever write another word without her? *The Old Pro.*

Re Aeschylean justice: 'And it came to pass that when they were in the fields, Cain rose up against his brother and slew him' – Genesis iv, 8. 'They had earlier said to each other "Come, let us divide the world". One had taken the earth, the other all the moveables on it. Now one said to the other, "The ground on which you are standing is mine". The other said, "Strip!" The first said, "Get off my ground". That is why Cain rose against Abel and slew him' – Talmud. Drama arises from the division of the spoils. Political visionaries always look forward, backwards, to the elimination of property, of interests, of religion, from which war, politics and art arise. When pottery began to be, decorated figuratively, timelessness was banished. The tradition of the new begins with dialogue and representation.

How many scholars acknowledge that ancient drama had to be rehearsed? When actors consider how to do or say things, their practicality institutes dialogue about the nature of the material they are being asked to perform. Ritual demands exact repetition; drama calls for innovation. Tragedy was more like comedy, in its secularising effect, than Aristotle admits: it too challenged orthodoxy. The *Oresteia* argues for peace as keenly as *The Peace* of Aristophanes. Drama implies the plausibility of the adverse case, hints at the unspeakable. Rehearsal is its education. Attic dramatists were said to *teach* their actors.

Stanley Donen told us that when Lennie Bernstein's wife was still alive, he was reticent about his sexual adventures. Once, in Boston, he picked up a sailor and led him back to the fancy Ritz Hotel, with the greatest circumspection, and in through the back entrance. After they had completed their anonymous business, and pleasure, the sailor put on his uniform and, as he assumed was expected of him, went discreetly to the door. L.B. called out, 'Hey, wait a minute! Don't you even want to know who I am?'

Democracy is the antagonist of truth. It requires hypocrisy in the face of all revealed Truths; it can neither embrace nor offend them. The politician trims truth with temporising. Alternatives are reconciled only in drama. Plato's attack on rhetoric not only rejects 'persuasion'; it casts doubt on the validity of any verdict, including a just one, which derives from advocacy. The majority vote has nothing to do with Truth. Truth requires a priesthood.

A couple of intellectuals plan to have their letters to each other published, perhaps after the death of one or both. Reviewers are touched by the subtlety of their mutual appreciation. Yet is there not an element of emulation in their competitive generosities? Someone claims to remember an obscure occasion when the two actually met (not recognising each other maybe) and each was disappointed by the other's personality.[24]

One could date the golden age of Attic drama as beginning with the ostracism of Aristides, which came about, allegedly, because the *demos* tired of hearing him called 'the Just'. Their capacity to be bored, even by heroic excellence, bears on the people's insistence on innovation in the drama and on its deconstruction of heroism. They tired of what they heard too often. Those who repeated pious formulae were likely to go the way of Aristides.

---

24 Almost forty years after this was written, Joseph Epstein and I, who had not and still have not met, began a year-long correspondence which amounted to some 175,000 words. Entitled *Distant Intimacy*, it was published in 2013 by the Yale University Press.

Many countries have had difficulty in surviving defeat; the British alone have struggled to recover from victory.

The wood fire crackles like a single-fingered typist, one crisp letter at a time.

The only centre party which could hope to create a constituency would have to be an *extreme* centre party.

A youngish woman with an undisclosed past and no 'connections' decides that she will begin life again. Under a new name, she takes a job in an anonymous town and there meets Denis, a mechanic, who finds her attractive. She experiences the stabbing pleasure of being penetrated ('known') for the first time. He is surprised by her 'innocence' and becomes devoted to her. 'Where have you been all my life?' She is comforted by his lack of curiosity about her past. Like a detective, she teases him into telling her about himself. A boy soldier perhaps, has a guilty history: there was a time in Aden when they were ordered to do certain things. She helps him to get over it. In her past solitude, about which she is never specific, she has read many books. 'You'd think you'd been to university,' Denis says, 'or was it a convent?' 'How about a prison?' she says. Denis says, 'Go on!'
    She decides to have a child, whom she insists shall be called Miles. She believes that, by giving life to a new baby, she can put herself straight again and atone for what she did when she was a girl. She reckons without the long vigilance of the dead child's parents who have been hunting her ever since she was released under a false name. She knows herself to be at risk, but she cannot tell her own child's father without disclosing everything she is seeking to be done with. In the last week of her pregnancy, she is run down on a zebra crossing by the dead child's parents. She is killed, but the infant survives. The murdered child's parents are caught and accused of careless driving. There is no evident connection between them and the dead woman. The report of their trial mentions the 'tragedy' of their son Miles having been strangled by a young girl many years before. The father of the new-born Miles forgives the 'careless' driver and shows him and his wife the baby who, by an odd coincidence, bears the name of the son they lost. They agree to become the child's godparents.[25]

---

25 *The Sunday Times* had just announced its sympathy for Mary Bell, who had

I love the tribute paid to Neville Chamberlain's courage on the grounds that he *flew* to Munich!

C.'s mother: at eighty-two what she misses most is physical affection. 'No one caresses me any more.'

The Alpha Link. A sequence of lethal accidents begins to eliminate a series of key personnel – scientists, inventors, intellectuals – whose bodies are never found or are in such a state of charred disintegration that identification can be established only on circumstantial grounds. One wife, who loves but was not loved by one of the 'dead' men, does not believe the evidence and hires an investigator who, after the usual scepticism, discovers the 'pattern' linking all these recent, apparently disconnected deaths or disappearances: the men (and women) are all highly expert in their fields of advanced research. One group (all said to have drowned after a helicopter crash) was developing a 'forbidden' neutron bomb. The investigator (a woman?) comes to realise that the Alpha people are planning world destruction of unnecessary civilian populations. When she decides to alert Russian intelligence, she finds the KGB top people unmoved and also strangely unsurprised. Quite soon, after a near miss in an accident, the investigator guesses that she herself is now in danger. The members of the Alpha link have in common a lack of interest in dated ideological concepts. They are all technocrats with a vision of an articulate society in which neither politics nor the arts will play a part. Their new Eden will have the clean and unquestionable 'science' advocated by Plato. One of the first projects of the new elite will be the development of an elixir of life. They mean to be the new immortals.

When the investigator is cornered, the Alpha people decide that, in view of the admitted excellence of her (undelivered) dossier and the brilliance of her deductions, she deserves to be recruited as one of the inheritors of the post-Holocaust earth. She makes a bold speech, denouncing the power-crazy evil of their delusions of divine right. They concede certain of her points, but refute others. They are polite, charming and implacable. The husband of the woman who first hired the investigator proves

---

been in prison 'without the recommended treatment' for something like twelve years. A journalist interviewed the mother of one of the victims and reported her distress at being contacted.

exceptionally seductive. He says that the discussion has been (key word) 'publishable', but also futile: the machinery for the cleansing of the world is already in irreversible motion. She can join them in their invulnerable capsule or not, as she chooses. None of them is going to do anything to her. She joins them.

What follows the volatilising of the Beta People is open to fantasy. The likeliest pay-off, after the establishment of the Ideal Republic, would be for certain 'guardians' to begin to disappear. Alternatively, the only thing which science cannot envisage or allow for might take place: the Second Coming. At the Final Judgment, the Alphas are sent to hell, which turns out to be the earth as it was before the bomb went off, in which the Alphas are now at the purulent bottom of the heap, with no idea how they got there or what to do about it.

The Last Time. When she told her lover, an American photographer, that she had decided to return to her husband, he recommended that one day she take a black man as a lover 'for the experience of being *really* fucked. Everywhere'. He looked terrible when he said it. He was disgusting. She was truly glad to go home. What was she ever thinking? Yet her lover's recommendation is lodged in her happily healed marriage like a shred of shrapnel which slowly works its way to the surface. Her husband is afraid that the past haunts and spices her imagination, but it is the future. (This is what *The Driver's Seat* should really have been about.)

Few women will object if you portray them in your novels as stupid; how many will forgive you if you make them ugly?

The wife of a young man who is often away on business befriends an old and lonely neighbour. The young man comes home one day unexpectedly and finds his wife sitting naked opposite the silent old man. They are drinking red wine. 'What were you thinking?' 'He decanted me.'

23.8.80. Lillet's wife Françoise is a strapping and independent lady who likes to climb mountains. They have five or six children and must be in their sixties. His grandfather invented the liqueur which bears the family name and made its fortune. Françoise recently conceived the idea of becoming an *au pair* girl. A woman of spirit and an excellent cook, she found a post in Scotland with a noble family. She went shooting with the Queen Mother when the royal family came to stay with her employers. Another day, another mountain.

'I toadily agree with you,' he said. 'Toadily.'

The clapboard boarding house in Provincetown, Mass. Our narrow bedroom was chintzily charming, colonially furnished. We had to go downstairs (mind your head!) for breakfast. Early birds were sitting in the narrow lobby, neat trays on their laps. We went and sat in the already warming garden. After a long wait, a handsome black boy brought us generous, overcooked ham and eggs. The place was nice as could be. It was a relief to get away.

Burgess writes of the 'sigh' of a tin as its vacuum is punctured; wouldn't 'gasp' be better?

25.8.80. A proof of *The Kennaway Papers* arrived from Tom Maschler, with one of his seductive letters, hoping for film interest. My interest comes partly from mere curiosity – but when was a writer's curiosity mere? – and partly from fear that James was somehow more important than I am. My apprehension derives from the simultaneous publication of our first novels. *Tunes of Glory* was taken very seriously; *Obbligato* was not at all serious and deserved no more than the indulgence it received. James was three years older than I and seemed to have greater maturity; he was certainly more of a Scot. He and Susie became, in a certain circle, mythical figures. John le Carré's *The Naïve and Sentimental Lover* promulgated the *mythos* and ruptured it at the same time. James had a militant flamboyance which I envied.[26] It seems now that the admiration which he gave to *Two for the Road* did not spring from detached professional admiration: he read the story for his own (and Susie's) and recognised its truth. He was like me and not at all like me. We exemplified an idea of dedication and professionalism. We both wanted to be artists and we were both lured by the cinema, with its gilded servitude. He was unlike me in the recklessness of his personal life. He assumed that being a writer involved divorce from domesticity. He fled from the pram in the hall to the unpromising haven of the screenwriter's Soho pad. Confident that he was a greater master of film technique than any

---

26 There is, in my introduction to a recent edition of *The Cost of Living Like This*, a brief account of our tenuous relationship.

of his scripts go to prove, he had the fruitful disadvantage of being a ranking Scot. He became a subject for local pride and patriotic promotion. His novels are *sui generis*. They show evidence of the many drafts to which Susie's book alludes. He was at least some kind of a Carlylean genius: his work was infinitely painful.

27.8.80. Irving Kershner called. He said that 'we' were touring in the Dordogne and he suddenly realised etc. I met him first in the 1960s, soon after I won the Oscar. He came to lunch at Seymour Walk (I remember only that we had strawberries and cream). He wanted me to do a screenplay from a novel by Isaac Singer. He passed for a serious film-maker. Since then he has had a long, uneven career. He told me, when we saw each other in LA, that he made a documentary about Caryl Chessman in San Quentin. It covered the last eighteen hours in his life. Kersh shuddered, eyes glinting, at the memory. He might have witnessed some sexual outrage; you would not have wanted to be there, but he had something over you because he was. There was a time when he was keen to do *Richard's Things*. It was on his recommendation that the Swiss producer Vuil came all the way to Brive to meet me. The uncomely Vuil drank B. and B. in a bar, tipped the hotel concierge from a thick Swiss roll of 500 franc notes, talked about a deal and went back to Geneva. I never heard another word.[27]

Kersh told me in California that he was parting from his wife because he wanted his children to have two homes. He arrived at Lagardelle about 4 p.m., in a rented red Talbot. He is tall and bony, with a small, baldish head, trim grey beard. His companion, Judy Wiles, took time changing her shoes in the car before declaring an English accent and the slim figure, and developed calves, of a dancer (retired). He has had a huge success: the sequel to *Star Wars* has outgrossed even that celluloid comic. He had a gross participation and is now a millionaire and can expect his millions to be refreshed every year for years to come. He proposes to retire sometime, but not before his current prestige has procured him a few more rolls of the dice.

Judy is a bright-eyed eager chorus-lady. Her father had been a theology don at Christ's. She mentioned him with uneasy pride, as if there was some notorious secret about him which I might have heard. She was an unlikely companion for a recently enriched and

---

27 I was told some time later that he had taken a heavy loss on a film he co-produced in Hawaii with Dino De Laurentiis.

divorced director. Kersh had a project he wanted to discuss. The discovery that we had a tennis court encouraged him to spring his proposal at once: a modern version of *Les Liaisons Dangereuses*, set in Boston. He had a title, *Dangerous Games*, and wanted it to be an 'R' not an 'X'; soft-focus, hard-edge. He claims a European company wants to back him. We then played three sets of doubles. Kersh was determined and vigorous. He very much wanted to win and made inventive line calls when, in the third set, Beetle and I began to beat him and Stee, which we did. Judy was impatient at the long delay before they went on to Sarlat. Kersh had not brought his money with him, but he means to please himself from now on. She dislikes California where, she says, there are only three topics: sex, money and how to keep young.

Kersh fears that he will die before he has had all the joy he can get from his percentage. He worked for over two years on *The Empire Strikes Back*. Often they got no more than seven seconds a day. He could never go beyond two takes, except in catastrophic circumstances, since it took hours to reconstruct the set-up. He commuted between two complete crews working on adjacent stages in order to raise the daily rate to a hectic twenty seconds. Eager to be seen as a thinking man, he said that he researched Icelandic myth in order to give the script body. When he retires, he intends to paint and enjoy music. He has an island place off Seattle, where he has played at the simple life for twenty years. 'That's all over now.' The islanders all went into the city by boat and saw the movie. They look at him differently. He means to invest his millions and live on the proceeds. There is something humble and adhesive about him. He takes advice, and gives it, with a wincing, eager expression which somehow alludes to being a *nebbish* and yet having all the luck.

Ron Mardigian says that Kersh is a 'mechanic'. He now has the air of a man who can wipe his hands on a clean cloth and never get them dirty again. He has commissioned a script about Britain after the departure of the Romans, all about Celts and Saxons. Who knows what kind of dialogue they will turn out to speak? He is also involved, he says, in the Malraux project which I discussed with Costa-Gavras a couple of years ago. Sidney Beckerman claimed to be producing it, but never had a penny in it. He is now out of *Man's Fate* altogether. Kersh says that he has a new angle on it. The Chinese are willing for him to shoot in Shanghai, but are uneasy, he says, about the anti-Chiang-Kai-Chek elements in the novel because 'they are eager for rapprochement with Taiwan'.

Money teaches the young how to age.

When D. decided to be an actress, she had to prove that she was
desirable and admired beyond her family circle, which was wholly
female. A lover was the easy evidence. She was frantic not for
sex but for proof that she could be something more than a good
student. Shame and sex are now linked in her mind because she
is ashamed of her theatrical pretensions and associates sex with
them. She is bewildered by her longing for the friend she had in
Geneva, since she is sure that she is not 'sexually Lesbian'. Might
it be that her friend was a surrogate sister, to whom she could
declare herself without inhibition because, being without sexual
appetite, there was nothing ambitious in her affection? Her friend
had everything that D. wanted, not least that there was nothing
desirable about her.

8.9.80. On the plane to NY, soon after we left Paris, an overweight
American tottered greyly to his seat ahead of us, face puttied by a
pain that seemed to cudgel him in no specific location. Pretty soon
there was a call for a doctor to make himself known to the cabin
staff. The first was a young man, probably French, with fair curls,
handsome face redeemed from banality by a blunted nose and attentive eyes. He was joined by a man in late middle age, with thick
glasses, grey hair and the creased been-here-before expression of
someone who has known many emergencies. They consulted
over the seat of the collapsed giant; asked quiet questions, received
even quieter answers. They called for the stock of drugs on board
and selected the likeliest treatment for their chalky patient. He
was accompanied by a ruddy-haired woman in her late twenties
(sickness had aged him, but he need not have been much older).
She had started the flight as a rather vivacious, hard-faced charmer
with a strong jaw and appraising eyes. Fear bled the vivacity from
her. She remained calm, controlling her distress by the discreet
manipulation of her mouth. From time to time during the long
trajet the sick man felt his way along the cabin to the lavatory.
He went like a cripple, bemused by dread that his condition was
not transitory. She was present, but touched him with no natural
solicitude; her dignity a little frigid; her eyes expressed resentment
and reproach. Solemnity had been forced on her and made her
older. He seemed older again. She might have been his nurse, but
then you looked at his hair and the young forehead and saw that
they were much the same age. Fettered by his pain, strait-jacketed

by the weight of the blanket they spread over him, he was made helpless by his helpers. The ice-pack applied to his head seemed somewhat sinister. She was vigilant but gave no sign of intimacy. Demeaned by his collapse, she did nothing to woo his recovery.

This Isn't Going to Work. A couple of high-flyers, working in the same New York office, happy to find that they 'mesh' when it comes to business strategy, decide to 'get together'. How about they specialise in mergers? They now find that they mesh as sweetly and excitingly in bed as they do in conference (they even like the same breakfast). They are happy together and take happiness for love. Who doesn't? They move in together and – hey, why not? – decide on a merger. There has to be more to life than going to work, doesn't there? 'Unless it's less,' he says. 'OK,' she says. On their European honeymoon, or coming back, still happy, the man is stricken like our fellow passenger. Neither behaves badly; she is concerned, he is stoical. Yet each realises how different the other is from the character which desire and opportunism (not always distinct) have fabricated. There is no quarrel and no overt sign or reason for disillusionment, but each is thinking, separately, 'This isn't going to work'.

Herb Ross's apartment on Central Park West is in the San Remo, a big old apartment house overlooking the lake. It used to be called the Twin Towers. There are two awninged entrances. To reach them I had to walk past the Spanish and Portuguese synagogue on the corner of W. 70th street. The San Remo is guarded by Irish security men. You cannot go up unannounced. A charmless young janitor called me simply 'Raphael'. I might have been a hairdresser. I was joined in the elevator by a young caterer who had come to measure for Herb's wife Norah Kaye's birthday party. Norah was due to fly in from LA to work on the new ballet season which she is running with or for Mikhail Baryshnikov.

Apartment 11D has a huge living room with aluminium shades and mirrored sills. It looks as if all the furniture and fittings were delivered on the same day. Herb said that he bought the place when property values were a tenth of what they are now, well, maybe not quite a tenth, but... He had aged in the ten years since he came down to the Wick with Jo Janni to talk about a film of Muriel Spark's skimpy shocker *The Driver's Seat*. He was wearing a huge coat that February day and seemed, on account of the raccoon muscle it lent him, a powerful man. He had credits only as a choreographer, which were not to the point. He can, and does, look back on the intervening decade with complacency. The apartment is a testimony to his long service and profitable conduct with Ray Stark, about whom he cannot say one flattering word. He rejoices to have been licensed by success to say goodbye to the man who gave it to him. In the same spirit of happy ingratitude, he says that he can no longer read Woody Allen (who scripted *Play It Again, Sam*). Woody is always writing the same short story, about how difficult it is to be a Jew who wants to fuck big Nordic girls. Herb has also had enough of Neil Simon, though not to the point of rupture. Grey and narrow-faced, he has the prescribed thinness of someone who has been advised to lose weight. He kept going to the bathroom to take pills.

The living room blazed with sunshine which the gleaming metallic shades could not resist. The air conditioning made it difficult to hear Herb's diffident speech. African masks hung at intervals around the walls of the ample room with its heavy brown freight of furniture. Herb had bought one or two of the masks himself as a matter of fact. They were not all old. He particularly liked a gourd with polished human features; 'contemporary workmanship'. The glass table at which we took coffee had a pair of couchant metal deer on it, their antlers high enough to hang the kind of cap, with feathers in it, that Herb would wear if that kind of thing was in style. He has long clean feet and never wears anything on them in the house. The big toe nails are opaque. He spoke intelligently and unaffectedly about the project, his enthusiasm only slightly diluted by the anxieties of Barry Diller. The Paramount chief had said that my script was 'beautifully written', which turned out to mean that it lacked sympathy. Herbert tried uneasily to accept my ironic view of the Sixties and Seventies while seeking to encourage me to a positive depiction of them. He has been weakened, slightly, by the failure of *Nijinsky*, for which he accepted responsibility: neither script nor casting had been right. The new Neil Simon play had been a modest hit though; he was due to rehearse some replacement casting that afternoon.

That night, he took us to dinner at Uncle Tai's, on 3rd Avenue. His afternoon had left him dismayed by the attitudinising and misplaced confidence of the actor whom Doc had imposed on the production. H. is more dependent on patrons, emotionally and logistically, than he cares to admit. He is not alone in resenting those from whom he has been glad to accept favours. He told us that Robin Gayley can no longer get any work, although he already has enough cash, real estate and royalties (from theme tunes) to take care of himself and Ellie. 'She fucks everything,' Herb said. He thinks that Robin's string of breasty mistresses is a blind. Rock music has now completely swamped the market; even Hank Mancini has fallen on harder times.

Her book on Shelley (a commission which I ceded to her) was published a few weeks ago. She decided at the time that it should not be reviewed in the *S.T.*; but after it received amiable notices elsewhere, she was irked to find that, during her absence, some tactful stand-in had not arranged to breach her embargo.

Bedtime Stories. The theme of adultery has been located, with salutary intelligence, by Tony Tanner as a principal motif in the novel. Any day now, it will found that the roof is often an important part of a building.

Paul Bailey, in a review of *States of Desire*, tells of a young homosexual in North Dakota who killed himself. His grief-stricken parents assured P.B. that they would have 'supported' him, had he told them of his homosexuality. But he could not tell them. Why? Might it be that he could not accept *their* sexuality?

Richard's Things was something of a failure at Venice. Once I had seen the final cut, I never imagined that we had any leonine chance. Tony Harvey radiates a kind of cheerful dismay. He cannot deal with the tragi-comedy of life; he is too sadly ridiculous himself. He had two women as his leading players and could not cope with the sex at all. T.H. promises that Alberto Moravia thought (and may have said in print) that the film was 'wonderful and extremely well written'.

The Spartans who opposed Lysander perceived that the total abasement of Athens would work against them. The elimination of the Other destabilises its opposite. Unselfishness is not without self-interest.

The Golden Age is incarnate in Midas; his touch homogenised everything and led to sterile opulence. There is no progress without small change.

Dionysos is the god of the theatre and the only theatrical god. He totes his own *agon*. In his progress, he is a god who demands to be seen, in different forms, and acclaimed. He embodies his own repertoire; not a force but a plot.

There is a waitress at the St Albert whose tables we do our best to avoid. She has round shoulders, dyed black hair chopped shapelessly short, bent thin legs under a heavy torso, a dripping nose, watery eyes. Perhaps she suffers from some allergy. She seems forever in a hurry, and yet she dawdles. Needing constantly to remind herself of what we have ordered, she consults the carbon slip on the table with a frown which doubles for a reproach. She does not smell, but her breath crepitates like a threat; her mouth never closes. Her clammy touch carries the taint of that dripping nose which no sniff wholly retracts. She has about her an air of frustrated impertinence, the menacing servility of a warder who dreams of asserting herself over those to whom she is bound, for the moment, to minister because they belong to the governor's party. I wondered why she grated so abrasively. Today I perceived an affinity between her and my half-sister Sheila, with whom I no longer correspond but who continues to telephone my mother from Canada. She says that she and Ted, her married lover, are going to settle in Ireland, where they mean to live on the interest on four hundred thousand dollars which she has made from real estate. She owns several houses and drives a Jaguar. She proposes to buy a new one when they get to Ireland. She no longer seeks to keep in touch with me, for which I feel only the pettiest guilt, though I am responsible for the *froideur*. She is a booming bore. I can excuse her faults, but not endure them. I am sorry that she is not the charming, intelligent Augusta which fantasy proposed. She has been ill-used and neglected, but not by me.

In the minds of our generation there has never been any reason to hurry. We have rolled out our youth as thin as it will stretch. We do not crave maturity. We have been keener to reproach others than to be responsible ourselves.

In Chekhov, characters resign themselves to marriage; in our day, to divorce.

13.9.80. In Paris in the September warmth, a young couple sat against the wall of a bank in the Boulevard St-Germain. The male had a bearded, thought-free Scandinavian face. The girl was in an ankle-length skirt, the uncomplicated accomplice. They held a little sign between them, applying for one or two francs to enable them to have a meal; Hansel and Gretel on the take. Their sign was covered in plastic.

15.9.80. One evening in 1954, when we were living in Montague Road, Cambridge, Beetle was badly scalded by boiling water from a kettle on the gas ring. John Nimmo was calm and kind. My memory is that he took her to hospital, in a taxi I presume, to have it dressed. Where was I? What did I do? I fear that squeamishness kept me from taking B. to Addenbrooke's myself. I have just asked her if she remembered what happened. She did: it was a saucepan, not a kettle; and I did, in fact, take her to the hospital myself. John and Dudy were staying on the top floor of Montague Road at the time. They fucked above our heads when we were in bed; it was no incentive to do the same.

The Hartleys have visited us many, many times, in Langham and in Lagardelle. Beetle is unaggressively determined that they not be asked again. We have known Patience for some sixteen years and she has never made a hospitable gesture; she makes taking seem to be a form of generosity. A couple of years ago, when we declared ourselves to be back in London for three months, she never had a spare evening. Geoff does all the glad-handing for his shy family; perhaps that is where their shyness comes from. He maintains his bonhomous style, but the effort needed to remain slim and boyish grows palpable. Working for a drinks firm is giving him an amiable double chin; he is chin-chin incarnate. This year they were not notably different from previous occasions, but they made us feel foolish for having greeted them enthusiastically. I opened two bottles of champagne when they arrived, but I avoided pulling a second cork on their last evening after Geoff, the sipping connoisseur, had declared that the Château de Tours 1971 lacked fruit.

When we first met, I liked his lack of pretence. Active and capable, he could strip down engines and instal and repair central heating. He had physical confidence that promised courage. He was a manager whose workforce, it seemed, both liked and respected him. When the factory closed down, circumstances forced him into the demeaning, perhaps more enjoyable, role of travelling salesman. He continues to be likeable, and to want to be. He likes to be overheard flirting with his secretary on the telephone. He threatened her with the sack because she called seven minutes later than agreed. Yet there is an edge of querulousness in him these days, a dash of bitters in his regularly filled cup.

Patience avoids comment and company. When she calls him 'darling', it sounds like an insertion by a scriptwriter anxious to establish their uxorious intimacy. She has lost her looks and, it seems, any interest in being desired; she has enjoyed, or endured, all she can take. Her withdrawal into middle age draws Geoff after her. She no longer says that anything is 'super'; he less frequently declares that other women are 'tasty'. She is taking what seems a slow revenge: packing her emotional baggage with deliberate coolness. Having decided to become an accountant, she seems to be playing a version of grandmother's steps, moving almost imperceptibly towards the exit. Once the children no longer make domestic demands upon her, and she is earning a reliable income, she may well retaliate for all the things which Geoff assumes have never bothered her. She does not have reason to hate him, but contempt needs no proof. Indifference is the faithful wife's retaliation against a man whose infidelity has been all words.

Godfrey Smith alludes to Ken Tynan's famous retort to Sir Beverley Baxter's scornful review of his performance as the Player King. What G. does not remark is that K.T. might never have been so insolent if, as well as a job which Ken coveted, Baxter had not had a knighthood. In that regard, he was a double for Ken's father and the perfect target for a bastard deprived of his birthright. Ken came back at him, a critical Oedipus, and claimed the other's front-row throne.

2.10.80. *The Climate of Treason* is riveting, but not very intelligent. Burgess and Maclean, Philby and Blunt seem more likely to live as comic figures than as infamous traitors. Yet in the case of the latter pair it is clear that they were responsible for the deaths of many men, some of them good. The fate of the Armenians sent to the slaughter by Philby is signally iniquitous. The laconic fastidiousness of the gentleman killer-by-proxy has stylishness on the page which it does not merit in practice. Indifference to the deaths of those whose names we find difficult to pronounce is a function of the covert snobbery which encouraged the quartet to place their consciences above common decency. If Blunt and the others had not thought well of themselves, socially, they could scarcely have sustained the servile vanity with which it piqued them to become the indentured labour of the unamusing Russians. Conceit and callousness (the ironist is always cold-hearted) sustain the poseur more reliably than any creed. We like to think that traitors must sincerely believe in the rectitude of their cause. We can endure anything in those who deceive us except frivolity.

Andrew Boyle is too busy indicting the climate to examine the fauna's social habits. He assumes that they were concealing both dark secrets and solemn purposes. He denounces what he lacks the wit to depict as absurd. The comedy of corpses requires a strong stomach, and perhaps a perverse appetite; but Boyle does his famous traitors the wrong kind of honour by taking them and their giggles so seriously. They are posturing humbugs. The cause was never a positive thing. Working slyly against his 'fatherland' enabled Donald Maclean to excuse his failure to confront his actual father. Flight to Moscow put an end to the painful pleasure of duplicity. He sustained his contradictions only by living a double life; once he 'came out', he was no more than a broken man. Philby was a far more conscious, conscientious villain. As an adulterous deceiver, he lived lies and lied to live. With his hermaphroditic passivity, Maclean was more interested in being seduced than in any virile sortie. He was never a free man or a figure of fun as Guy Burgess was when he cut loose. Emotionally parasitic on the masters he affected to serve, even in Moscow Maclean insisted on being victimised by those to whom he had sold, or lent, himself.

Burgess's cover had always been the too loud revelation of his doings, shrilled in a register which made them incredible and amusing. He hid in the open, with his flies undone. He was so appallingly outrageous that he came to be the prize in a fancy game of pass-the-parcel. If no one much wanted to undo the last layer of wrapping, few failed to come to the party. Donald never matched Guy's abandon. He was bad-tempered and soft, torn between all the poles to which he might have attached himself: a Scot in England, a married queer, alienated and ambitious: he was, it seems, as eager for success in the Foreign Office as he was to betray its secrets. The double life offset disappointment in his straight career with little-do-they-knowingness. When the turncoat has to come out in his true colours, they cease to become him.

What could have been a prettier or more characteristic proof of Philby's need to find something to betray, when resident in the land of his dreams, than his liaison with Melinda Maclean? Such an intrigue seemed ideologically neutral and no business of the Russians. Yet Kim was never so revealingly bourgeois as in sexual matters. The adulterer enjoys the property of another by purloining his wife: what he does to her, he is also doing to *him*. During the Spanish Civil War, while pretending to be on Franco's side, he validated the pretence by enjoying an aristocrat's mistress. He never acted like some ideological Mumby and attached himself to a hard-working proletarian with laborious knees. He was an unfeeling *casseur* whose pleasure was deceit and conquest. The situation which pleased him best was one in which the woman had to harm someone else before she came to him. Deceit had to be at the heart of everything. The lovers were guilty from the start. Their conspiracy demanded sophistication in which sincerity was a discord. The adjacency of the husband gave the situation piquancy which doubled for passion. The woman had to accept Kim in a hurry; duty was always calling. The deceiver had to be able also to deceive himself; a serial Aeneas, he stammered with every Dido. Kim not only seduced his ladies, he also had children with them. He made his cover-story more romantic than was strictly necessary. Do the innocent attribute rarer pleasures to deceivers than they actually enjoy? Spying is an amalgam of routine and fear. In a bureaucratic context, it entails putting one more, invisible, name on the c.c. list. Yet the sense of escape and of being trapped, the double bind of the institutionalised enemy of the institution, makes every minute doubly charged.

Praise from those whom you are betraying is a more handsome tribute than any tick in an honest margin. The whore's faked orgasm carries a similar charge of self-satisfaction. Drudgery is made divine when performed at the expense of an unsuspecting master.

Plot is to fiction what riddling is to poetry. Treachery, dissidence and adultery – all alien to the Platonic system – are of the essence of fiction and drama. E.M. Forster's 'weariness' with regard to plot takes on a sly complexion if, as Steiner would like, Morgan is to be linked with the Blunt affair. The wish to dispense with plot is like the wish to be done with 'cover', as spy or as homosexual. Forster could be glossed as wanting a society which no longer 'needs' fictions (or female heroes). His long silence as a novelist seems to coincide with slothful yearning for a society which has no call for the ambiguities of bourgeois art. Forster craved narrative in which nothing had to be made up. There was small choice for the homosexual in pre-1960s society but to produce art which was, in some regards, furtive. How else was dissidence to be expressed?

Communism could be imagined as making 'plots' as anachronistic as private property.

The manipulations of the ruling class are enacted with curt tenderness. I recall being taken out to lunch by Alan Maclean[28] and 'Auntie Marge', after they had read *The Earlsdon Way* and were bent on bending me from my decision to eschew humorous fiction of the kind that they (and their reader, Jack Squire) had so enjoyed in *Obbligato*. Hospitable and well-intentioned, they feared, very nicely, for my prospects. I would 'make no friends', they warned me, if I persisted in the caustic mode. By satirising the Tories and making fun of another publisher,[29] I had crossed an ideological line. My return to the fold would take no more than a minute; I had only to put *The Earlsdon Way* back in a drawer. How could I not prefer their continued patronage to relegation from their list? They took it for granted that the integrity which really mattered was social, not aesthetic.

When I first met Alan, it was four years since Donald's fugue. Alan declared their brotherhood almost as soon as we met. A nervous, chortling man, he supplied an appropriate nephew for Auntie Marge; he lent her status, she lent him her beard. He was literate, but not very interested in literature. Had he been a spy, he might have behaved pretty well as he did as an innocent. He was appalled when the only copy of the manuscript of *The Earlsdon Way* was filched from his office. Someone had stolen his briefcase during the unguarded lunch break. I suspect that the briefcase was lifted by a member of the Special Branch. He must have hoped for juicier reading than my second novel. The panelled Macmillan offices gave the place the aura of a department of state. It was staffed by dull, magisterial persons who might as well have been running the country.

Alan was penitent, to the tune of fifty pounds, when I had to rewrite the whole book; but that did not inhibit Macmillan from rejecting it when it was done.

---

28 Since Alan was Donald Maclean's brother, the Foreign Office had been obliged to dispense with his services, although no suspicion of wrong-doing attached to him. It is fair to assume that Harold Macmillan arranged for him to be accommodated in the family publishing business, in which he was to have a long and successful career.

29 I transformed Victor Gollancz into some kind of a Shavian eccentric, but the source remained obvious.

Iris Murdoch has persuaded her readers that Eros is the rightful ruler of the human heart. Because 'love' makes no sense, offers (and brooks) no arguments, it takes primacy over all other motives: I can't think, therefore I am in love. The peremptory powers attached to Eros have their political correlative in the 'right' to express any opinions and desires; the more uninhibited, the more 'authentic' they are. Anarchy is eros introduced into politics, terrorism its promiscuous expression.

'Guess who's in there,' Beetle said, when we were shopping in Sarlat before lunch. She seemed at once pleased and unexcited. It turned out to be the Gooddens, whom we used to see socially when they lived in Dedham; they later moved to Bath. I thought Leslie looked older, Robert rather well; Beetle thought the reverse. I asked them to join us for lunch, but they had just bought a Boursin for a picnic and disappeared in friendly haste. They may not have realised that I was proposing a Sarlat restaurant and feared that we were going to haul them off to Lagardelle. I may not have made it clear and I may not have meant to: Beetle and I enjoy our *tête-à-tête* lunches at the St Albert. What are the Gooddens to us? The kind of amiable people, nicely placed but not quite snobbish, whom we might have been pleased to know, if local society had meant anything to us. Had we never left England, they are just the sort of people who would have lent grace to our table and *poids* to our Christmas card list. They have the undemanding civility of those too shy and too well brought up for enthusiastic overtures. Happy to assume that the surface ran deep, they would never favour you with intrusive intimacies. They have the decisive, slightly defiant togetherness to be found in couples one of whom has been married before. Robert has retired from running the RCA, but he has retained the confidence of his office. If sensuality had administrators, he would be head of the department of finesse: he relishes the good things in life (he introduced me to Restell's wine auctions), but he is arty and crafty enough never to shout the odds. Leslie is so nice that you cannot help wondering if she is as nice as you think she is. It is no kind of hardship to guess that we shall never see them again.

Of All People. A married man who once had an affair with a very pretty girl who treated him with gleeful cruelty, but to whom he has not given a thought for many years, suddenly recognises her in the street of a city to which he has had to go on business. He is only a little pleased to see Harriet as a provincial and unattractive middle-aged woman and is about to turn away, but then her face changes, as she meets her husband (or lover?) and he sees that smile she used to give him, sometimes. The vision of her happiness is an assault. He would like to kill her. He has no time to represent himself to her as the successful and happy man he considers himself to be, but he wants her to recognise him as what she refused to let him be: something *essential* to her life. He elects to be her death. He waits calmly for her to be alone again, follows her and, in a quiet place, says 'Hullo, Harry, remember me?' She frowns and then she says 'Of all people!' and then he kills her, without resistance, as if – he tells himself – that was what she wanted. He catches his train and goes home to his wife, who finds him 'heaven' that night. No one ever connects him with the dead woman or with the place where she died.

14.10.80. Guy Lee was quite exultant over the death of Roland Barthes ('that Frenchman who got himself killed crossing the road'). He regarded Barthes as a charlatan and his critical ideas as pernicious. He supposed B. to have introduced unbridled subjectivism into the objective business of textual criticism, which is scarcely the case. Guy embraces obsolete causes like old friends. He is in favour of capital punishment and becomes quite flushed when he talks of the misplaced tenderness devoted to criminals. He thinks he is a lucky man to be where he is, but his gratitude does not stretch to tolerance. He is at once contented and captious.

The scholar, with all his dead masters, learns to be inhuman through the conquest of sentiment. Regard for the truth leads to a selfless narcissism. The idea of a pitiless master who awards rigorous servility the only marks worth having is common to the academic and to the apparatchik.

It is almost a year since the death of M. Lacombe. A month ago, young Bernard, who now runs the property, very capably it seems, put his cows in the field adjacent to our orchard and vegetable garden. One of his heifers again jumped the fence (which should have been electrified) and ate some of Beetle's crop and a swathe of rosebuds. I called Bernard in an access of unworthy rage, but he was already up here and had recovered the errant beast. '*Il a mangé un peu de salade?*' Beetle thought the comment charmless. I shook Bernard's hand with scant warmth. A year ago, I would have done anything to abate his anguish.

Oddly enough, Freddie Ayer seems to have become very interested in aesthetics. Is it that he cannot believe that they can possibly be as dull as Richard Wollheim has made them?

Shelley exemplifies the man who, with comic earnestness, ruins the lives of everyone with whom he comes in contact. He existentialises a rhetoric of freedom which is blown to tatters by the same careless winds to which he addresses his odes. If he had been a philosopher of liberty without seeking to embody it, his work might have been well received; but he took his metaphors for places to live in. The consequence was that he was blown away by reality. Byron accused the world of being 'ill-naturedly and ignorantly and brutally mistaken' over Shelley. Shelley himself was good-naturedly ignorant and mistaken; he never took the world, or other people, into any kind of accurate account. Once he had disdained to be a deceiver, he drew his energy only from indignation. It has been argued that he observed nature more closely than Leavis gave him credit for, but he simplified 'society' and its complexities like a Bennite. Less of an actor than Byron, he gave himself an unplayable messianic role. He then set full sail, on a stormy sea, in a craft with little keel.

Frankenstein's monster, embodying lethal power without imagination, is the objective correlative of everything that Percy B. refused to acknowledge in the ambitious vanity of man, something on which his wife was an expert.

The Athenians, as Perikles boasted (in a *funeral* oration), were can-do people. Nothing was forbidden as long as it was successful. Rhetoric, as Plato lamented, was bound to displace fixed standards in a society loud with argument and bargaining. His case against rhetoric seems logical: the public speaker brings sentiment into judgment just as the sophist soils philosophy with opportunism. Plato plays much the same trick here as he does against the poet: he makes it seem possible to accept democracy, and its arts, on con-dition that certain apparently contingent practices be abandoned. His proposal is itself cunning and rhetorical. While it is true that persuasion can be employed disreputably, it cannot be eliminated without a radical alteration of the social and judicial system. The extirpation of triviality cannot be achieved by trivial measures; once taken, they never result in trivial changes. Plato's reproaches are systematic, not casual. His seemingly modest reforms can never be effected unless the whole relativistic, Protagorean fabric of democracy is dismantled. All tolerance carries an element of comedy. There can be no good arguments in favour of democracy; it is a practice not a theory. Its virtues can never be established logically as right or necessary. It produces nothing better than wealth and individual happiness. Plato's ideal state is a logical response to contingency. Taken as a practicable blueprint, *The Republic* has had unremittingly bloody political consequences; read as a satire, it remains a work of genius.

Plato's determination to say nothing disparaging about the gods detaches them from human affairs. They are more like the distant and indifferent deities of Epicurus than anyone chooses to notice. They may be the guarantors of the justice of the state, but they cannot affect it. If there were room for their discreet intervention, his state could not be as ideal as Plato would have it. Only a fallacious form of justice would leave room for the machinery of appeal which, by its nature, concedes that human judges can be fallible. Abolition of the apparatus of appeal is an inexorable feature of totalitarian societies. In logic, there are no reprieves.

21.10.80. On the boat coming back from Ios we met an architect and his woman and a little girl. They seemed like a family, spoke French and offered us some wine at lunch. They joined us for coffee under the big blue windows of the empty first class (a faster boat had left an hour before us). It turned out that he was a Yugoslav, she was not his wife and the little girl was not their daughter. She sought to attach herself to us and became a flattering nuisance. He was dark, self-assured, discontented and aggressive. He had not had a good time with the lady, who turned out to be the daughter of Jean-Marie Drot's second wife. Drot is the rotund French TV director who built the first and finest pleasure dome on the headland on the right of Mylopota bay. Although an exile, the architect came from an important family. He retained a proprietary air. He would make no prophecy about what would happen after Tito. He said that it was a myth that the goat had denuded the Greek landscape. There were several parts of the world where the soil had not been eroded or the hills deforested despite the presence of goats. He had recently formed a *co-opérative* of building trade specialists with a view to constructing houses and even factories without the obstacles created by traditional bureaucratic formalities. The French do not make it easy for him to work, even though his scheme for job-creation gets an unofficial wink from the functionaries who block its realisation. At once resentful and smug, he was so weary of Marie-Thérèse and her child that he abated his churlishness and turned his charm on us. He wanted us to dine with them in Athens, which we declined to do.

The next morning, we came on them outside the Archaeological Museum, in the café under the corrugated plastic roof topped with vine-leaf chaplets, where they no longer squeeze fresh orange-juice. The little girl presented herself to us in the clear hope that we would take her into our lives. Presumably he is thinking of marrying Marité, who bored and irritated him, because it would give him an irrefutable claim on French hospitality. At once tough and garrulous, she was tenacious and *sans illusions*. Carrying a vision of her future in her eyes, it would be no surprise if the little girl was called Cassandra.

5.11.80. How rarely, in the diaries and notebooks of the famous, is there any mention of the great events which historians assume were present in everyone's mind! The plunge of Icarus did not splash Breughel's ploughman. No more has Reagan's election changed our day. The arrival of what one dreads is seldom as dreadful as its anticipation. At least in a democracy there is a change of programme. There was a reminder of how we take things for granted in Jimmy Carter's announcement that he would collaborate in the handover of power, quite as if there was a possibility that he would not. The dollar rose by 10% and the market jumped for joy. It is hard to escape the feeling that it was not wicked of the American people to reject the advice of Harry Evans and William Rees-Mogg and Peter Jay, even if it is unlikely that Ronnie will be able to provide them with more than twenty-four hours in a day. Americans are concerned less with practical politics than with the repeal of mortality. The most pampered people on earth are easily persuaded that they have had a raw deal. The main hope, when a man of little brain and much rhetoric is elected, is that he will prove not to mean what he said. If he genuinely believes the cant he has been happy to peddle, Reagan's presidency threatens us with a bumpy ride. He has the short temper of the charmer who cannot imagine why anyone should not think well of him.

6.11.80. I had lunch with Alan Sapper, the secretary-general of the ACTT and president-elect of the TUC. Paul has been trying to get into the union for more than two years. David Deutsch advised me to do what his father did more than thirty years ago: take the secretary-general out to a good lunch and make my pitch. I have never really believed that bribery worked or that I was capable of it. I decided on Au Jardin des Gourmets, where my father used to take journalists in the days when they could be made pliable with a bottle or two of Gewurztraminer. I was delayed at the *S. T.* and arrived ten minutes late. Sapper was already there. We had never met but he had the instant affability of the public figure. He had already planned his menu, apart from the wine. He preferred claret, he said. I chose a Léoville las Cases 1970, which he approved.

In the flesh he was less fleshy than his photographs. He wore a dark suit and flashed no sign of working-class solidarity. He had a moony face, slightly bulbous eyes, puffily lidded and made sly, if only by the shape of his skull. He lisped slightly, voice sleeved in saliva secreted too copiously in the shining cheeks. He was at once smug and unpretentious, though he did come it rather oenologically: he did not like white Bordeaux except for the best Sauternes. He had had a Russian dessert wine in Odessa which was almost as good as Château d'Yquem. He brought the Soviet Union in with a tray of glasses, so to speak. I took the opportunity to twit him on his admiration for that charmless society. He clearly preferred its system to the capitalism from which his members made their often fat living. I asked if he was a member of the Party. 'Yes – the Labour Party.' He seemed to add the last words as a prudent afterthought. He studied to be a biologist and, so he said, became a TU official and political activist because he wanted to do something for his fellow-men. My purpose being to collect not to correct, I was only a little ironic in alluding to the hereditary aristocracy in the ACTT. Its consequence was that those outside the charmed circle of initiates, such as my son Paul, could not even *apply* for a job in the cinema. I pitched it so gently that I feared that I had not made my point. In the event, he made a note of Paul's name and said that something would be done by the beginning of the week. It was all absurdly easy, except that nothing has yet been done.[30]

There were no awkward silences in our side-by-side conversation. I did not fail to quiz him on the state of England or to declare my support for Shirley. He said that she had been a 'disaster' at the conference, which suggests she may have been quite effective. He is a Bennite, avid for ideological prospectuses (how nice that he had chosen his lunch, not a cheap one, before his host had arrived!). He is hostile to the EEC, not because it has been

---

30 Nor was it. Paul managed to get his union card only five years later, no thanks to Alan Sapper.

unrealistic but because it has 'caused so much human suffering'. I should go and look at Corby, a steel town reduced to penury 'at a bureaucratic stroke'. He ducked the question of whether there was any market for overpriced steel.

The previous morning, after tennis, Patrick Sergeant had conceded that the EEC was anti-socialist, which supplies the real reason for Sapper's humane rage. He would not have to alter his views or his performance in order to become the full-time servant of a one-party state. He would, no doubt, accede gleefully to an enabling act, introduced by a Benn government, which would relieve the British people of the obligation ever to think again. He is not only a fellow-traveller, he is also a fellow who travels and has tasted the fruits of privileges which, he maintains, are fairly shared in the land of the Gulag and of penal psychiatry. He reserves his animus for the compromises of the open society. With his appetite for good food now and apocalypse later, he really wants a disarmed Britain, out of the EEC, deprived of further choices, committed irretrievably to a socialist future. He is a smiling fanatic, prepared to force his message down your throat, lubricated by the claret of your choice. He asked curiously about Shirley, the Catholic 'right-winger', quite as though he had never thought about her at all until I spoke amiably about her. He regarded her principles as evidence of some disreputable disease. If only she had abandoned them, how much she might have achieved!

The solemn puerilities of politics were never so obvious as in Sapper's irreversible admiration for success and power. I left the restaurant slightly elated at the seeming success of my ruse and ashamed that I had been so hospitable to a smug *apparatchik* in a dark suit. I was better able to understand the disgusted bemusement felt by Goronwy Rees and others when listening to the famous traitors. Marxism sounds so callow and so full of vindictiveness that one hastens to dismiss it. Yet Sapper's words, benign and rancid at the same time, remain in the mind. There is nothing in the complex web of British society and culture which he would not send to history's jumble sale. What disturbs me is the degree to which I could find good reasons for not denouncing such a man, the silly hope that one could get along with him. Yet his smile is that of Arthur Koestler's Chinese executioner as he says, 'Kindly nod'.

She has no colour at all, her eyes dark in that long, sallow face; a sort of smile appears only furtively. One is as little embarrassed to talk to her about death as one would be to discuss expenses with an accountant. She has become the accredited expert on catastrophe, acquainted with all manner of grief. It seems to keep her almost young. She has the sad hope of a martyr who has been exquisitely tortured: pain is her familiar. Her aptitude for suffering has, it seems, made her attractive to men. Her need gapes like an unstitched wound.

17.11.80. Tony Harvey phoned last night to say that *Richard's Things* had been enthusiastically applauded at the NFT. After the screening, however, he had been blackguarded by a man whom he took for some provincial lecturer. This man had sneered at the photography, the script and the direction. He said that more trouble should have been taken to coordinate the elements and over the stitching of the script. Tony was offended and angry and wondered who this strident person might be. Derek Malcolm told him that it was the film censor. Mark Shivas said that it was an old friend of mine and so, in a manner of speaking, it was. For who should this malevolent person be but Jim Ferman, whom I have known for twenty-five years? I was sufficiently vexed, and ill-advised, to call the Fermans' number as soon as I put the phone down on Tony H. When Monica answered, I asked to speak to 'Jim Ferman'. My voice was apparently unrecognisable, even though I have spoken countless times to Monica, often to ask them to come down to the Wick for the day, which they often did. She kept asking who wanted to speak to her famous husband and I had to say, 'Freddie Raphael'. I put the phone down, thinking it a good moment to leave them to stew and not wishing to spend my thunder on a secondary target. I dialled again a few minutes later and Jim, honey-tongued, answered. He affected bewilderment that I had not said hullo to Monica. I asked him why he had vented his dislike of me by seeking to destroy someone who had been out of work for several years. Jim denied that he had said anything offensive. He could not believe that I believed what I had heard. I asked whom *he* would choose to believe, someone who was a friend or someone who was not a friend. And which was which, he asked. I said that Tony Harvey was my friend. Jim found it convenient to conclude that in that case there was nothing more to be said. I do not know who hung up first or which of us imagined that he had trumped the other. I wrote a letter to Monica in which I apologised for my incivility to her but was unrepentant over my approach to Jim. Mark Shivas called to say that Jim had called him, after our conversation, and told him that he had approached T.H. only because no one else was talking to him. He had not attacked him, but had been led to discuss the film and speak his mind. I knew that Jim had long been saying sour things about me behind my back and I was sure that T.H., although mildly mad, had not much exaggerated. He generally took even lukewarm praise as fervent endorsement. Mark said that he had, by chance, sat next to Jim on a flight to Milan three weeks ago and that J. regretted that we no longer saw each other. I was slightly mortified, but I have never been close to Jim, although I have done him a few good turns.

19.11.80. Sartre should really have said that hell is having to *work with* other people. All the same, my trip to England last week did yield an enjoyable conference on the Byron film. I suggested solutions for a number of editorial problems which had puzzled the others. They were responsive and agreeable. I wonder if they realised how important their presence was: there are times when there can be no performance without a gallery.

Paul came to lunch at the canteen. We ate exhumed fish and dead peas. David Turnbull came by and said that the little Cambridge film was going to be repeated. He is pale, timid, genial and not at all likeable. Frank Cox offered to drive me to the Albert Hall, which was the landmark for my rendezvous with 'EEtv', the Anglia TV syndicate. We went by way of the Kensington Hilton for tea. Since the lounge was rather full, we had to sit near the piano, where a woman in a black dress was playing *La Mer*, capably. We were quite animated after our meticulous deliberations and began to talk about Koestler and the Jews. I was in full flow about the Khazars when I found the pianist standing at my elbow. Frank thought she wanted my autograph. 'Excuse me,' she said, 'but I couldn't help overhearing your very interesting conversation...' Had she some clinching pro-Koestler point to make? 'And I find it very difficult to concentrate on what I'm doing.' She spoke civilly, but where other than in England could people who were paying £2 a head for tea and cakes be expected to adjust their volume to suit someone who was being paid to entertain them? We were not being loud and there was plenty of other noise in the room.

The scene at EEtv was solemn, smoke-ridden and tedious. The consortium was having a dress rehearsal of the confrontation with the IBA. I spoke briefly and was deputed to repeat the performance on the big day. The helpfully severe head of the mock Board was an elderly, blue-eyed, black-irised man called, I think, Sir George

Middleton. The anxiety of those who had worked at length on the application rendered them depressingly malleable. They were hard men being instructed in the production of soft answers. Michael Rice, the pop-eyed, sandy-haired PR man whose offices we were using, does a lot of business in Saudi Arabia. Framed water-colours of Riyadh and adjacent places, all blue and ochre, brightened his walls. Pretty blondes were in debbish attendance. Business, I could hear D.H.L. saying, is no good; but it certainly supplies a second home without tiffs or obligations. Money eliminates guilt.

The next morning, there was another session; post-mortem before we were dead. It was enlivened by John-Julius Norwich. He rides a little folding bicycle around London and has the unintimidated posture of a man who never has to repeat his name. One would not be astonished to see him, one summer, wearing a T-shirt with VISCOUNT across the chest. As we left, he remarked to me, in his Oxford and soda tones, that the richest member of our syndicate, a hunched, fat, frowning industrialist, was not only very boring but 'so *ugly*'.

All generosity betokens a bad conscience; all reconciliation surrender.

Compromise allows the established order to prevail. The determining moment in my life was when I was re-admitted, conditionally, to the Charterhouse society which had demonstrated its malice and its untrustworthiness. The condition was that I should trust and respect my enemies. I fear that I did so. The successful outcome of my humiliation seemed like a victory. Had I been evicted without reprieve, I might have been less of a trimmer. I should have been forced to avail myself only of my creative powers. Diplomacy and its pleasures have lamed my capacity for being incautious. I have spent my best efforts trying to remain in a game I do not like but cannot bear to lose. I have wasted my life in cowardly accommodation with forces which, had I exerted myself, I might have overcome. It would have been better to crawl to another place rather than to take on the values of those who have poodled me. Too thankful for small mercies, I have failed to outgrow the nursery in which they are granted or withheld. Cavafy was right; it is too late now: *Allous topous then tha vrees*. You will not find other places.

A superb, golden, frosty morning; scabs of frost reformed on the windscreen a few moments after I dosed it with warm water. All our troubles seem so far away. John Lennon was shot dead by an autograph-hunting junkie this morning (last night in NYC). Showbiz passes random death sentences. The revenge of the public is strangely punctual when it comes to those who shame it by exacting an excess of admiration or – more significant – who trick or train it into questioning its values. Lennon ended like the Jesus whom he was execrated for claiming to have outdone; like Gandhi, whom he admired; and like the pariah who fails to be humbled by fame and fortune. Lennon's notoriety was too enviable not to arm some sorry Erostratus. His killer declared that he wanted to be known as the man who killed John Lennon. No wonder pulp fiction used 'equaliser' as a synonym for a revolver!

When I first heard of her in 1950s Cambridge, Monica was recently separated from a music don called Beament. She wore fly-buttoned 'slacks' and rode a hand-painted red bicycle. She favoured lurid make-up and talked very theatrically (she knew Miles Malleson). Her allure derived from her wanton reputation. Jim came to Cambridge, as a graduate student, after he had been in the USAAF (he sometimes wore flying boots) and at Cornell. He seemed a man among many boys. He drove a second-hand MG convertible, an enviable symptom of mobile maturity. America was distant and glamorous. Neither precious nor pretentious (as Bob Gottlieb was), Jim had a certain *sérieux*, a white smile, soft voice, thin hair, palely freckled handsomeness. He was not a load of laughs. Tony Becher and I were quick to dub him 'Grim Jim'. He became a recurrent character in my gossip column in *Varsity*, where I distributed unmalicious bladder-blows. It did not occur to me that he was a Jew. Never an actor, he moved in theatrical company. Leslie Bricusse was sufficiently impressed by his New York credentials to recruit him as his successor as President of the Musical Comedy Club, not least because Jim had regarded *Lady at the Wheel* with patronising disdain. He meant to trump us with the rather good idea of a musical based on Max Beerbohm's *Zuleika Dobson*.

Thanks to an introduction from Monica, he teamed up with Peter Tranchell, a camp musicologist don, who had written several numbers for the Footlights. ('It's spring,' said one of his naughty lyrics, 'and we are feeling ourselves again!') Peter and Monica were said to have honoured a version of the compact between Mme de Merteuil and Valmont. *Zuleika* promised to be much more sophisticated than Leslie and my and Robin Beaumont's jejune

Riviera revel. And so, I believe, it was; I never saw it, because I was on my travels. Peter Woodthorpe had a big success in the comic lead. The show appeared certain to transfer successfully to London.

By the time it was being rehearsed with a professional cast, Jim and Monica were an item. In her late twenties, Monica had always been much too old for any of us to dream of marrying her, but Jim was, it seemed, man enough to do so. We saw them both one evening in the Nimmos' flat in Ashley Gardens while the London cast was in rehearsal. Monica was in a black fur coat. Neither she nor Jim had a word for me or Beetle. A week or two later, *Zuleika* opened in London and was all but a hit. It flopped without serious casualties. Had Jim been a lyricist of talent, he might have learned lessons and proceeded to better things. In the event, he became a trainee TV director. Ted Kotcheff was his mentor.

We met him and Monica again by chance, on our way into the Festival Hall to buy some tickets. We sensed, and warmed to, their happiness (Monica was pregnant). I recall the radiance of the sunlight on the doors and the Portland stone. They seemed too good, and too happy, not to know. We did not see them regularly until we came back from our long travels and bought the Wick. Jim was by then an established TV director. I had had several plays on ITV, had written the script of *Nothing but the Best*, which would soon be in production. I was successful enough not to feel unsuccessful. Since petrol was cheap, they came not infrequently to the Wick at the weekend. Lucy (then called Louli) was nice enough, but little John-John never failed to make Sarah cry; impervious to pain, he was happy to cause it. His parents took no notice. Because they lived in a mansion flat, off the Finchley Road, we visited them only for dinner, without our children. The company was often somewhat smart: David Mercer, the Bakewells, the Midgleys, Austen Kark and Nina Bawden. Jim went through the motions of being affectionate (escorting us down many flights of stairs to our car), but he had no capacity for warmth. Beetle has not forgotten his awkwardness when, by chance, they came to share a taxi. Presuming a pass obligatory, Jim managed neither virile boldness nor gallant discretion.

In the early 1970s, it did not occur to me to wonder whether his career was prospering. We took the Fermans to be much like ourselves, interested in the arts, alert to social issues, concerned for their children. Monica was an eager gossip. When we made our sorties abroad, she was the one who typed long and amusing letters. Jim was always busy in the cutting room, often till the early

hours. I suspected (wrongly, no doubt) that his nocturnal per-
fectionism might be a cover for amorous occasions. He certainly
made his work his home; Monica her home her work: she was a
devoted mother and a generous hostess. Her roast lamb was worth
driving to London for. She had a part-time job at the Festival Hall,
during which her old nanny came to care for the children. We
never tried to account for John-John's frantic aggressiveness.

Jim's meticulousness gained him a reputation for going over
budget. I had to persuade Stella Richman to have him direct *The
Trouble with England*. We were in Provence during the shooting.
Some time later, I met Ian Bannen in the street, outside the London
University Senate House, and congratulated him on his perform-
ance as Mike in my play. He looked puzzled. When I mentioned
The Trouble with England, Bannen said: 'Jim Ferman wrote that.' (Yet
Jim had proposed, quite seriously, that I play the part of Mike.)

When Harry Gordon, who was living in Hamilton Terrace,
heard the story, he said that I had either to face Jim with it or to
accept that our friendship would collapse. Harry, whose honesty
also took the form of telling me any bad things which mutual
friends had said about me, reported that Jim had accused me of
having 'sold out'. Harry was amazed by Monica's obsessive concern
with Strontium-90 and the imminence of global catastrophe.

By the mid-Seventies, Jim was more or less unemployed owing
to the righteous extravagance of his productions. He was convinced he spent more money than his colleagues only because
he was a perfectionist in an imperfect world. He had bungled my
attempt to introduce him to the movies by insisting to Jo Janni that
there was only one film he was prepared to make, David Storey's
Flight into Camden, a novel of such resolute gloom that even
Stanley Kubrick would have had difficulty promoting it. The truth
was that Jim had neither the flair nor the charisma to be anything
but a TV journeyman. By 1975, even that modest furrow was no
longer available. His last hope was that I would, or could, procure
The Glittering Prizes for him.

I had scarcely seen him since January 1971, when the Fermans
came to visit us at the Wick and I broke my little finger keeping
goal in the Digings' garden. Jim was kind, Monica resourceful
with the witch-hazel (no apt specific for a dangling finger). After
Jim had driven me to Colchester Hospital, Beetle – in a state of
shock – finally flew out, verbally, at John-John, who had once
again distressed Sarah, by breaking one of her toys. Monica may
have phoned a day or two later to see how I was, but Jim called

only when his version of *Mayerling* was about to be screened. It was his last show. He told Beetle that the writer had failed to deliver the goods and he had had to rewrite the whole thing.

Soon after we began shooting *The Glittering Prizes*, he became the Film Censor (did he ever know of my remark that he would find it difficult to go over budget *watching* films?). He and I must have spoken at some point, because I recall him saying that he had wanted to ask my advice about taking the job. I am sure that I should have advised him to take *any* job. No reference has ever been made to the money which I sent him when he was down on his luck and which he promised, *reproachfully*, to repay as soon as his temporary difficulties were resolved. His only just not offended letter represents the only time he actually put pen to paper in answer to all the occasions on which I wrote to them.

When I lost my cool, though not my temper, a few weeks ago, it was nothing more than emptying an emotional trash can in which there was never anything worth keeping. He never liked me and there was never enough of him for me to like. He was very clean and he never raised his voice, which gave him the lineaments of a tolerant and balanced man. The manic behaviour of his son, his own pedantry (oh the slowness of his cogitations!), the steady denigration of all those whom he envied, especially writers, all his repressed resentments never added up to anything recognisable at the time.

By chance, we heard him, *qua* censor, on the radio at the weekend. No one, unless he was Professor Higgins, would now guess him to be American. He has the tones of a man who has learnt English from the best recordings. He speaks with dignity and without the smallest personality. His well-turned sentences are calculatedly disarming: failing to be anything but reasonable, he is the very best next thing to a nobody. He works long hours at a job which yields neither revenue nor applause. The task of balancing the shamelessness of movie-makers against conventional morality may be thankless, perhaps demanding; but it is a high-wire act performed no more than a couple of inches from the ground.

18.12.80. I watched the little Cambridge film last night. I looked as though I lived in a cupboard with old clothes, my face an unmade bed. My mouth was loose and yet inflexible. I seemed bowed down by a sense less of guilt than of humiliation; yet I was not humble, petulant rather. I had no complaint about my voice; I speak well enough, but I look somehow *diffused*. While glad that

I do not have much need to look at myself, I can see that I could direct myself, as it were, into presenting a more agreeable figure. I could cultivate a quiet courtesy which would make me appear tender and humane. No wonder politicians and public figures can be schooled to look like convincing examples of sincerity. The little film was evocative, straightforward and rather modest.

Because Conti was in it, we went to see *They're Playing Our Song*. Tom was cute and Lucy Arnaz was ballsy and every line might have been made with a ruler. There were some good jokes, more than there were laughs. Neil Simon is in the business of converting truth into falseness. An orthodontic Midas, he is forever turning gold into fillings. He is so apprehensive of reality that he cannot rest until he has given it the ring of falsehood. He resembles a Bricusse with talent or a Woody Allen without it. Beetle said that she knew the show was not going to be for us merely by looking at the faces in the foyer. The tunes were weak but you remember them because they were repeated as often as an SOS. The only moving part of the show was the scenery; there was even a motor-car on the set.

Tom has bought himself a Rolls. He keeps a chauffeur's cap under the dash in case the revolution comes and he has to pass for his own chauffeur, an easy imposture. He once avoided a speeding ticket by playing the part of a man in such urgent need of a pee that the cop let him go.

I did *Desert Island Discs* with Roy Plomley. I heard Jonathan Miller describe it as 'the OM of anthology programmes' (*With Great Pleasure* was no more than the CH, he said). Steiner still thinks that Jonathan will end up with the genuine OM. I suppose that a society which gives a man a knighthood for garbling his words on TV[31] may well go all the way to honour a medico who panders to its conceits without requiring it to do anything more than say 'Ah'.

On Christmas Eve, I hared to Cambridge in the little Merc to do some more present-buying. I rewarded myself with the latest volumes of Wittgenstein's notebooks, published thirty years after his death. Evelyn Waugh said of himself that if he had not been a Catholic, he would scarcely have been human. If it were not for

---

31 I do not recall to which celebrity this sneer referred but it was not to Jonathan, who was not knighted for a decade or three after this entry.

W., I should certainly be less humane. What philosopher has ever argued more strongly against self-righteousness while being convinced that he was never wrong? I never saw the man, but I cannot pass Whewell's Court without thinking of him. Heffer's had a copy of *Oxbridge Blues* on a wire stand, the only fiction so dignified. I felt like a successful author for a moment.

On the way home, the road was dry and empty. I must have been doing around 120 mph when I saw a cop ahead. He signalled me into a lay-by for a chat. I made no pretence of innocence, but confessed that I was 'dreaming'. He looked like an ex-NCO in the military police, so I said it in my best Cambridge accent, the only rank I could pull. I had the Contiesque inspiration to say that I was in a hurry because my mother was coming from London for Christmas and I knew that if she spent long with my wife, the two of them alone in the house, the whole family would have a gritty few days. There was a tiny movement of the little microphone which was bracketed across his upper lip like a stiff moustache. The day had been saved. He never suspected that I might have been drinking, perhaps because of the speed with which I slowed down when I spotted him. We parted with mutual assurances of seasonal goodwill. In fact, Beetle was, as I knew she would be, very tactful with Irene: she even filled a stocking for her as well as for the children on Christmas morning.

1981

6.1.81. My grandmother's housekeeper, Winifred Stanley, was the Françoise of the Raphaels. The white-winged domestic of the Lord, she subscribed to *The Watchtower*, which she kept on the kitchen table in Dorset House, as if, in a Jewish household, its rigorous Christianity was appropriate only to the servants' quarters. She never chided the family for its lack of religious punctuality, but she did observe the High Days and Holydays for us by sending out New Year cards, in early October, lest we forget.

We could not maintain the Wick if it were not for the Smiths. Jack's 'Certainly' promises that he is willing to do whatever he is asked; but he is moody and has little finesse. He has been handsome and is still very strong. His father could lift a heifer off the ground, like Milo of Croton. Isabel is from County Durham, untiringly kind to the children if we are out. Jack would, I am sure, die to defend us and our property. He would also watch us being carted off to a concentration camp by his policeman son; neither he nor Isabel having any knowledge of why, both would presume that there had to be a good reason.

The IBA hearings were so mortifying that, even if we had been awarded the franchise, I should still regard the interview as a laugh-free farce. I felt rather ill, having had no more than a glass of water at lunch at Langan's, where I could scarcely bear to look at Patrick Garland, who wanted a play from me for Chichester next year, not because he was repulsive (his pinkish-yellow fleshiness reminded me, agreeably, of Guy Ramsey) but because he was eating fish in a rich sauce. In the intervals between my going to be sick, we got on quite well.

The EEtv people had laid on limousines to take us to what turned out to be our own funeral at the IBA holy of holies in Knightsbridge. The building had the cramped pretentiousness of a company that is all front office and no product. A clutch of ladies in hats and shapeless coats filled the lobby. It occurred to me that if they constituted a rival group, there was no hope for us. In fact, they came from some suburban Women's Institute whose idea of uplift was to inspect the premises of the inspectors of cultural degradation. With patronising graciousness, Lady Plowden, in an autumnal silk dress and half-glasses, came to welcome us in the wings before flitting back to her throne. Filing in, like candidates for a chorus line, we were arranged, or arraigned, in a decided batting order. The IBA was already installed at a long table opposite us, their names in front of them. The nervousness on both sides was that of elderly people in a public baths, afraid that their robes would fall open and reveal nothing much worth seeing. The presence on the Board of an ex-headmaster of Charterhouse, a cleric and an Oxford philosophical lady (Mary Warnock) gave the occasion an air of polite nightmare. We were reminded that the proceedings were 'confidential'. The only good reason for secrecy was the fear that it might become generally known that nothing interesting or intelligent was going to be said. The behaviour of Mr Pursell, the vice-chairman of the IBA, was particularly sharp, more like that of prosecuting counsel than of an impartial monitor. In my innocence, I assumed he was doing his duty rather than making sure that one of his nests remained feathered.[32] The most dismal aspect of the thing was the dread which the Board manifested (and our side too hastily allayed) that our programmes would be too 'up-market'. The spectacle of a collection of clever people seeking assurances that we would not let the British public down by screening anything that demanded intelligence, or might foster it, was enough to make one book an early flight to a world elsewhere.

After we had received the bad news, we all had lunch in a Pakistani restaurant around the corner from Rutland Street. It was the Monday after Christmas. London was as it had been before ITV was thought of; one could park where one pleased. I bought a silk dressing-gown in Sloane Street and bags of books at Truslove and Hanson. The changes in the franchise decided upon by the

---

32 Pursell was a director of Guinness. The Guinness pension fund had some 200,000 shares in Anglia Television. If our syndicate had been given the franchise, the shares would have been, if not worthless, greatly reduced in value. Since Pursell had no direct control over the Guinness pension fund, it was later claimed that he could not be held to have had an undisclosed conflict of interest. It was, however, true that, at the time, the main Board of Guinness had complete discretion over the use to which the pension fund could be put (including collateral for Guinness itself). Hence any fall in its value would be disadvantageous to Guinness's fortunes.

IBA did not leave the impression that we had been singled out for rejection; no other candidate, whether more refined or more glamorous, had fared better. The Board was there to discourage anyone from making waves. Fat, ugly Gordon Claridge, whom I shall rejoice never to see again, dissociated himself from any future plans. He was eager to draw a line under EEtv, which he had joined in the hope of cash and from which he now meant to extricate himself, and his investment, with whatever could be salvaged from a suit against the IBA on account of Pursell's alleged duplicity.[33]

There is something awe-inspiring about a man interested in only one thing. It hardly matters whether it is mathematics, sex, bridge or money. How superb to be sure that nothing matters except what matters to oneself! The monomaniac has the singularity of a natural object; the dandelion that never dreams of being a rose. It was typical of a man with a legendarily beautiful mother that John-Julius was so disgusted by old Claridge's ugliness. It was almost touching to see a man's greed undiminished by age or satiety. Claridge has the complacency of a Jonsonian humour; he has done well and wants only to do better. In line with the abstract habits of modern management, he has no interest in any investment for its own sake. Trees that can be shaken are worthy of his husbandry; if fruitless, they merit the fate of the cherry orchard. He has no sentiment. His rumpled clothes and jaundiced, baggy skin are the travel-worn portmanteau in which he totes his avarice. He lives alone, an abacus which lacks even a playful click as it does its accountancy. His embarrassingly prolonged last words to the IBA were as vacuous as those of Martial's lawyer. He damaged our cause more than anything except Peter Hall's half-heartedness. It is unlikely that I should have long endured the corporate taste of the others, even if we had been allocated the end of the rainbow; but it might have been amusing to see how much gold is really there.

On TV last night, Bernard-Henry Lévy criticised the fascist strain in French political thought. He dared the others to ask him what

---

33 Forbes Taylor, who had been a regular soldier, was not disposed to accept a dubious decision. He was one of a party of Scottish nationalists who, in 1952, removed the Stone of Scone from under the throne in Westminster. His indignation with regard to Pursell was aggressive enough to come to the notice of Willie Whitelaw, then Home Secretary. Forbes received a personal phone call from Whitelaw advising him that it would not be in his future interest publicly to question a verdict which was not going to be changed.

right he had to do so. They implied that he placed undue emphasis on anti-Semitism, but they were too *rusé* to fall into the trap which his dandified insolence had laid. He is the Jew in its most provocative guise: handsome, articulate, clever, and *richissime*. He has the 'need' (Jim Ferman attributed it to me) to dominate all social gatherings. Honouring neither party nor ideology, he has the public-spiritedness of the gregarious solipsist. He advocates the Rights of Man, since they demand the openness to talent of all the careers. Confident that equality will confirm his superiority, he is an unbuttoned fellow whose mirror supplies all the compliments he needs. He does not wait to hear what anyone else has to say because he has so much to say himself and says it so much better. He calls for no revolution because, however much he despises the old guard, he would not be deprived of the system whereby they can be goaded into giving him their attention. His good news is, above all, that of his own epiphany.

26.1.81. Shirley and her friends have finally taken to the lifeboat, though they have yet to lower it. They seem still to hope that their divorce from the Labour Party will not be made absolute. They nurse the residual hope of the conceited that no party can be complete without them; hence that Foot cannot really give them the boot. The sound of Trades Unionists bleating for blood does not obscure the fact that clever people are taking a principled and painful step. If the quartet are in truth as negligible as speakers at the special conference declared, how come they formed part of the cream from which the last Labour government was clotted? How can the Party be undamaged by a departure so delayed as to seem like inverted *arrivisme*? Labour's own selection procedures must be defective if such defections are unimportant. The problem remains of how the putative chiefs can recruit enough Indians to merit their plumes. More people are likely to wish them well than will join them on the war-path.

Granted that a number of CSD candidates could be returned at a general election, any new party based on reason and moderation risks desertions when it hits a bad patch. The quartet may attract temporary, disillusioned support, but where will they find loyal, come-what-may adherents? A party of rational principle does credit to its sponsors; but what lure does it offer to unreasonable men and women? Without some appeal to prejudice or resentment (the unplaned planks on which both Tories and Socialists rely), no brave new faction can hope to survive. No one will denounce a party standing for decency and fair play; but where are its thick-and-thinners to be found?

Third parties tend to come a bad third. What then is to be done? Jenkins and co. are unlikely to make the kind of impatient error which took Mosley into the cul-de-sac of fascism. They have small appeal for public schoolboys who have failed their A-levels or for street corner paranoiacs with William Joyce's gift of the gab. What drove Mosley to extremism was messianic virility. He was at least somewhat feared; Shirley and her friends are more likely to be mocked.

Mosley's example shows how easy it is to be right in one's criticism of conventional politics and how wrong in tactics. In order to maintain a head of steam, Mosley had recourse to a loutish constituency which dismayed respectable people (Harold Nicolson an egregious example) who might otherwise have stayed with him. Mosley's Keynesian programme, never clearly formulated, now earns him applause for foresight at a time when Keynes' own reputation as a medicine man is in decline. Robert Skidelsky's suggestion that Mosley was driven to militancy by the machinations of the Communists ignores the significance of Mosley's own declaration that he was a fascist, a deliberate call to arms which recruited both allies and enemies. What malign quirk impels Skidelsky to make a martyr out of a posturing mountebank? Professorial perversity, the wish to display paradoxical boldness, may furnish the answer, unless it is determination to be exempt from any accusation of being 'prejudiced'. The lure of Mosley was that he made obeisance to his virile totem an alternative to serious thought. He played the routine right-wing trick of giving the strong the impression that the weak were about to deprive them of their birthright, which could be redeemed only by the greater subjection of the already dispossessed. Skidelsky affects to be dispassionate with regard to 'the Jews'. He recalls the judge in the Deep South who declared, when seeking election, that on the colour issue he would seek to 'tread the narrow line between partiality on the one hand and impartiality on the other'.

Skidelsky seems seriously to believe that 'the Jews' were in a state of war with Hitler first and then with Mosley. There is no shortage of those who accuse Jews of being cowards because they did not defend themselves; Skidelsky is at least original in making them guilty because they did. 'The Jews' neither had nor defended their group interests during the 1920s and 1930s. The hard-faced men who did well out of the war, in Germany and in Britain, had no common Semitic features, although there were Jews among them. The fate of Walter Rathenau, the classic *bouc-émissaire*, a good man by general standards, showed very early how symbolic was the role of 'The Jew' in the demonology of the *entre-deux-guerres*. Eliot's now regretted line, 'The jew is underneath the lot', shows only what a cheapskate, in-crowd-pleasing metic Tom was, the impotent smiler with the pen-knife. His line is no more evidence of Jewish iniquity than were the Protocols of the Elders of Zion, to which Skidelsky adverts without mentioning that they were forgeries.

Can any bold new leader, with a lisp, rally troops to his standard by saying that, while he may eventually raise it, he remains more or less loyal to the cause from which he may soon divorce himself? There is something decorous in the hesitations of the worthy, but they do little to encourage others to expose themselves above the parapet. In search of a slogan, the CSD has saddled itself with a parlour-pink sampler on which the words 'Perhaps' and 'Soon' are picked out in pale threads. If Labour were now in power, and the manoeuvres of the dissidents were actually endangering the government's majority, there might be a prospect of significant change; but if that were the case, which of the quartet would risk his seat in order to challenge the Left?

Suppose that Marx is right and that the efflorescence at the top is the reflection of movement at the base, what omens can be read? The most plausible is that we are witnessing the amputation of manual workers from the political process. The Unions are increasing their hold on the Labour Party, but the price will be that the party itself loses its standing on the parliamentary front. The Foot-men and the Bennites will, for a while, appear to have taken the tiller, but they will find themselves without a ship of the line from which to fire a broadside. They will all be in the same boat and it will be a very small one. The detachment of the proletariat from the Fabians implies the end of a common cause binding workers and intellectuals.

The collapse of manufacturing industry inclines the meritocracy to seek advancement in businesses without a large workforce. They will therefore tend to the Tories. The traditional working class will feel bewildered and betrayed. They will lose faith in the intelligentsia, including any who remain in the Party. Waverers, such as Shirley, may be motivated by fear of some 'totalitarian' takeover, but their vacillations can also be read as apprehension at the emergence of an uncontrollable, non-Fabian, working-class party, especially since economic theory seems responsible for the number of unemployed. The working class does not have theories; it has interests.

Emphasis on principle is noble, but ill-advised: the CSD needs to offer a practical programme for economic sanity and development. Its problem is not merely the unemployed but also the unemployable. The hard cases are less intractable than the thick heads. Shirley's educational system has done its comprehensive best for the unteachable, but the social consequences of an unrepressed urban proletariat, which is cowed neither by the cane nor by the sermon, are vandalism and the menace of nihilistic violence. The National Front has yet to trade on this situation, but who can promise that it will not? The emigration of the Labour Party's Fabian elite may prompt applause, but the rankest of the rank and file are likely to lapse into reactionary rage. The working class is not socialist because it has placed its hopes, until now, in socialism. The disintegration of the Labour Party will reveal some pernicious termites in the foundations. If the least favoured *couches sociales* lose contact with the civilised voices who, whether out of conscientious ambition or worthy opportunism, have for so long spoken up for them, if their sense of abandonment is accompanied by a realisation that the present unemployment is not cyclical but a permanent condition of life, the solidarity of racism and reactionary militancy may prove irresistible. There will always be some politicians who will share, or claim to share, the frustrations of the rabble, but they will not become dangerous until they have nothing to lose.

The success of the CSD and their allies could provoke a recklessness which has not been seen since the eviction (or elopement) of Oswald Mosley in the 1930s. Enoch Powell's failure, whether from scruple or squeamishness, to mobilise those who applauded his excesses, but could not support a prig in a Homburg hat, is no guarantee that no demagogue will ever rouse the disappointed, especially if he figures famously in the media. Even if denied such access, a sufficiently clever and shameless man might command the streets. Once in power, he could jettison any residual propriety. It is odd that no punk politics have yet to erupt. It remains possible that there will be an upsurge of those who, suffering from the contraction of British complacency, are still infected with the latent jingoism of a race which once assumed its moral right to rule the world.

Old political vanities die first at the top; they can remain, green and fruitless, springing from below ground level, like suckers, all thorns and no roses. The elite which believes in (because it presides over) reason is likely to underestimate the bleak rage of those who, further down, have been trimmed of their antique faith, but have no compensating confidence in their intelligence. The recourse of the Polish workers to the religious pole, their renovation of Catholicism, is not open to the British working class for whom the Church of England sets no moral example and offers no social refuge or leadership. The British are, it appears, committed irrevocably to a secular society. Happy as this may seem to a positivist temper, the despair of the proles will more probably issue in destructive vandalism than in sensible retrenchment.

28.1.81. The not improbable scenario is that the first violence will take place in black quarters. The failure of many of the black unemployed even to register for benefit is some measure of the detachment of blacks from society. The figures signify the rise of a separate and rejected mentality among the marooned immigrants: they are powerless to rise and have nowhere to go in a society which has renounced any kind of formal culture. A demanding educational scheme at least offered steep, reliable ladders to higher places. Its well-intentioned levelling may lead to a Gadarene frenzy, a nihilistic explosion without hope or objective. If blood is shed, and it almost certainly would be, the trauma will become incurable. An unapologetic party of (white) 'self-defence' could easily arise.

Lévi-Strauss remarks on the relative paucity (hence the repetitiveness) of the symbols of any given society. Men play again and again with the same counters, especially at a 'pre-scientific' level, when observation is partial and undisciplined (a feature of unfavoured classes). In cases of social unrest, reconciliation requires the mediation of some kind of magic formula. The inadequacy of the vernacular (in modern terms, the triumph of the cliché) renders public debate ineffective. The bewildered are forced back to atavistic loyalties, however ridiculous or alarming. The present Tory government resembles a shaman whose spells are failing to achieve advertised results. The sin, it then has to be said, lies with the people. The wisdom of the wise, we are told, is threatened by the malice of the foolish; the powerful are being lamed by the powerless. The Tories are resolved not to regard unemployment as a 'real' problem; the real problem, they insist, is inflation. They have recourse to laying especial emphasis on the gravity of the one thing which they may eventually be able to remedy. Inflation is immoral; it must be chastened and put in chains. The truth, however veiled, even from their own eyes, is that the Tories believe that the working class deserves to be punished. They are glad to see it demoralised and demeaned. Unwilling to admit their sadism, even to themselves, they convince themselves of their Hippocratic mandate.

If there were any evidence that Mrs Thatcher had a dispassionate scientific view of the way the world works, her tactics might seem timely. In truth, as with many 'strong' leaders, there is sentimentality at the heart of her heartlessness. She believes in the responsible mission of the bourgeoisie and she imagines that the greed of the entrepreneur can supply the best, if not the only, means of creating prosperity. She craves the dependence of the lump on the ingenious ruthlessness of the boss. She wishes the workers to be subservient to a single source of income, not to the state but to honest capitalism. The paradox is that, in seeking to repel Marxism, she is creating, to the best of her nostalgic ability, the circumstances in which the Marxist model will have its best chance of resurrection. By polarising workers and management, through eliminating governmental mediation, she is succeeding, intentionally or not, in sharpening the class antagonisms of an obsolete manufacturing society.

For decades it has been demonstrably untrue that capitalism leads inevitably to the impoverishment of the workers. Marx has been empirically refuted by the growing prosperity of the lower classes; but when a government congratulates itself on the acceptance, by an intimidated workforce, of wage increases below the level of inflation, it is applauding a trend which will lead the disillusioned masses into violent conflict with the bourgeoisie to which, for a while, they seemed eager to attach themselves. The absence of immediate signs of discontent persuades the government that its measures are effective, perhaps welcome. For those incapable of self-criticism, incompetence smacks of impartiality. Not knowing quite why it is doing something persuades the government that it must be acting out of principle. Since no one is happy, it seems certain that they are not doing anyone any favours.

The Tories' cleverest young man declares that, in the medium and long term, reflation would prove disastrous. Being far-sighted glorifies his closing his eyes to the dimensions of the disaster actually in train. He knows, surely, that the government is betting on the cyclic revival of world trade. The hand on the tiller is steering no purposeful course; only the usual change of the prevailing winds is going to put the country back in the race. Meanwhile the skipper talks as if her tactics are likely to procure a change in the weather or at least to put her in the best position to profit from it, if it ever comes. This is a version of Lévi-Straussian primitivism: the impotence of the powerful prompts a myth in which doing nothing is a form of purposeful command. Drift is passed off as a rarefied form of steering. Magic replaces causation, mantras trump reason.

The rejection of Keynes seems like a scientific reappraisal, but it is, in practice, more like a retreat from at least partially effective management to superstitious fantasy. Thatcher's realism is a modern name for shamanism. Inflexibility is not a feature of strength but of intellectual feebleness. Belief in cosmic solutions and disdain for pragmatic patchwork is the mark of the ideologue, not of the enterprising. Capitalism can be justified only on the strength of its achievement in creating wealth. When it is defended on *moral* grounds, its advocates are always shysters. Wanting to make economics a matter of morals, Mrs Thatcher affects to be not cleverer but *better* than Keynes. Such a notion introduces ethics into mathematics and rhetoric into logic.

Our neighbour Christiane, once so pretty, has become a painful sight. Ever since she borrowed money from me four years ago she has had a bad conscience. Now she proposes to pay us back in dozens of eggs, the only currency on which she can lay her hands. Norbert does not know of the loan, which was supposed to be for a couple of weeks. Norbert's mother has always been unkind to Christiane. When Martine (the Barats' second daughter) was born, the *mémé* refused to look at her because she was not a boy. '*Fausse couche!*' she said. 'What good is that to me?' She accuses everyone of stealing from her. On the eve of Marie-José's wedding, she forgot that she had bought her a present and said that Christiane had taken money from her room. She resents everything that goes out of the house, even a pot of goose fat given to Martine. Now seventy-six, she has been a scold ever since her daughter-in-law arrived. Christiane takes her coffee in bed and cares for her when she is sick, but the old woman regards her with nothing but suspicion. Norbert lacks the nerve to oppose his mother; he applies himself only to the land. He and C. have no time to themselves. The *mémé* never leaves them alone. If Martine had been a boy, all might have been different, perhaps.

The most regularly genial man in St Laurent is Robert Jouves, the *menuisier*, a resourceful (and expensive) craftsman. He too has his parents-in-law living in the house, but he repairs to his adjacent *atelier* where he works in cheerful solitude. He has the perkiness of an undieting jockey, cap tilted slightly back, face cocked to the sun. His happy expertise allows him to be untroubled and uncriticised. His wife – a large, brassy woman with overdone hair – is ambitious for her children, who are the same ages and sex as our own. Bernard is in Bordeaux, studying medicine and finding the work very hard. The girl, Christine, is shy, pale and pretty. Having got her *Bac*, she is at university in Périgueux. Jean-François is a spoiled boy in Stee's class at the *collège* in Belvès. He used to infuriate (and amuse) us by cheating at football in the scratch Saturday games in the village. He came up and worked very hard at the tape which they made on Sunday, a version of *Maigret et les gangsters*, part of a *projet* for their French teacher. Stee is increasingly aware of how thick the peasant children are. We may well have to move to a more stimulating environment.

21.1.81 Anthony Blunt, it is said, never liked the idea of going to the Soviet Union, evidence that he cared little for its actual state. The disdainful man does not expect to be happily at home anywhere. The traitor is more richly and deliciously occupied in subversion than in anything constructive. Like the secret policemen whom he serves, he is more concerned with punishment than with ideals. He despises the follies of those whom he betrays more than he believes in the merit of those to whom he delivers them. He cannot bring himself to leave his duplicitous occupation, not because he is dedicated to an ideal but because he is addicted to the secret joys of two-facedness. A sensualist finds satisfaction in adultery; the idealist in treason. Deception may be painful, but the pain is exquisite; it spices the dull days which are a part of every straight life. Serving two masters helps us to salt and pepper. How do I know? I write screenplays.

On my way to LA, via Toulouse, I had three hours between flights. I walked round and round Roissy to bank some exercise against the sedentary time to come. Milstein was checking in, with Carol, whom I have not seen since she cooked a single duck for us and them and the boring Harlechs. I clapped Milstein on the back, one-handedly. He turned with a show of instant cordiality. 'Hul-*lo*!' It was a salesman's response, unsuspicious and unflattering. He looked lankly grey, his complexion fumed by some sunless agency. If only because he is unamusing, he passes for a serious person. They were going to Paris for a typical reason: someone had lent them a flat. Dick would go to the ends of the earth for a rent-free holiday in Ultima Thule, no matter what the natives were like. Carol has thickened and wore a thread-thin scar around her right eye. She has an air of wistful defiance, as if pleading for the right to do something that she knows that you know she has done already. They toted between them, like unadmitted luggage, the invisible baby of their unhappiness. It makes them at once pathetic and displeasing. They displayed the politeness of those without spontaneity. It occurred to me that I had intruded on their rare privacy (he is always at the office, she at the typewriter). However, they came eagerly to have a free cup of coffee. Carol is weary of advising women of how to be good wives, good mothers and good to themselves. She despairs of concocting new recipes for having your cake and cutting everyone a slice. They had been invited to go to Bali at Christmas, five days to go there and back. It had been rather far, but the experience was wonderful. The memory of what they had not had to pay for was better than any Dramamine and more enlivening than any aphrodisiac. They were enveloped in complacent melancholy. The shallowness of Milstein's intellect and the urgency of his opportunism have procured him a glamorous life without joy or depth. He has much to be proud of and little to be pleased with.

As for Carol, having now got everything she ever asked for, she seems to have concluded that she must have asked for the wrong things. I felt a sort of vindictive tenderness towards her, as for a public figure who has some petty, incurable blemish. We saw Christopher Chataway once, small and furrily furious, only just under control, a minor minister late for some unofficial appointment, officious with diminished importance. I recalled how he had once tripped and fallen on a bend, when well-placed in some important race. What Carol has done, the private thing in the public eye, cannot be mentioned but accounts for that sly smile. She has manifestly done her own thing. She takes the kind of modest pride in her first adultery that another woman might in her first baby. If she once feared that she had the uncreased banality of a child-bride, she has now joined the unblushing grown-ups. She is as aware of Milstein's deviousness, his insincere usage of sincerity, as she is of her own. (Yes, she had noticed, she once told me, how feminine Milstein sometimes was.) She has ambition without character, a dangerous condition: those who are not full of themselves require frequent topping up. They feed on dramas and become addicted, and seemingly devoted, to energising company. I liked her better not because she is any nicer but because she is more interesting. She has turned into someone for a novelist to betray: there is not necessarily more to be said for her but there is certainly more to be said about her.

The Mardigians have a crossbred spaniel/poodle called Zeus. Its brother Apollo died. They live a modest life in an immodest town. Although often apart, when working, they seem to rely on each other's company. Each with children from earlier marriages, they have had none together. Ron spends all his time reading crap scripts. He often tells me of their deplorable effect on his literary diet. By choosing to represent writers, he is limited, intentionally or not, to the lower end of the pecking order. Without any talent for falseness, he settles for efficiency and sincerity. Loyalty is a painless habit with him. Discontent is no part of his winterless life. Merle admires his thighs. His son, Brad, who is sixteen, lives with them, a handsome, not tall, dark young man who drives a VW Scirocco that wheezes dryly before it fires. While I was staying with them, he was picked up by the cops outside his school and roughly handled. He had no ID, so they handcuffed him and searched him, not believing his story that he was on his way to his car. It might have got heavier, but the school janitor vouched for him. He reacted, at the time, with tears and an unstoppable flow of words, but shrugged the incident off when I asked him about it. The young, it seems, no longer draw revolutionary conclusions. The same day that the cops picked him up, another sixteen-year-old was shot by a gang of teenagers. So many people are done to death in LA that murder is now for Angelenos what the plague was in the fourteenth century. The population is divided between the lucky and the unlucky.

Bel Air is no safer, so the statistics promise, than Watts. Stanley Donen nevertheless resists Yvette's wish to be taken to some of the exciting black discos to be found there. The blacks, alone of all the ingredients in the unmolten melting pot, seem incapable of making it. Their anger cannot be assuaged nor, it seems, sublimated. In Beverly Hills, there are rarely any blacks at social gatherings unless they are the diplomatic representatives of financial interests in the separate world of black music and film. Even Sidney Poitier, the nicest and most able of black successes, has fallen back on the cushions of a black 'artistic community' which lacks the militant menace of the Sixties and Seventies and has settled (yes, yes, understandably) for honouring the tastes of an uneducated, socially apathetic black audience. Its resentments have been sublimated downwards into crime. It is more rewarding for blacks to be on relief than to take the lowest paid jobs, which are the only ones available to them. Men regularly desert their families (i.e. the females they have impregnated) and take to the structured world of street gangs. Rape is a vengeful form of hunting. One of the main hunting grounds is the car park at LA airport. Women come back to their cars after having been observed to say farewell to their men and are grabbed by the ankles from under the car and then assaulted. I remarked that it required some agility to rape a woman under a modern motor car, but the intention seems mainly to be to terrorise. Vengeance has replaced hope.

John Fowles. What he would have us take for his tragic sense of life is a function of unsmiling determination never to let his brown teeth be seen in public. Unable to be brief, he will never be witty. The paragraph is the smallest denomination in his literary currency. The pockets of his prose bulge with cumbrous tetradrachs. Like some extra-terrestrial creature who has made a forced landing, he has Henry James's ponderousness without the Jamesian *sérieux*. When he talks of the pleasures of narrative as an almost abstract discipline, there is condescension in his modesty. A joiner, not an artist, he is always seeking to impress with the skill of his carpentry. The factitious teakiness of his final product is calculated to conceal from the reader, until he happens to weigh it, its balsa provenance. His novels are like the meals of two-star chefs, delicious until consumed (the last courses not without some dutiful effort). Only when the fattened diner leans back does he realise that he has consented, expensively, to take part in the production of what will soon amount to nothing but shit. The thing does not keep. All is vanity. The *patissier*'s refinement declares itself in the lightness of what looks to be solid and durable.

Maschler's magnification of Fowles' fame has suited them both: no artist has been misrepresented, no rare talent debased. Tom can be, and is, accused of having commercialised refinement for his vulgar purposes, but neither the fame nor the money is displeasing to his ungrateful author. Fowles lacks the honour to take open pleasure in his own imposture. He is the counterfeit who rings true and against which, like a deceptive tuning fork, all gold is tinny. Tom is the merchant of bluff; it gives him more satisfaction to sell a fake than the genuine article. He has the terrible, because insatiable, gift of the prospector: he can sniff gold even if he does not appreciate its refined uses. My lack of sales has disappointed him only because I have failed to do him proud. He has been vexed by my reluctance (in truth, my inability) to involve him lucratively in the movies. It is not enough for him to have been a remarkable publisher. Conscientious and conscienceless, he is drawn to books which he may not understand and does not always make profitable. Yet the cinema has always enchanted him (I wrote my first script at his instigation[34]); film attracts him as a brothel does a man who passes one every day on the way home to a happy marriage. While deploring my Hollywood involvement, Tom would love to have a hand in it. He boasted of his friendship with John Calley, but who boasts of such a friend cannot have many.

After Calley backed out (his favourite way of backing), Tom succeeded in promoting *The French Lieutenant's Woman* and now boasts of the false rumour of his having an affair with Meryl Streep (the result of his having borrowed her borrowed cottage for a weekend, when she was not using it; no surprise there). He tells me stories about the biz with the eagerness of a midshipman informing Nelson of the thrill of weighing anchor. La Streep's absence from the last weeks of shooting alerted him to the influence on morale of the star's daily twinkle. He was disillusioned to learn that the mechanicals were interested less in the beauty of Karel Reisz's work than in their prospects for another job. Tom received $50,000 for his packaging skills and treasures it as a man might a baby he has managed to father late in life. He bounces his cash on his knee and waits for it to take its first steps towards earning interest. He cherishes the hope of a large, if belated, family of fat cheques and he expects you – however many you may have had of your own – to be as exhilarated by his commonplace achievement as he is.

20.2.81. LAX. Dirk Bogarde was already in the first-class lounge with Tony F. and a young man for whose benefit Dirk was sharpening some of his old saws. His elegant consonants and unabrasive vowels cut through the dull air like a cheese-wire. He believed, he would have it known, in entertainment. He

---

34 Karel Reisz read it and passed the comment that it had 'the wrong values', rather a scrupulous response to a débutant's effort. Forty years later, I renovated the old script and turned it into the first episode (directed impeccably by John Madden) of the television mini-series *After the War*.

viewed with dismay the full-frontal vulgarity, in every sense, of the American taste. He has something of the datedness of colonials who, from their rugged outposts, deplored the decadence of the central government in whose name their writ was officially signed, but whose lack of spine contrasted lamentably with their own unbent standards. It was typical of Dirk that he should be slagging the show which he had just done, with Tony Harvey, into which no press-gang had forced him. Despite his fastidiousness, he is rarely unwilling to serve under any colours. He takes lamentable jobs because he is anxious about his income and he defends himself on the grounds that he must keep himself before the public. I did not go up to him or show any signs of recognition. He had, no doubt, aged (he must be in his very late fifties), but the voice, so well modulated, so serviceable and so cared for, was like a cosmetic which smoothed the wrinkles out of his persona. He worked his creamy malice into every crevice, a precious panacea. His face is indeed older; the veins map his discreet excesses with faint red graphs; the eyes poached and pouched in their white whites. Alert to flattery and to slights, he never loses the apprehensive vanity of the homosexual (or quasi-homosexual) of the era when gay actors had to court their public and cultivate a press whose treachery had always to be feared. Good opinions were solicited by the carefree style of men forever on their guard. In Dirk's case, the portcullis was always apt to descend; boiling oil always on the hob. The charm of his tone sheathed his readiness to respond to the unkind cuts of the careless or the spiteful. As an actor, one of his *points forts* lay in the depiction of a kind of hounded cunning which could transform itself into tart, but elegant, retaliation. He was forever on the run from being identified with Simon, in the Pinewood *Doctor* series, which won him the unsuspecting admiration of the shopgirls without whose fantasies no great career can prosper and from whose company he could never run quite quickly enough, for fear that he might lose it.

Penny told me, with a hint of intimate revelation, about the death of Bunny Garnett. He was eighty-nine. She did not live far away and spent a good deal of time with him in his cottage. She had had a *tête-à-tête* lunch with him only a week before the stroke which felled him. What she didn't tell me was part of what she did. There was pride in her discretion. Bunny was notorious for his susceptibility to ladies. He was always making offers to women. Saki told me, in Taos, of how, quite recently, Bunny asked a young

American woman to come and stay with him in the Lot. Saki advised her to go; it was a rare chance to do something she might never do again; but she didn't do it. I have no evidence that Penny, neither plain nor beautiful, had anything but an *amitié sentimentale* with the old man. If she rendered him some kind of sexual service for kindness's sake, well then she did. Perhaps she merely took her clothes off (Bunny was quite a nudist in his younger days). I cannot help contrasting Garnett's death in his rural over-ripeness, attended perhaps by a sympathetic young woman, with my father's in that grim hospital. The stock figure of 'dirty old man' sanctions the repression of the old for showing signs of vitality. Disgust with desire is the common reaction of middle-class women who have traded their bodies for security and wish no longer to honour the bargain. It is easy to imagine Penny, neither sexy nor indifferent, doing whatever would please the old man and not harm herself. Her lack of beauty means that she has no solemn sense of what she might be *worth*. She can proceed according to impulse and goodwill. Tenderness is an aspect of not thinking too carefully about how clean things may be or what anyone might think.

Imagine an expat woman, in a nice marriage to a nice man with two nice children (at the local school), who by chance gets to know an old man who lives alone. She has a multitude of friends, but they all see her only as the nice woman she undoubtedly is, and nothing else. By loving an old man, without anyone knowing, she escapes the fear of derision and of disappointment. If she doubts her beauty, he does not. To be seduced, however far that goes, is another act of kindness, not of vanity. She need not dread her inadequacy, as she might with a younger and more demanding lover. Her marriage is unthreatened. Her love of the old man has a purity, whatever she does or allows him to do, which leaves everything in her life as it was before, but with a secret ingredient which is her *petit bagage*. What she loves in her Bunny is the tranquillity which he inspires, the ease with which he broaches the dread topics, sex and death. She might well hope that she can be with him at the moment of his dying, that final flutter of his breath like a last gift to her. First Pan, then Silenus, Bunny, it may be, had the charm of not taking things too seriously; but if he was flighty, he was not facetious. He was not much of an artist, but is one of the durable oddities of Bloomsbury that they accepted the transience of art along with that of life? In the long run, it is not only we but everything that is dead. *Vivamus atque amemus* was moral enough. Roger Fry said that not even the greatest masterpiece was worth looking at more than about three times. The demoralisation of art, the emphasis on its decorative and life-enhancing qualities, was what made the 'immaturity' of Bloomsbury and its promiscuities so abhorrent to Leavis.

A man and a young woman found dead on the Isle of Skye have been identified as a 'suicide' and his mistress. The dead man had been dead before. Some ten years earlier, his clothes were discovered, like Sergeant Troy's, on a Dorset beach. He was presumed to have drowned. His wife and father-in-law (or father) have now identified him as the dead climber on the Scottish island. I know nothing more of the facts. We are left to wonder whether he always had a mistress and planned to make his life with her after faking suicide. By what means did he live after taking on a new identity? Had he discovered happiness with the second lady or – more interesting – had he become disillusioned and more enamoured of death than of the woman he had 'died' to be with? Was he tempted, surreptitiously, to take his 'love' with him to the destination which he had already scouted? He had 'died' the first time, it might be, because he could not face the pain and drama of a divorce and of the 'explanations' which would precede it. He may have felt a violent passion for the second woman, but he knows her to be both less fine and less 'worthwhile' than the 'widow' he left behind. He can be seen as a victim even when he set about to victimise others. After the 'suicide', he may have been tempted to check the warmth of his own obituaries. He wondered whether his wife really cared for him. He might even be touched by her grief and almost – ah, almost! – wanted to go home again. His desire for the new woman and his pleasure in the freedom he has given himself are tarnished by the loss of what he was sure he never wanted, until he lost it. The temptation to return grows into an obsession, the 'love' which he must hide from the second woman as he did her existence from his wife. He had imagined that he would leave the worst part of himself behind him, like his old clothes on the beach, but he now finds that what he brought with him is too skimpy to keep him warm. The Cavafy-like irony emerges of the futility of flight from oneself. Probably, the second death was a banal misfortune. Even so, the man's mock suicide had deceived the world, but he was incapable of the quite simple task of leading his love to safety (the bodies were found two miles from a refuge). Without premeditation, the couple 'found death', as the French say. The island of Skye is oddly apt: *Caelum non animum* etcetera.

Mary Moss died. She was sixty-three. When we knew her in London, in the mid-Fifties, she was plangently vivacious and a little too shameless (the low-cut dresses) for the prevailing climate. She was John's second wife; his friends had liked the first one. Mary was the very type, they thought, of the 'continental' seductress. In fact Polish, she met John when he was a colonel on the Control Commission in Germany. Their affair was sufficiently scandalous to lead to his recall. John told me how he had been roused from their compartment in a *wagon-lit* by an important knock. 'Are you Colonel Moss?' 'Yes, I am.' To prove it, he opened the door wearing only his regimental tie.

They returned to London. Mary was not only 'naughty' (a word she pronounced as if to prove that she was English), but also an excellent cook and hostess. She was a very good bridge player. My father and I partnered the Mosses for several seasons in competitions. We did especially well in those where a female was a necessary element in the team. Mary was our best player. John's flamboyance often threatened to throw away our patient games 'in the other room', but Mary carried him with ease and grace. Our big moment was when we won the Crockford's Cup. Thanks to the citizenship gained by marrying John, Mary became an English international. Her skills at the table supplemented their income. John had not lost the fortune he had inherited from his father, but it was barely enough to support the *rentier* life. He became a half-commission man for insurance and mortgage brokers.

After the economic situation in England became stringent, the Mosses went to live in the South of France. They found an apartment in Cannes and later bought a new bungalow in a development near Cagnes. They enjoyed themselves among those who shared the same rock pool in which they were happy to paddle. When Mary began to suffer lapses of memory, and no longer drew trumps with the same assurance, their fine-weather friends dropped them. She has, we now hear, been dying for eight years during which John, who had never worked in his life, devoted himself (not always patiently, he told me) to dressing and washing and caring for the naughty lady who became, by the slow end, an insensible and virtually speechless vegetable. John looked forward only to the moment when they woke up in the morning, when he would say 'Good morning, darling' and she was able to say it back to him.

11.3.81. *La Giaconda.* Victor, a literary man in his middle years, goes to a publication party, where he meets a clever, pretty and − as they always say – talented young female to whose work he later gives a good notice. 'You deserved it,' he says, in reply to her 'I'm not sure I should say this, but thanks!' Victor has been married for some years, she for very few. She has recently had a baby. There is something reassuring in her maternity. Both intelligent and, it seems, happy, she reconciles marriage and modernity in a way which reflects agreeably on Victor's own domesticity. Some time later, the marriage of an architect acquaintance, whom he neither likes nor much respects, is said to be in trouble. Adrian is a reformed *coureur*, possibly bisexual, whose betrayal by his wife has given him a cold menace. The coldness comes of the fact that he does not want to break with his (rich?) wife and the mother of his children (India and Guy). Adrian has been living in a resentful limbo but is soon rumoured to be involved in a rather chilling affair with a woman with whom he is said to do all kinds of things, although the two have no social connection. Victor is unsurprised and unaffected, until he discovers that the woman in the case is the same girl to whom he gave that nice notice, and of whom he thought so well. Now that he knows that she is not at all the girl he took her to be, he falls instantly and angrily in – what? – 'love' with her, as if she has been deceiving him and deserves whatever he would now like to do to her. Imagine her smile when she discovers this. Imagine the conditions she sets for allowing him to do them.

The *Guardian* columnist. Affectations of candour commission her notion of herself as the most attractive sexual traffic warden on the block, the bubbliest babe who ever clinked glasses with her secret self and then published the secret. *Santé*! Prescribing herself for everyone, she spreads her legs in so liberal an invitation that one might expect her to be available on the National Health.

The Sponger. A writer is plagued by an old friend who never calls him except, as if it were an afterthought, to propose some project which will prove profitable to the caller. 'Do me one small favour. It'll take you three weeks, tops!' The fun of talking to Dickie lies in guessing what his real purpose will turn out to be. Since he never takes offence, there is regular pleasure in turning him down, if only to discover what the next thing will be. He calls one day, as he always does, 'just to catch up'. The narrator waits, with his usual unkind patience, to see what the one small favour of the day will be. On this occasion, the conversation reaches term without any proposition being advanced. He realises that the other man has really called only to tell his old friend that he has a two-picture deal with a major company. He truly has phoned this time only to keep in touch and to promise that he will never ask for a favour again. Bastard!

27.4.81. *Any Questions* took place on Good Friday, in the same week as the riots in Brixton, after which Willie Whitelaw (a character straight out of Aristophanic nomenclature, though no one has remarked it) did a walk through the lawless black borough. A man with his disastrous teeth is well-advised to be tight-lipped. The broadcast was from a prettyish place near Maidstone. I drove there in spring sunshine in the little red Mercedes 280SL which, like a well-preserved actress in her thirties, still attracts the eyes of the young. I was almost down to the A13 when I came on a young policeman erecting a DIVERSION sign on the roundabout where I was supposed to turn off for the tunnel. I got out of the car, submissively, and asked him how I was now supposed to get to Maidstone. I was correctly dressed and spoke in officerish tones. 'Your guess is as good as mine,' he said. I looked at him and then I said. 'Now look here, I'm supposed to be making a broadcast and I have to be there by six o'clock. Suppose you see if you can make a better guess than I.' My tones must have sounded as if they came from a good regiment. He gave me detailed, courteous directions, after which I reached the tunnel without delay. It did not require very quick wits to apply this anecdote to Brixton. I managed to bring home to an all-white audience the kind of courtesy which the blacks of Brixton must encounter in their daily commerce with the police.

The panel had dinner before the broadcast at the Great Danes Hotel on the M20, the kind of huge roadhouse which once grew fat on adulterous couples, such as Byron and Claire, who repaired to it to avoid metropolitan scrutiny; a club-house for indoor games. There was a large car park, bald as an airport runway. An old Humber was depositing Muggeridge and Denis Healey. The staff were attentive, but nervous; they might have been at an audition. I went and talked to Kitty Muggeridge who had the air of dutiful boredom common to wives of garrulous public figures. I let her know, as if she didn't, that her witty remark about David Frost ('He rose without trace') has been printed in the new Penguin *Dictionary of Quotations*. She did not ask me if any of mine had. Malcolm had a bad conscience, he told me, over his failure to answer my letter asking why he had such a bad opinion of Byron.

He would do so now: Byron had initiated the habit of living a lewd life in public and taking pleasure in the publicity attendant on kissing and telling. He was not interested in B.'s devotion to liberty and tolerance.

Malcolm is now an old man, thin and blue-eyed; the jaundiced crustiness around the blue seems to presage the opaqueness of death. Does he really believe in his own saintliness? Apart from a spurious modesty and a show of interest in other people (a PR exercise in Christian forbearance), he is much more smug than S. Mugg, his media moniker. He was so polite and flattering that I must somehow have given him the impression that I had the goods on him. He attributed to me a *bon mot* about how a Graham Greene novel without God is like a Wodehouse without Jeeves. He promised that I said this on TV when we were discussing *The Honorary Consul*. He is an able publicist for his new faith. Having disparaged all comparative moralities, he embodies the arrogant humility of those who declare they have higher standards than other people and then live in the proud penitential confidence that they can never live up to them. I was flattered by the old boy's recollections, but not entirely seduced, even when he invited me, and my wife, to visit him in Robertsbridge whenever we were in the country. We were, he said, to 'propose' ourselves.

At lunch with us on the previous day, George Steiner had recalled doing broadcasts to Europe with Healey who had 'the most perfect French accent of anyone whom I have ever en-countered in a non-*Francophone*'. I repeated this to Healey, who showed more amazement than gratification. He reacted without warmth or interest, remarking that George had become 'some kind of a polymath', which he made sound like a social disease. Healey and his wife were of the same discontinued line, like a pair of Toby jugs. Healey was smaller than I expected, especially the head. He is of an ill-advised colour, sanguine as a blood-blister. He either intimidates his medical man into silence or does not listen to his orders. The famous brows are less hirsute than expected. He speaks in a gentle Yorkshire accent. He wore a blue suit and an Apex tie. I affected to think that he was advertising cheap flights, but it seems that Apex is the name of his union. He was both cheerful and gloomy over dinner. His failure to win the leadership had made him less morose than reflective. Minded to retire, he wonders why, with so many things that interest him, he contin-ues to hustle for power. He spoke generously of Shirley, whose courage he acknowledged while declaring his determination to cast her into oblivion, if he could work it. He reserved his animus for David Owen, who, he said, saw himself as the next PM and was high on his own vanity. I remarked that Owen seemed to have the grievances common among those whom fate had particularly favoured. He liked that enough to shoot me a look, as if canvassing for the franchise, from under those blue-seeming brows.

The dinner (trout or steak) was so agreeable that the subsequent broadcast lacked devil. The Conservative Detta O'Cathain was businesslike and broadminded for a henchperson of Mrs Thatcher. We lacked a villain or even a rogue. The need to be cautious diminished Healey as soon as he was in front of an audience. He had told us at dinner that he once made the mistake of saying in public that someone was 'out of his tiny Chinese mind' (a catchphrase, whether he knew it or not, of dear Hermione's). He had been berated for racism, even by the Chinese embassy. He has an excellent mind and a quick intelligence, but he has learnt that the electorate must never be allowed to see them at exercise. He smiled at my remark that Mrs Gandhi and Mrs Thatcher had in common 'the ability to combine dullness with menace'. I suspect that he more envied me the chance to say such a thing *coram publico* than wished he had said it himself. As Shadow Foreign Secretary, he cannot afford to take an incautious view of the lady who rules India, whatever kind of a villain (as Malcolm indicated) she may indeed be.

Steiner is so touching a mixture of brilliance and effrontery, of subtlety and crassness, that I am always defending him even though he is, in many regards, better placed than I am. John Peter was anxious that I should convey to G. that he was misjudging the situation on the *Sunday Times*. I have always thought that G. was being paranoid in his fears that he was about to be jettisoned from the roster of retained *savants*. His articles have an urgent, if alien, density which distinguishes them from the more amiable contributions of the *indigènes*. Since he was scarcely a regular contributor, he could not be accused of overloading the pages with a cargo of sophistication. He might vex the foolish or tantalise the merely adequate (by questioning their adequacy), but he could hardly endanger the circulation or – despite his boastful fear that he is not worth the price they are paying him – dismay the accountants. It does, however, appear to be true that Harry Evans now questions G.'s place in the literary scheme of the paper. The wind of his breezy disfavour may have reached George through

John Peter, who was G.'s pupil at Oxford. John's conviction that he has been ill-used inclines him to recruit other malcontents. He seems especially resentful of John Whitley, who has refused to honour the agreement, to which Harry Evans had set his seal, whereby J.P. would work four days a week, having the fifth free for the composition of a study of the drama which, in John Carey's winking view, is 'extremely important, innovatory, epoch-making; in brief, not bad at all'.

Meanwhile, James Fenton continues to take his role as public executioner with saturnine seriousness. He prowls ·around the office like a one-man host of Midian. A weave of enthusiasm and antipathy, aping the grand manner of Levin (all that flannel about 'my masters' etc), he promotes plays such as the laughter-free comedy *Make and Break*, which have small merit but fancy provenance. Fenton shaves his dark head rather close, as if fearful of catching something from casual contacts; he looks both silly and sinister.

Peter Wood's allegedly smart NT production of *The Provok'd Wife*. The most inventive moments took place in the interval when the curtain did not come down and the set-dressers did their stuff around the recumbent John Wood. When on his feet, he overacted as usual, while Dorothy Tutin did a breathless impersonation of her mother. Dotty is an actress of great limitations; she has never done anything very bad and she never lends herself to a risky enterprise; she plays safe boldly. Expert at getting a certain kind of laugh, at the expense of her own vanity ('Pretentious? *Moi*?'), she has become a star with a remarkably limited orbit. In the museum of the National, she is an unstuffed exhibit. The place combines superb professionalism with the cosy parochialism of an amateur company which supplies its own ovations. Loud and obvious, John Wood expects to be congratulated on the subtlety of his shouting and the generous thickness of his ham. He is ugly and plays the gallant, crude and plays the charmer. Magnified in that small pond, he sports the lineaments of a big fish.

T. became disgusted, he says, with the art world, particularly the effect on it of Christie's and, even more so, of Sotheby's. Both seem impervious to exposure and ignore all press reports, however damaging, presumably because they do them no damage. It reassures more clients than it alarms to be in dodgy hands. T. is a clean, blue-eyed, rather elegant person with an aura of chaste nuttiness. He is completing (or has at least begun) a study of the relationship between neo-Platonism and the iconography of the Eastern Church. He has actually read the *Enneads*. He has two teenage daughters who had just given their first all-night party, for which their parents had agreed to go into temporary exile. He was suffering from a loss of virginity which troubled him more than he had expected. His children are trilingual, having had two years at a *lycée* in Paris before being forwarded to their grandmother in Marbella in order to be hispanified. T. has the very slightly shifty complacency of a man who has cut corners for the highest motives. I had asked him to value two of the icons which I bought from old Martinou, in Pandrosou Street, in the late Sixties. The shop is now run by an odious man, as suspicious as Martinou was trusting. The last time I was in there, the new manager enraged me by asking me to leave the shop because I was carrying a big plastic bag. He feared either that I would pouch something or that I would knock over some of his overpriced junk. I responded by ramming my fist within an inch, or two, of his nose.

T. confirmed that Martinou had sold me what he said he had, four of the last set of icons ever to pass through his hands; the churches and monasteries had all been stripped. Back in the 1960s, uncertain which to choose, I remarked that I wished my friend Nikos was with me. Martinou loaded a stack of icons into my arms and told me to take them to my friend. What I wanted to keep I should pay for, the rest return. He demanded neither address nor deposit. There was something superb in his polite condescension. His gesture conveyed disdain for the muscular tyranny of the Colonels. His gaze conveyed the primacy of intuition over any formal scheme. It was a gesture at once mercantile and, almost, affectionate. What Englishman would match, or understand it? Our bond was between our untouching hands. Even T.'s ascetic unworldliness could not compose such a Mediterranean mixture of sacred and profane, trust and calculation.

T. reminded me of the English émigré masseur who had kneaded me at the Beverly Wilshire. His metallic cleanness had something unsalted about it, like a diet biscuit. Bryan Forbes told me that he drank his own urine, a faddist's beverage which, in due time, enabled you so to refine your liquid intake that you pissed pure H_2O. T. knows more about icons than anyone in London, but speaks no Greek. He has the dedicated myopia of the monographer who, in his own field, knows it all, and nothing else. He is busy discovering the roots of all religion, but has small interest in philosophy. He claims to be a Gnostic, but (and?) was unamused when I told him how Michael Ayrton, when filling in the space after 'Religion' in the form for enrolment in the RAF, had written 'Gnostic'. The recruiting sergeant frowned and said, 'Better put C. of E.' I offered T. a fiver for his valuation. His eyes did not roll upwards (they did not speak Greek either). He pocketed it without a quibble.

The BM requires one to have a pass before taking anything beyond the door. They fear Irish donors, I suppose. The head-vase which I bought at Sotheby's for £120 one wet boring winter afternoon was queried by Charles Ede because he had never seen an example with a fillet of the same kind on the black roll of hair above the forehead. Although at first anxious on the same grounds, the BM man recalled another example and could find nothing wrong with mine. When I compared it with other examples on crowded display, it was clear that my ignorance had spotted a particular beauty. It is one of the finest small fifth-century pieces I have ever seen. Had there not been another with the same features, I should have been told that mine was inauthentic. It is not advisable to have anything unique if you want people to certify its originality.

A Wittgensteinian gloss might consider what is meant, in such a context, by 'looking at something differently'. The same piece, regretfully or jeeringly repudiated, would have seemed valueless. Bereft of its antique provenance, ownership of the same vase would become a matter for commiseration and the kind of frowning reappraisal which concludes, 'Of course one can see now...' See what? The article is stripped of its rank and appears a blatant imposture. Yet the thing would have been exactly the same object if that other filleted head-vase had been pinched by the archaeologist's assistant or broken by a careless peasant's plough. The destruction of the one would entail the devaluation of its sibling. As it is, the warrant of the BM is so widely accepted that Ede can now give a 'replacement value' for something which, taking it to be unique, he regarded as literally priceless. (Cf. Steinbeck's *The Pearl*.)

Making Up. A man in hospital is surprised by a visit from an old friend from whom he has long been estranged. He realises that it must mean that he is going to die. As if to avert his fate, he refuses to be reconciled. 'Flowers? What do I want flowers for?' An unfinished quarrel is a symptom of vitality. The other man catches wind of the sick man's fear and, after a moment, realises that the kindest thing he can do is to match his intransigence. 'You don't want them, don't have them.' The wife comes in as the visitor leaves scowling generously, his unwrapped flowers in his fist. 'Whatever's wrong with him?' she says, and then: 'You're looking better!'

13.7.81. I still hang around the big gambling table of the movies despite my secret promise to myself to emigrate to literature. My reconciliation with John Schlesinger threatens a further postpone-ment of my exodus. On the day of Sarah's show, I took him to lunch at Langan's. We started late (I had been recording my talk on Maurice Cowling for the Third Programme) and finished at tea-time. John is grizzled and bearish; his new film[35] has been sourly received by Ned Tanin, whose feet, in small socks, I remember on a desk at MCA in Piccadilly when Gareth and I were trying to set up *What About Us?* Tanin accuses John of having spent $20m on a turkey. John believes the film is funny and will prove successful, or may. Was it worth undertaking? That quibble, if potent, would disqualify most contemporary production. When have there ever been so few new films we have any wish to see? John wore a rather unused green suit, with a gilded gloss on it. He has, it would appear, decided to allow distinction to license undisguised weight. He makes no further pretence to dieting. We ate copiously (though he refused a pudding) and drank a bottle of champagne. He had brought me 'a book', *Gorky Park*, a thriller which has been 'bought for' him and which had gushing reviews. He has also come back to the idea of a film about Lord Lucan. He is more interested in the 'crime and punishment' aspect of the story than in the satirical possibilities I once pointed out to him. I confessed that I had been unwilling to have *A New Wife* sent to him sooner because I did not fancy being turned down by John Schlesinger. He smiled and admitted that he had refrained from approaching me for rather similar reasons. There was pleasure on both sides at our *rapprochement*. We always had a good time together. Work proceeded rapidly and efficiently in the days when I used to go to his Peel Street house for conferences and salads. He was amusing and amused. If he assumes that his preoccupations must always be paramount, there is a good measure of self-mockery in his conceit. I shall resume working with him, if I do, with relief and enthusiasm, but I should be deluding myself if I imagined him to be someone of commanding intelligence. He does so want to be

---

35 *Honky-Tonk Freeway.*

taken for an artist, but never at the price of setting himself to create a work of art.

At Sarah's graduation show, Amanda Redman told me that after she had shown her breasts to the camera, Liv said to her, 'There! I don't know how you can do it. You have completely destroyed your career – no one will ever respect you again.' Liv has been in England recently, playing the idealist on behalf of UNESCO; noble sublimation of her shame at neglecting her own child. That she had no leading man on *Richard's Things* made the situation worse. She had no one who could flatter or flatten her. She now declares herself to be a writer and says that from now on she will prepare, and perhaps direct, her own scripts. I hated her pretentious book and, alas, she lived up to it.

Mark Shivas is now into American TV. He is doing a big production about Maria Callas, from Arianna's fanciful book. No one has ever been more opaque to me than Mark. He is civil, even affectionate, in his nervous *renfermé* way, but I cannot read him. I am unable to provoke him to candour or to impatience. We had a marriage of convenience and it has ceased to be convenient. He came to Sarah's show and has been as genial as he knows how. He makes no pretence of being an intellectual, though certainly quite intelligent. He confesses, with a small smile, that he was fired as a front-man on Granada's movie programme because he failed to smile enough on camera. He keeps his troubles to himself, either because he is a Stoic or because they do not trouble him. He has a modest style (he dresses rather drably), but a BMW has replaced his antique Morgan. He advances without seeming to advance himself.

It seems that my picture with Stanley Donen has fallen on stony ground. Lord Grade has collapsed to the tune of £50m or so, a tune unlikely to be reprised. Stanley loved him when he was a rich old hoofer who liked to kick up his heels, but who knows if their romance has survived? I agreed to do the thing out of sentimentality. There are worse motives and better excuses. Even as the balloon goes down, Marty Starger remains full of gas. Everything he has touched in the movies has turned to dust. Yet his offices are glassily palatial, walls covered with happy pictures of Lew with and, once or twice, without the cigar. Starger has made so many wrong decisions that he has become irreplaceable; who else could be persuaded to be the head of something on the verge of decapitation? That such a man should need an expensive staff is unsurprising. Dan Rizner drives a new Mercedes sports and a feeble bargain. He was about to be head of UA, but then needed bypass surgery (*triple*) and the Board wouldn't wait to see how he came through, or if. He survived, but his chances of ever being top dog did not. He has now become a carrier-pigeon that tries to bark, or at least growl. He was embarrassingly urgent in proposing that Gerry Lance's sidekick in *Songbird* be given greater prominence. He gave me a little bearded smile, but it is unlikely that he saw the whole irony: he is the dauphin of the last king; he will never make the grade and nor will Grade. Starger has had the luck to make a putz out of a limey, but American banks are involved and they are unlikely to forget a face with that much egg on it.

14.7.81. After thirteen weeks, the Hollywood writers' strike is over. What a way we have come from the aggressive naivetés of Clifford Odets! The cry of 'Strike!' no longer heralds Lefty, but rather hefty fees for lamentable material peddled in a wider range of rubbish. After aping desperate measures, the rich members of the Union will become even richer and the poor will be compensated only if they hold office in its bureaucracy. The rallying calls concern only cash. The writers will seek neither to influence the taste of their masters nor to supply them with a better class of garbage. Appeals to solidarity on the part of those dedicated to self-seeking and credit-filching cannot fail to amuse. The only art to which the Hollywood writer is devoted is amassing wealth. His agent is his prospector and the client works where the pay-dirt is most paying, and dirtiest. He is never concerned with principles. Questions of conscience are for losers. To introduce the vocabulary of the working-class struggle into this quadruple-garaged world is twenty-one-carat effrontery. 'Waiting for Righty' is the name of the only game that counts.

At least with Americans it was certain that a settlement would be reached: where there are dollars there are deals. The English lack such simple lubricants. Their present difficulties prove that where money is lacking principles thrive. The collapse of Tory policies was always likely; no political scheme has been successful in practice since the time when military muscle gave Christianity its prosperous allure and allowed God to gain British nationality. He seems no longer to sport that particular passport. British resentment declares itself in the disobedience of His servants. By resorting to vandalistic orgies, they denounce not only the present government but any routine opposition to it. All political solutions are despised by a mob which refuses to channel its rage into any version of uplifting idealism. The inadequacies of the Left are as much exposed by the littering of England as are the miscalculations of the Right. No political organisation, even of extremists, seduces the mob. In a modern glass-house, what is more satisfying than to cast the first stone? The government proposes to punish the young for its own failures. The bad meteorologist blames his barometer. British vanity has made it a matter for self-congratulation not to use one's imagination and to persist in the belief that their glorious national character will prevent the English suffering the fate of other nations. The dislike of immigrants has at least something to do with British shame at the presence of those to whom unkept promises were made. The anger of the blacks is compounded of boredom and contempt for the puny hypocrisies of a 'society' without ideas or wealth. National penury embarrasses moralists who would like to believe that agitators and the pill have been the causes of all the trouble. A free society, in which a parade of alternatives is part of the meaning of freedom, must deliver the goods in order that the stock of possibilities be shifted. When a significant proportion of the people, however well-heeled by comparison with the wretched of the earth, cannot take part in the exchange of goods, the deprived do not consider themselves obliged to respect the glassed prospects offered to their gaze but beyond their grasp. The smashing of shops is a loud resignation from conventions which are accepted when the merchandise on show is accessible in exchange for money.

A society which depends for its vitality on the greed of its citizens for 'necessities' and pleasures (why else do so many work at jobs they detest?) should not be surprised, though it always is, when the denial of satisfaction leads to explosions of uncontrolled demand. The sight of desirable goods teaches the habit of en-titlement. In affluent times, money mediates between desire and possession. Money civilises greed, but cannot banish it; it is part of the same nexus. In the past, slumps led to contraction of advertis-ing in those parts of the press which catered for the lower-paid. Television advertising keeps images of luxury and delight in front of the eyes of those on whom officialdom enjoins restraint. The poor are teased by the spectacle of plenty. The parade of goods is, however, essential to the idea of society to which the Tories are committed.

Is there then something to be hoped for from the Socialists or the SDP? Almost certainly not. Where the Tories flatter the successful, the Socialists are determined to chasten them. They will replace (or more probably add to) the grievances of the poor by provoking the sullenness of the able. The result of Bennite policies would be that only the governing *apparat* will enjoy the big cars, foreign travel, and grand apartments which money could once buy. In old England, men grew rich and famous by getting the market right or making lucrative conquests. Statues might then be built in their honour. In ideologically rigorous societies, secular or religious, the statues are of those who guessed which line the party was going to follow.

Louise Purslow rang to sound me out on the subject of the Reith Lectures. Various functionaries in the BBC are asked to advance their candidates. She proposed 'cinema and television' as a topic. I suggested something more trenchant: 'Public and Private Arts'. I was also called by the President-to-be of the Cambridge Union who wants me to speak, next term, against the government cuts to the arts budget. He assumed that I should be opposed to the economic starvation of the Good Cause. I found myself ambivalent. There is a strong case for the maintenance of the National Theatre and Covent Garden, because the state there declares its capacity to mount worthy spectacles, as it does with the Changing of the Guard. We do not look to such places for new ideas but for new productions. Nothing has ever happened at the NT which could be called revolutionary; and why should it? *The Romans in Britain* may have shocked but it clearly did not *rally*. The best effect of the production, to which wild centurions will never drag me, is likely to be the humiliation of Mrs Whitehouse. She made the elementary blunder of confusing the representation of an act with the act itself. If her logic were applied elsewhere in the West End, the villain of *The Mousetrap* would be arraigned for murder and the director for incitement to the same. Inability to distinguish between the portrayal of an act and the real thing is fostered by the television to which she has become so furiously addicted.

The authentic national theatre is taking place in the streets. The rioters hoard their cuttings like pros. TV news runs their rushes for them. It has now displaced school as the means of comprehensible education. It moralises, but it cannot teach morals. It prompts acceptance or rejection of people, not of ideas. The viewer decides first of all whether he likes the speaker. The newscaster mimics the messenger in the tragedy; but he is by no means one with his message: we react to what he says according to the personality, the *playing*, of the mouthpiece on duty. What enrages us or leaves us indifferent when delivered by one presenter can appal or move us when delivered in a different style or tempo.

Television can teach everything except how to be intelligent. The viewer accepts it as the kind of mirror in which he wishes he might be seen. The camera will not look at him unless he personifies the things which entertain (or horrify) his peers. Television favours what we have more or less seen before. The series has triumphed over the 'single play'. TV is the medium of protraction. The citizen as star must find a plausible place in the continuing story of the continuing story. The masses are forever auditioning for parts in the unmitigated national theatre which can be put on without a licence or public funds. You are nothing if you are not on TV. Respectability, the dated virtue that kept the streets safe and the vocabulary clean, has no famous dividend. Whereof one cannot speak entertainingly, thereof there is no future.

Television's ceaseless parade of toys would excite the least acquisitive child; it promises that we have a right to things because we can see them. We feel guilt at what we cannot afford; resentment follows guilt. The stones thrown in English cities are for two birds: the society from which the throwers are excluded and the partition which keeps them from the way of life they cannot abide to see lived by others. The problem of the government is to generate an inhibiting morality which can replace both religion and the class system. The Tories cannot play the red card of the Future and they lack the conviction for a fundamentalist withdrawal to capital punishment and St George.

The regression to Islam in (predominantly) Muslim countries appeals to the essential character of the people. The constant talk of an 'Arab nation' is an indication less of the cohesion of all Arabs than of the sense they all share of the unreliability of the *patriae* to which they have been assigned, often very recently. The rejection of colonial geography is rendered plausible by the promise that there is an older and more valid allegiance to which the people can have recourse.

Return to official Christianity has its supporters, at lofty and basement levels (Sissons and Whitehouse are provisional poles), but Christianity is now too demanding for the English. They have become so accustomed to mouthing what they please that harder tack would break their teeth. Can there be some non-metaphysical rallying cry? Back to what? The rock on which British greatness was founded has crumbled. There never was a wise and reliable ruling order; there was a snobbish oligarchy and an ill-used working class with delusions of imperial superiority. The wealth, to which the British found an early key, was due to the belligerent adventurism of younger sons and the inventiveness of non-conformists and outsiders. It generated new liberties but served, at the same time, to confirm the privileged in their vanities. Christianity became so efficient an instrument of domination that, with the collapse of empire, it lost its appeal for the under-class. It is hard to *believe*, but not difficult to argue, that the forces of resentment will now prevail. Incapable of building anything, the under-class experience destruction as a kind of inverted creativeness; they may have no hope, but they do have despair. If they cannot charm other people, they have been amply instructed in how to intimidate them.

When the British go abroad, they cannot speak to the natives, but they can piss on them. All the spray-paint vulgarities in Biarritz are in English.

The post-war decade seemed to allow culture and responsibility to oust metaphysics without frivolous or immoral consequence. Marriage remained the modal sexual relationship. That it no longer required divine sanction did not desecrate its centrality. The defeat of privilege did not appear to destabilise society. Only a posturing reactionary such as Evelyn Waugh could claim that Attlee's England made him feel as if he was living in an 'occupied country'. The diminution of cant seemed to have cleared the air and somewhat to have flattened the horizon. In spite of all that, the vanity of the British remained intact, to their later undoing. Free of their traditional mentors (and the wealth that backed them), they continued to believe themselves uniquely qualified to pass judgment on the world. Tired of Attlee's modesty, they came to applaud whatever ingratiating verbiage would sustain the illusion of mastery. The best television in the world replaced the Grand Fleet. Pundits became its admirals, piped aboard by their signature tunes.

As soon as architecture was refined to respond only to the supposed needs of a building's users, it lost its magic. Functionalism has no inspirational register. Without pretentiousness, art supplies nothing finer than what polls tell us that the public wants. We are then sentenced to live in ticked boxes.

The indifference of white kids to the racial issue is at once reassuring and slightly disconcerting: they have passed the point at which they can be bothered to feel superior to anyone else. They will not have it that anyone is in a worse state than themselves. They are against only whoever deprives them of what they want.

Today there is talk of people 'starving' in Hackney. No doubt there are people in a distressed state, but to say that they are starving is wishful greed: it purloins words that apply literally to millions and millions to describe those who cannot afford all the burgers they would like.

17.7.81. The best-known writers of the post-war period may have been closet *littérateurs*; but they have, in public, laid emphasis on what they have in common with the common. We have been persuaded by the bookish that books are not all that important. Quality matters less than popularity. The very English belief that simple prose is the proper reflection of common sense implies that all complexities are pretentious and likely to have alien origins. One may congratulate those who downgrade Chesterton, Shaw, Strachey, Galsworthy, Priestley, Wells (none of whom has lasted very well), but the elevation of disparagement as an art form, practised by applauded journalists such as Levin and Clive James, is no sure sign that we live in a golden age. We consult them not to discover their opinions of this or that programme or play but to be entertained by their merciless capers. They are today's lord high executioners whose functions are particularly devitalising.

The idleness of the purchasing public has made the bestseller, by definition, a good book; a book cannot be good unless it sells. That vulgarity was always implicit in Graham Greene's suggestion that it was better to be among the big battalions, even if some of their doctrines were unpleasing, than to be humane and ineffective in some cranky and righteous clan. His division of his own work into 'novels' and 'entertainments' was more conceited than modest: it promised that when he was really doing his best, he was a serious man of letters. He relished playing the double agent, like his friend Philby. It is hard, in both cases, to know which register delivered the greater reward.

Making it easy (or even easier) for artists makes it difficult for art. Its social value has little to do with its encouragement and much more to do with its digestion. To sponsor literature, as a cash crop, is a recipe for its decline. The hatred of art and the sense that it is alien and parasitic are the likeliest consequences of giving it special budgetary status. Visual arts are best preserved by putting artists directly to work, in the Greek style, for the embellishment of the city. Walter Benjamin got it wrong: the mechanical reproduction of art is infinitely less degrading than its replacement by discussions and appreciations by posturing pundits.

The degradation of art is seen most insidiously in the shift from interest in artists' work to prying into their more or less secret lives. This has had the paradoxical effect, in the case of Lytton Strachey, of elevating his importance as a writer in order to justify voluminous curiosity concerning his sexual activities.

A library burned in the riots will not, we are promised, be replaced. That'll teach them, though it is not quite clear what. The punishment of a 'community' by removing one of the means of education means that it will become dependent on the stimuli which have led it to destruction. If the government is really planning to use old army camps as detention centres, might it not find it cheaper and more expeditious to surround the least favoured districts in its decaying cities with barbed wire?

27.7.81. George Fischer said that he had approached Isaiah Berlin several times to do the Reith Lectures. He always claimed to be busy. What can he have been doing? Berlin is the Jewish Morgan Forster: the less he produces, the more unassailable his eminence. Isaiah told G.F. that he couldn't contract to do the lectures in 1983 because he might be 'gagarr' by then.

The Romantics Festival. My morning, afternoon and evening with Alan Bates were enjoyable and alarming. I was suddenly seized with stage-fright which Alan's own show of nerves did little to relieve. He was anxious over whether to wear glasses and afraid that his readings of Byron were too unintelligent or too banal. He has a 'pad' at 122, Hamilton Terrace. It has a kitchen like Schlesinger's in Peel St; a spiral staircase up to a studio hung with paintings by his brother, Martin. He has another brother who was a stage designer, very talented, he said, but never able to meet his deadlines. He abandoned the *métier* and went to teach in their native Derbyshire. He never sees Alan, whose success inhibited his own. We read my Byron script and then took a Miles and Miles car to the Queen Elizabeth Hall for our permitted one hour of rehearsal. We managed no more than a third of the text. Alan fretted about 'costume'. I insisted on taking him to lunch (at the Savoy Grill) before we returned to Hamilton Terrace. We should not have had anything to eat before the show otherwise.

The lack of interest of the organisers in what we were doing did us too much honour. We had been instructed to start promptly at six, since the hall was needed again at eight. We pushed through the curtained doorway, like instrumentalists without instruments, and onto the stepped stage. The audience was still coming in. Uncertain of our running time, and with no one to introduce us, I thought we had better start. I got as far as 'Byr–' when Alan decided he did indeed need his glasses. He delivered his rehearsed ad lib., claiming that his vanity was second only to Byron's, and put on his specs.

I began again and had read a sentence or two when a surly voice called out, 'Can't hear a word'. I tried to make light of it, asking whether it was my words which were inaudible or the noise of the incoming feet which drowned my voice. I said I would begin again. Sensing that the audience did not wish us well, I considered with dread the many pages which lay ahead of us. The laughs came reluctantly, but they did come, from a hall almost full, despite the bad weather and the awkward hour. I never quite lost my apprehension that we were being greeted with muted resentment.

When we finished, almost exactly to time, at 7.30, we received civil enough applause to get us off the stage without embarrassment. We dithered about taking another call. 'Now or never,' the stage manager said. So back we went. This time there were loud cries of 'Bravo!' My mother said later that they even shouted for more, but I never heard it. As we were saying goodbye, Alan said to me, 'It went very well. We should do it again somewhere. The Grand Theatre Buxton possibly.' David Hughes reported in the *Sunday Times* that our evening had been 'the highlight of the festival', about which he said amiable things. He did, however, refer to 'cheap jibes' on my part. I cannot recall any. Can it be that he doesn't know much about Byron, who delivered more than a few?

30.7.81. The Sullivans left early this morning. At Lagardelle, John was recognisably the same pawky person whom I met on the stairs to Howland's rooms in October 1950. His face still looks as though they didn't have one his size; it now hangs in sags and folds on the lank-haired armature of his skull. He is prized in Santa Barbara, not least for his willingness to absorb a large workload. His extraordinary energy seems to be running down. He resents, where once he gloried in, the six courses he is obliged to teach in order to keep the number of classical students up to the mark required by the quota on which the faculty's finances depend. He talks a lot about philosophy, but has no obvious instinct for it. He argued that 'compulsive' and 'involuntary' had the same meaning, a view refuted by a simple example such as the fact that I feel impelled to take a book with me into the lavatory; this might be said to be a compulsive act, but it is scarcely involuntary. I suspect that Johnpat (as Judy calls him, from a distance) thinks philosophy rather smart and craves the cachet of membership in its fraternity.

While Beetle and Judy and Stee watched the royal wedding, John and I lounged in the *tepidarium*. He told me of his only homosexual experience. He had a gay graduate student when he was at Austin and accepted an invitation to visit him in Phoenix, Arizona. He was greeted by his thirty-five-year-old pupil and 'two raving queens'. They introduced him to their community, took him to bars and even threw a party for him to which women were invited. John tried to 'put the make' on some of them, without success.

When the evening ended, he was ensconced in his host's four-poster. He turned off the light, but shortly afterwards it went on again. One of the queens had brought him a nightcap. He was naively touched by such solicitude and quite unprepared for the kiss on the lips which followed the emptying of glasses. 'I love you,' said the soulful fellow. John said that he found himself responding, like any appalled virgin, 'But you hardly know me.' The lover was undeterred. He proved his feelings by going down on John, who offered his lack of rigidity as a symptom of his irrevocable straight-ness. The lover desisted without, as they say, any hard feelings.

The next night, John's host drank too much and had to be put to his own bed. John had nowhere to sleep and found himself climbing into one half of a let-down or roll-out sofa, in which his lover was already lying. Compulsive, was it, this choice of couch, or involuntary? John realised that the other had a hard-on and, anxious for unprodded sleep, he quickly gave 'two or three strokes', in order to produce the desired effect in the shortest possible time. His bedfellow repaired to the bathroom and made no further call on his benevolence. As he was telling this story, which reflected rather well on his Latin generosity, Judy called down from the terrace of the sitting room that the carriages were rolling away from St Paul's.

Index